# Race Winning Strategies

# Race Winning Strategies

## Smart Lessons with Deep Dakron

# Tom Linskey

SHERIDAN HOUSE

First published 1995 by
Sheridan House Inc.
145 Palisade Street
Dobbs Ferry, NY 10522

Illustrations by Tadami Takahashi

*Library of Congress Cataloging-in-Publication Data*

Linskey, Tom, 1953–
    Race winning strategies : smart lessons with Deep Dakron / Tom Linskey
        p.      cm.
    ISBN 0-924486-88-0  (alk. paper)
    1. Yacht racing.    I. Title.
GV826.5.L47    1995
797.1' 4—dc20                                      95–20732
                                                          CIP

Production/Design: Lorretta Palagi
Composition: Kathleen Weisel

Printed in the United States of America

ISBN 0-924486-88-0

 CONTENTS

 FOREWORD

Why do we race? Of the many mysteries of sailboat racing, this is one question for which I've always had an answer: We race because it's fun and challenging and, whether we win or lose, racing to win is a reward in itself.

The next question, of course, is: How do we win? As in most races and regattas, there is no single correct answer but rather a multitude of choices and paths that can lead to success. But speaking from 30 years of experience, I will venture that winning is a direct result of exercising a muscle neglected by too many sailors: the mind.

When I began racing at the age of 12 I spent whole summers on the water and developed an intuitive sense of how the wind worked and how to make my boat go, but that didn't mean I could win regattas on any regular basis. Like most sailors who were boat speed and kinetics artists, I was good but far from great, and despite winning some events my ups and downs were all too apparent on my score sheets.

This was in the mid-1970s, which seems like antiquity now, but almost all of the verities of sailboat racing back then hold just as true today. What I lacked was consistency and a thought-out approach to racing and regattas. About this time Dave Ullman, a Newport Beach, California, sailmaker, was dominating every one-design class he stepped into. Dave seemed to win national championships so effortlessly that his awestruck competitors nicknamed him "the Wizard."

During the Canadian Olympic Training Regatta (CORK) at Kingston, Ontario, in 1974, I stood next to Dave one evening as we pondered the results in the 470 class, a doublehanded spinnaker-and-trapeze Olympic class dinghy in which we were racing each other. Well—Dave was vying for the lead with a couple of Frenchmen and I was barely above the fold in the two-page printout of results. The race that day had been very windy, and Dave, of a diminutive height that somehow added to his mystique, remarked that he was exhausted. "Me too," I said. "I've never hiked so hard, and my arms are about to fall off from pumping." Dave threw me a look of pity and said, "Mentally," and moved off.

In 1977 I went to work for Dave as a sailmaker and, being young and tall and skinny and able to fly a spinnaker, began crewing for him in the 470. Finally I would witness the Wizard's magic first-hand! After my first race with Dave, in light air, I returned to the beach in a state of utter mental exhaustion. Some magic. The man was nonstop rapid-fire questions! Where was the most wind on the course? Did the boats on the right have more or less wind than we did? What about the boats on the left? And their angle: Were they higher, lower, or parallel? And the wind: Was it right, left, median, or moving in a persistent shift to one side? And what are the compass numbers? And what's the wind doing further up the course? And what are the relative positions of *all* the boats? Dave, who wanted no surprises, meant *all* the boats. Where are they, where are they headed, what's their sail trim, can we cross that boat—that dot of sail—in the far left corner? My skipper, relentlessly gathering and monitoring information and therefore our odds of success on the racecourse, was making me exercise my mind like never before.

And it worked. Together we won three world championships in the 470, the first team in the world to do so, and though we finished third and second in our two attempts at Olympic selection, in 1984 I was fortunate enough to be chosen as a spare member of the U.S. yachting team for the Olympic Games in Los Angeles—the highlight of my life. I'll never forget the opening ceremonies, marching into the Los Angeles coliseum—the athletes from the other countries had formed ranks, but the U.S. team poured pell-mell through the tunnel and into the spotlights and incredible stadium roar. In the mixup I found myself, Forrest Gump-like, shoulder to shoulder with track and field legends Edwin Moses, Dwight Stones, and Carl Lewis. You never know how exercising your brain can transform your racing—and your life.

While all the high-tech advances in equipment these days do make sailboat racing sexier, it's important to remember that technology is no more than a tool, something else we can utilize on our way to mastering the real thing: the art and science of racing strategy and tactics. Such is the focus I've tried to bring to this book. It's the basics of racing, and the polish you put on the basics once you learn them, that will win regattas for you again and again. Even at the Olympics and world championship level, the sailors who execute the basics best are the ones who go home with the medals.

A word about the characters in this book, of whom I've grown perhaps too fond—the struggling club racer, Deep Dakron; his rock-star tactician, Scratchen Sniff; the sailmaker extraordinaire, Kent McBatten; the yacht club know-it-all, Zig Zag Brooke; and Deep Dakron's long-suffering crew: the Kid, the Mumbler, and Lisa Quick-Cam. You already know these folks. You've raced them in regattas big and small, you've overheard them in yacht club bars, you've asked them questions in sail lofts, you've yelled at them while approaching leeward marks. It's one of the tricks of writing that real-life situations—real on-the-water racing—can sometimes be better portrayed through the use of fictional characters and situations. I hope I've succeeded.

May you finish every race and regatta exhausted—and victorious.

Tom Linskey
August 1995

 PART ONE

# SKIPPERS AND CREW

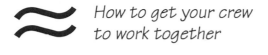 *How to get your crew
to work together*

# SKIPPER CONFIDENTIAL

"That's him! That's Zig Zag Brooke," a voice whispered.

With a gasp and a numbing sense of unreality, Deep Dakron recognized the famous man and his famous look: faded crew shirt with monogramming, weathered foul weather bib pants, beard and Topsiders gone silver with salt, one finger stirring a rum and orange.

"He always picks the middle stool at the yacht club bar because it doubles his chances of handing out advice," the voice confided. "Go ahead, ask him."

Deep Dakron took a step forward then hesitated, undone by the presence of the yachting legend. "Tell me again why he stopped racing," Dakron said under his breath.

Dakron's confidant spoke in hushed tones. "For years, Zig Zag Brooke and his *Obfuscator* were the scourge of the club racing circuit; he had the dubious distinction of winning more weekend and weeknight races than anyone in the world. Brooke always steered his own boat, up until he began to get old and started to zigzag too much. Before long a young hotshot took over the helm and he was bumped upstairs to the windward rail, but with Brooke in the position of Owner/Check Writer, *Obfuscator* continued to win. Then the worst possible thing that can happen to a racing yachtsman happened to Brooke."

"You mean . . . ?" Dakron gulped.

"Yep. Zig Zag's checks began to bounce. He took a bath selling *Obfuscator*, fell behind in his yacht club dues. Lost his charge privileges at the bar and his name went up on the notice board. He's gone a tad sour since, but he's still as sharp as ever. He stopped racing but never stopped thinking about it. Now he haunts the yacht club bars every weekend, picking up post race hors d'oeuvres and low-priced drinks, and dispensing free advice. A bit mysterious, though; people swear they've seen him at three yacht clubs simultaneously."

Before he knew it, Dakron was seated next to the great man.

"And what's your reason for losing this weekend?" Zig Zag Brooke growled without preamble. "Everyone's got an excuse to lose. That sanctimonious book by Mr. Conner, *No Excuse to Lose,* had it all wrong, because unless you're a millionaire, a paid professional, or a fanatic, you've got at least one damn good excuse for losing a sailboat race. What's yours?"

"My crew," Deep Dakron said simply.

"The perfect alibi," agreed Brooke. "A crew is the most important equipment on the boat. Crew members are temperamental and difficult to keep tuned, they take an inordinate amount of feeding and watering, they're a maintenance headache, and they're darn hard to fix when they break down. What's wrong with your crew?"

"They **don't listen**," said Deep Dakron.

Brooke grunted. "If they're not listening it's probably because you're not telling them anything interesting," he said. "As the skipper, you're in the role of both teacher and game show host. In the face of competition from more stimulating leisure time activities, such as baseball, golf, and video games, you've really got to work to make your subject—your 'program,' if you will—come alive for your crew. It's up to you to motivate them to participate in your 'class,' or race."

Dakron looked doubtful, but Brooke, staring into his drink, continued.

"I attacked it on two fronts with my old crew. The first way I'd get my crew to listen was by giving them something enlightening to listen to. Coming into any maneuver I'd be supplying key details that would get them focused on what they had to do. For instance, I'd say, 'Let's remember that it's windier (or lighter) out here than we realize,' or, 'We've got chop/current/a powerboat wake to contend with here,' or 'We're going to have a boat close on our lee bow after we round this mark, so we'll need the genoa and main sheeted in quickly. Don't worry about cleaning up the spinnaker sheets or the pole, just get everyone on the rail, hiking.'

"You get my drift? Then I'd spell out exactly what I wanted to achieve—we want to round this mark with full boat speed, or make a tight rounding to shut out the boats astern, whatever—to give them an immediate goal. Nobody was allowed to just go through the motions on *my* boat, no sir!"

Dakron didn't doubt it.

Brooke sipped his drink and went on. "The second way I got my crew to listen was to call on an individual instead of addressing the group at large. Teachers know that if you pose a tough question to the entire class their collective response will be to shrink from it and think, 'Gee, I'm sure glad teacher isn't calling on *me*, otherwise I'd have to listen/think/answer/act.' But if you direct your comment to the person whose area of responsibility it is, that person has no choice but to listen, and respond. And if he doesn't know the answer his neighbor will often bail him out, so you've got at least two people listening and thinking about something at once, which on most boats is pretty darn good."

"Sounds like you used to talk your crew all the way around the course," observed Dakron.

Brooke shook his head and sipped his rum. "Nah! I save the conversation for the bar. When racing, just a few key words and phrases to the person whose attention you've caught is all it takes. Now, how else is your crew malfunctioning?"

"They **don't think for themselves**," said Deep Dakron sadly.

"A common complaint, at least from the skipper's viewpoint," said Zig Zag Brooke. "But consider the possibility that you may have squelched their initiative by yelling at them once too often. If they seem to be waiting to be told what to do, maybe it's because they don't want to suffer any further damage to their pride or their eustachian tubes. You've got to turn this scenario around by showing them how much they can contribute to winning by thinking for themselves.

"Whether you run your ship as a benevolent dictatorship or a repressed democracy, each crew member should be encouraged to exercise his or her own initiative. This is not the Navy; nobody should be waiting for orders. As part of a team, each member should know, prepare, and follow through on his or her responsibilities with a minimum amount of nouns, verbs, and adverbs from the skipper.

"And a person's individual initiative should extend beyond his own sphere. A crew member must always be thinking ahead to the next thing that can be done for the boat, the sails, the rest of the crew and the skipper in order to win the race. The initiative of the individual, even if it's slightly misguided and must be gently redirected, ultimately benefits the group effort. Once they know that, and once you start encouraging them instead of chiding them, your crew members will begin to think for themselves."

"But they **don't work together**, either," Dakron complained.

Zig Zag Brooke stirred his drink with one pinkie. "It's up to you, old scout, to instill an *esprit de corps* in your crew, any way you can. Brings to mind an out-of-control spinnaker drop/leeward mark rounding my crew and I pulled off about ten years ago. It was blowing 20 and we were coming in on two wheels, way too hot and way too close to the mark, and I'd delayed the chute douse to grab the inside overlap on another boat. Just when disaster seemed inevitable, I stood up and screamed, 'We're gonna do a Hoolie!'

"Well, my crew ran with it, screaming 'Hoolie! Hoolie! Hoolie!' at the top of their lungs. They yanked the spinnaker down and muscled in the main and jib and scared the hell out of the competition besides. It was the best 'disaster' rounding anyone had ever seen," Brooke said modestly.

"But what does 'Hoolie' mean?" Dakron asked.

"Doesn't mean a damn thing!" said Zig Zag Brooke. "The point is, I galvanized my crew by giving them a rallying cry. Modern society teaches us how to work against each other—observe the dog-eat-dog of rush hour—but not how to work as a team. I advocate forming 'mini teams' onboard to accomplish shared jobs, such as the bow man and the keyboard man reaching an agreement on the communication, steps and timing of a basic matter like topping up the spinnaker pole before the hoist and lowering it after the spinnaker is dropped. Encourage them to experience the difference between each person struggling by himself, like they do now, and then have them try it working together, say, as a 'pole topper unit.' Teamwork really works: no more conked heads, swearing, or shouting back and forth. A lot of crews don't work together simply because they don't realize that they *aren't* working together. They may think they are, but it's up to you, Skipper, to get them to *really* work together."

"Like Fred Astaire and Ginger Rogers," said Deep Dakron, "but my crew are about as in synch as Tonya Harding and Nancy Kerrigan. What do you do with a crew who, lost in an intellectual discussion about whether Iron Butterfly or Deep Purple perfected the drum solo, find their feet dragging in the water because you've tacked, and they're now hiked out on the leeward rail? They just **don't pay attention**."

"We've arrived at the crux of your crew dysfunction," Brooke said gravely. "Skipper, have you forgotten what it's like to be a crew member? To be brutally honest, crewing can feel like a secondhand experience even during the best of times. Even though it might be the crew's contribution that has won the race, it's the almighty skipper who has the buzz of steering the boat, and grabs most, if not all, of the glory of winning. Then, during the worst of times, crews are relegated to the role of ballast and scapegoat by an unappreciative lout of a skipper looking for any excuse to bruise. Ask yourself: If the job description of crewing appeared in the classifieds, who would apply for such a position?"

"Low pay, and not a lot of benefits," Dakron agreed. "But crews do get a free lunch, and cold beer."

"So, unless you're crewing a dinghy or you've landed a plum role on a glamorous big boat, crewing can turn out to be a thankless and/or boring way to spend your weekend. As skipper, you should realize that to stay healthy the average crew needs both creative 'work' and nonresponsibility 'play,' or else it'll lose its enthusiasm—and here's your problem—and stop paying attention. If there's not enough work, either physical or mental, to perform at certain points in the race, go ahead and let 'em take a break, drift off and recharge their racing batteries.

"It might help to ask one of your crew to make sure the rest of the 'off-work' crew don't disturb the 'cone of silence' around the helmsman with their chitchat. Also, one crew member could watch for upcoming 'work' for the rest of the crew and ready them ahead of time, so the skipper doesn't have to. Who of your crew would make a good lieutenant?"

Dakron thought hard. "I guess my best officer candidate would be the Mumbler. He's a bit hard to make out, but he's the most intelligent regular I've got."

"The Mumbler?" said Zig Zag Brooke. He stared into his drink and sighed. Where have all the good crews gone?

# CREW CONFIDENTIAL

"**U**m, er, ah, excuse me. Er . . . could you, um, I'm sorry, but would you mind if I asked you one, uh, ques—"

Zig Zag Brooke swung around from his seat at the bar, annoyed.

"Speak up, son!" he barked. "These yacht club bars are too damn loud! I'll never understand why sailors raise their voices when they exaggerate. They only make their stories harder to deny later. Now what is it *you* want to have me believe?"

"Um, er, ah, if I might ask one question—"

"Fire away!" Brooke boomed, reaching for a sip of rum and orange. "Any question at all! Is there a sailor born who doesn't thrill to the opportunity to parcel out advice?"

"Er, uh . . ."

A look of recognition passed over Zig Zag Brooke's face. "I know," he said. "You must be the Mumbler. You crew for that fellow Deep Dakron. What's the name of his boat, *Sna*something."

The Mumbler, nodding vigorously, said, "Fu, fu, fu."

"*Snafu*, that's it," Brooke said. "If I remember correctly, that's the boat where the **skipper yells** quite a bit."

The Mumbler nodded even more vigorously, rolling wet eyes heavenward.

"A yelling skipper isn't much fun for anyone," agreed Brooke, "except for the crews of nearby boats, who always seem to get a kick out of it. The worst part about a yelling skipper is that it rarely improves the crew work, or the outcome of a situation. Besides the numbing and alienating effect on the crew, yelling exposes the inadequacies of the skipper, not the crew. Usually it's the skipper's own lack of preparation, anticipation, or communication that he or she is really yelling about."

"Oh!" said the Mumbler brightly.

"But that doesn't mean a long-suffering crew should just hike out and take it," Brooke continued. "I suggest one of two responses: **close your ears**, or **industrial action**."

"Ahhh!" exclaimed the Mumbler.

"If you can stand it, the close your ears option creates fewer ripples onboard," said Brooke. "It may help to think of the skipper's mouth functioning similarly to a pressure relief valve on a boiler. Visualize the pressure building up inside your average insecure and unstable skippers: during the race they're worrying themselves sick about boat speed, tactics, strategy, and most of all, because they're the skipper, they're worrying if anything will be left of their reputation after the weekend is over.

"Sooner or later all that pressure has to blow, and when it does, remove yourself from ground zero and let it blow over. Slipping in a succinct comment afterwards may alleviate your suffering and let your skipper know just what a cretin he or she has been."

"Hmmm," said the Mumbler.

Brooke gazed across the bar and said, "I remember one windward mark rounding in *Obfuscator* when I really let loose at my crew. 'EASE THE JIB! EASE THE MAIN! WILL SOMEBODY EASE THE GODDAMN SAILS!' I screamed, even though my crew were easing them just the way they should. After I calmed down I heard one of my crew mutter, 'Can't we get that thing tightened up?' meaning my pressure relief valve—my mouth. Well, after that I realized I'd been crying 'wolf' lots of other times too, and that comment put a clamp on my needless blasts."

"Ahhh," breathed the Mumbler.

"The other crew defense, industrial action, should be taken only if you find unbearable pressure building up as a result of the skipper's ravings. As jib and spinnaker sheet technicians, crews hold an awesome power in their hands. Just the hint of an onboard strike or work stoppage is enough to bring skippers to the negotiating table.

"My favorite example is the dinghy crew member who refused to come in off the trapeze until his skipper stopped yelling. 'Go ahead and tack,' the crew said, 'and we'll flip.' Well, the skipper stayed on port tack a lot longer than he would have liked, and when they finally did tack to starboard labor/management relations were viewed in a new light."

The Mumbler had another question. "Uh, er, ah," he said.

Zig Zag Brooke said, "But what do you do if you've got a skipper who **doesn't communicate**? By 'communicate' I mean give the crew the *why* as well as the *goal* of upcoming tactics and maneuvers so they can prepare and contribute to the effort. Usually it's simply because the skipper hasn't thought out what he or she wants to have happen, and thus can't verbalize any coherent plan to the crew.

"Skippers can get so mesmerized by the helm and the telltales that they forget about things like windshifts and marks and other boats. It's your job to make them think about the problem at hand, work out a plan, and communicate it. Maybe they have a vague notion of what they'd like to see happen, but that's a long way from informing the crew.

"Help the skipper and yourself by doing a quick bit of interrogation. Where do we want our boat to be during the approach to the mark? After rounding the mark, how do you want the sails set? Where do you want the crew weight? What's the timing for the spinnaker hoist or the drop? What's the choreography; who goes where, when? What signal do we listen for? Will we be tacking or gybing right away? Do you want us to call the distance to the mark, the positions of the other boats, the inside overlap, the wind, the tide, the course to the next mark for you?"

The Mumbler nodded. "Ummm," he said.

"You could feed the skipper all the questions and pass the answers and 'the plan' back to the rest of the crew. Of course, if all your attempts to drag some sort of cohesive plan out of your skipper fail, I'm afraid your race is doomed to mediocrity."

Brooke reached for his drink and then added, "I suppose you could use hand signals, if you wanted."

"Oh!" said the Mumbler. "But, but—"

"No!" said Brooke in horror. "Don't tell me you've got a skipper who not only doesn't communicate, he also **doesn't listen**? The most despicable double standard of skipperdom. No wonder good crews are leaving the sport in droves! But to be fair, it could be that your skipper doesn't make the effort to listen because all he or she ever seems to hear from the crew is a mumble, sorry, I mean a jumble of chitchat.

"The first step is to lower the volume of chitchat and direct relevant suggestions to the skipper or the tactician. Typically, many crews scatter comments on the order of 'We've got to get down to that mark,' and 'Sure aren't going very fast,' instead of directing a specific question or suggestion to the skipper: 'What do you think about sailing five degrees lower?' or 'Let's try easing the traveler down two inches and sheeting the leech harder.'

"Remember, too, that just because a skipper doesn't seem to be listening doesn't mean that he or she *isn't* listening. Skippers have to concentrate on steering, so if you do manage to get a grunt out of them you can consider that a reply; they're probably mulling over your information."

After another long silence, Brooke squinted at the Mumbler and said, "You know, you seem to be a darn good listener, but you haven't contributed much to this conversation."

"I would have," said the Mumbler, "but I didn't think you would listen."

"Um, er, ah," said Zig Zag Brooke.

# HOW TO STEER YOUR SKIPPER

"**B**e silent, and steer!" cried the renowned super-duper tactician Scratchen Sniff, walloping helmsman Deep Dakron with a fly swatter.

"Ouch!" Dakron wailed, and the crew grinned.

"The skipper shall steer the boat and the crew shall steer the skipper," Sniff declared. "Steering the boat is the *easy* part. We have the hard job out here."

"Huh!" said Dakron, cringing as Sniff's fly swatter rose again.

Sniff addressed the crew hiking on the rail. "Okay, team, here's how we're going to get our skipper around the first mark first, for once."

The crew stared back with an all-time drought of confidence.

"First, we must answer that perpetual question of the skipper, **how am I doing?** This is the only way we can keep him from looking at everything but the telltales and get him to concentrate on making the boat go. And let us not forget that other little mystery of yacht racing: Even with a helmsperson who is concentrating, sometimes everyone but the man on the handlebars can feel that the boat is being steered wrongly. Skippers either never look at the telltales or else get so wound up in them they turn into zombies."

"Harumph!" Deep Dakron snorted.

Sniff waved his swatter and said, "So it's up to us crew to put the helmsman back in the groove when he comes ungrooved. Sometimes a cheery, supportive 'Keep her moving!' will work if the helmsman is just distracted, but it's usually more constructive to describe our boat relative to the competition: 'We're going a bit high and slow here,' or 'We're going a little too low and fast—pinch her up a touch more.' If we don't reassure our helmsman now and then, he'll start looking around for how am I doing? feedback himself, and you know what that means."

"Remember that time he almost tacked us?" said the Kid, laughing into his sleeve.

"Next, we crew must **paint the picture** for our left-brained—or is it scatter-brained?—helmsman so that he stops looking around and steers fast," Sniff continued. "Ever since the Egyptians first raced their dhows down the Nile, skippers have wanted to know the three w's: WHO (Who are the other players in the race?), WHAT (What does the wind look like?) and WHERE (Where is the next mark?).

"We must paint the skipper a mind-picture of which boats are where (especially noting the movements of the top dogs) and how they're spreading across the course and how we are placed relative to them. Talk in boat lengths early on, when the boats are clustered, and then talk in zones of the course ('Boats A, B and C are on port near the port-tack layline; D, E and F are in the middle of the course heading to the left'). Which boats are converging with us, and which boats are splitting away? The goal of WHO picture-painting is to do such a thorough job that the skipper never gets any nasty surprises.

"With WHAT, the wind information, due to the nature of the wind there will naturally be some surprises, but we can minimize them by doing three things: Tell the helmsman whether we are headed or lifted, check up often on the angle and velocity of wind our competition has, and look for wind signs (wind on the water, other boats, clouds). Everyone should watch the wind, and we should keep updating the helmsman in all three wind areas.

"With WHERE, all we have to do is make sure the skipper is clear on where the next mark is. You can use the clock analogy—for example, the mark is at 11 o'clock—or talk in degrees from the present course—as in, the mark is up (or down) 15 degrees. And distance, too; use boat lengths when you're close to the mark, yards or minutes when you're still at a distance.

"All this commentary doesn't have to come from only the tactician. Everyone can and should contribute, as long as they consult their brain before opening their mouth. I remember one race where we had a five-year-old on board. Out of nowhere the little boy pointed and said, 'Look at the big boat!' Everyone turned and saw a freighter bearing down. We tacked and crossed its bow, and the boats around us found themselves becalmed when the ship passed."

"Maybe I should recruit a five-year-old as tactician," said Deep Dakron.

Sniff swatted him, but Dakron spoke up again, bravely. "Does this mean that the helmsman never gets to look around or say anything?"

"Not at all," said Sniff. "Some helmsmen are actually pretty fair sailors, and it doesn't hurt to have their opinion, once in a while."

Dakron looked around, and opened his mouth. "If that's the case, then I don't think we should be going *this* direction when the mark is over in *that* direction," he said.

"Be silent, and steer!" Sniff snapped, giving him another *thwok* with the swatter. "The next way we steer our skipper is via **truth doctoring**."

"Is that like wrestling your conscience, and winning?" asked the Kid.

"Sort of, but it's more closely related to public relations," said Scratchen Sniff. "Crews, think of yourselves as onboard spin doctors. Truth doctoring is the art of feeding your helmsman only those things that you feel he should know, which often means softening or withholding ugly realities which may upset him. For instance, if it happens that we are hammered by a certain windshift, but we should keep going toward it to both cut our losses and get into the new wind, we could say how great we look to make him carry on. And if it happens that a boat to leeward is tearing us to shreds, but we should hang on a bit longer, such as occurs after a leeward mark rounding when it's more disastrous to tack into a mass of spinnakers than to hold on another twenty seconds, we won't tell the skipper how bad we look underneath the genoa."

"Why not, for heaven's sake?" said Deep Dakron.

Sniff explained, "Because if we do he might fall apart, or do something rash with the tiller. Sometimes it's necessary to put the helmsman on a truth diet for his own good, and the good of the race."

"I knew it!" Dakron howled.

Sniff gave his helmsman a love tap.

A few tacks later, he resumed addressing the crew. "The last way we can get our skipper to relax and steer fast is by **taking care of business**. A winning effort comes from getting all of the details right. This means looking after all the distractions that helmsmen worry about: *Is the chute packed? Is the spinnaker sheet in the pole? Who is on the halyards? What's the course to the next mark? Is it a port or starboard rounding? Is my Coke still sitting on the bag of ice or has it rolled off into the corner?*

"The better we see to the details, the less we have to listen to the helmsman fussing. And finally, he'll understand that all he has to do is be silent, and steer."

Here, Sniff lowered his voice. "And sometimes we might even catch ourselves about to make a teensy weensy mistake, and correct it before the helmsman catches us. Once again, if we do our jobs right, there'll be no nasty surprises for the skipper."

"Here we are," said Dakron, closing in on the windward mark. "How are we doing?"

Sniff made a victory sign with sailing-gloved fingers. "We are in first place," he chortled. "Everyone, let's get ready for a bear-away spinnaker set."

After the spinnaker was up, Dakron glanced back at the fleet. "Why is everyone else rounding the mark to starboard?" he asked.

Scratchen Sniff's eyes popped. Frantically, he checked his pockets. "Whoops. Say, who has those sailing instructions, anyway?" he said.

"Give me that fly swatter," said Deep Dakron.

*Learn to use a racing language of specifics*

# SPECIFICALLY SPEAKING

Deep Dakron was in the groove. The slight weather helm transmitted a steady flow of signals, like an electric current, from the tiller up through his arm and back down through his seat, grounding him positively to the deck. Dakron's internal balance sensors were tuned to the angle between the headstay and the horizon, and his hand automatically moved the tiller extension to maintain the correct angle of heel.

It was all working. *Snafu*, his Meltdown 34, was moving quickly up the first beat of the Olympic course, sailing slightly higher and faster than his immediate peer group. Then, the buzz of conversation from the windward rail penetrated Dakron's concentration.

"Oh! Ooooooh! Heh-heh, look at *Frazzle*. They're cooked!"

"Parboiled!"

"Deep fried!"

*"Pssst.* How about those guys in the left corner? Looks like we're gonna be history next."

Deep Dakron shifted uncomfortably and asked no one in particular, "How are we doing?"

"Just steer!" two crew members snapped. Then:

"How can they point that high?" someone wondered.

"They're on the other tack, dummy."

"No, they are on *this* tack, buddy boy."

"Oh. So they are. Uh-oh."

Dakron cocked his head onto his shoulder and tried to reenter his trance-like state. He hit a wave, his boat speed dropped, and the windward rail buzz started up again.

"Anybody else think those guys are getting to us?" someone whispered.

"Nah! Well, I dunno. We don't seem to be going as good as we were."

"*Pssst,*" another voice hissed. "You talk about the boats on the left, take a look at the guys on the right."

"What boats? I don't see any . . . *no way.* How did they get *there?*" a voice gasped.

Dakron's mind snapped. The tiller extension slipped from his fingers and *Snafu* rounded up, the genoa shaking. "Would somebody please tell me," he said, "WHAT THE HELL IS GOING ON."

For the first time since the race began, a dead silence fell over *Snafu.* Then, from his trimmer position at the leeward genoa winch, the Kid, a lanky, shy 15-year-old, coughed and spoke up. In thirty seconds the Kid gave Dakron a detailed verbal picture of *Snafu's* position and speed relative to the boats nearby. Then he went on to describe how the fleet was spreading out over the racecourse, and *Snafu's* placement on the racecourse, noting some differences in angle and wind velocity between *Snafu* and the competition.

Dakron now had a mental sketch of what was going on, but his mouth, as did every mouth on the windward rail, hung open, speechless. No one had ever heard the Kid utter a complete sentence, let alone so many in one day, and so eloquently. What was more, the Kid was speaking in a foreign tongue, a language of specifics; he talked in boat lengths, in degrees of angle, he spoke using quantifiable numbers to describe the fleet distribution and wind velocity, and never once did he slip into the subjective, noninformational "We look good" or "We look bad."

And not only that, the Kid went right on talking.

"When I crew dinghies, one of my jobs is to keep track of the other boats and feed that information to my helmsman, a constant flow so he knows what's going on behind his back. We've got a system for nearby boats, so he doesn't have to watch them every second. Instead of saying, 'Smith is below us and Jones is above us,' I'll try to be as specific as I can with boat lengths and numbers and say, 'Smith is two boat lengths *down* and three lengths *forward*, and Jones is three lengths *up* and one *back*. This sort of puts the boats on a mental grid for my skipper—and for me. Then if something changes we pick it up right away, because we've given the situation a quantifiable description in the first place."

Dakron stared, slack-jawed. *Quantifiable*. He never dreamed that the Kid knew any five-syllable words, or that he could pronounce them, much less use them in a sentence.

The Kid continued, "Then, I keep an eye on boat speed and tell my helmsman how he's doing with his pointing and footing. I'll say, 'Jones has come *forward* one boat length, and *down* one in the last twenty seconds, but Smith has gone *back* one and *up* one.' So he knows he's going higher but slower than Jones, and lower but faster than Smith. Every so often I tell him who is making what we call the *net gain*, whether the boats that are sailing high and slow or the boats sailing low and fast are making the overall gain in the conditions. And I'll keep comparing their pointing angles relative to us: If we're outpointing them, I'll say, 'We are *bow up* on Jones a couple of degrees.' If we're pointing lower, I'll say, 'We are *bow down* on Smith a degree.' If we're pointing even, I'll say, 'We are *parallel*, or *same*.' Besides comparing our boat speed and sailing angle to our competition, we tend to spot shifts and puffs and lulls real quick that way."

No one said a word, and the Kid continued.

"Then, as the race progresses and the fleet spreads out, I'll update our placement relative to the fleet. I try to estimate whether roughly equal numbers of boats are to our left and our right, or whether it's more like 80% of the boats are on our left side and 20% are on our right. This helps us keep tabs on how the race is shaping up and helps keep us out of corners, or at least makes us realize how high our risk factor is getting if we start to sail off by ourselves. Besides all that, I keep an eye on boats in the extreme right and left corners. Are they headed or lifted relative to us? And most important, do they have more wind, the same, or less wind than us?"

On the windward rail, a few heads nodded. The headsail shivered, and Dakron pulled the tiller toward him.

The Kid said, "If I do everything right, if I keep looking around and updating my helmsman and myself, he can put his concentration into driving the boat fast. Besides, I can't feel the boat like he can, because I don't have the tiller, and I have a lot more free time to look around than he does, so this way we can both do our best at our jobs. I find that when I have the responsibility of describing a situation it makes me look more closely at it, and look more often, and then saying everything out loud helps me to keep it all straight in my own mind. From there, we both talk about what we should be doing tactically, weighing things up. Crewing this way is a lot more fun for me, because I contribute more to the winning."

The Kid noticed for the first time that Dakron and the crew were staring at him, and he flushed a deep scarlet. He looked down and pretended to rub a spot on the top of the winch.

Dakron thought, the Kid should be steering. We'd win then. Or at least the Kid should be calling the shots. Keeping tabs on the fleet. Feeding me information. Constructing that winning mental grid in my consciousness.

"For Pete's sake," Dakron said, "why haven't you ever said anything before?"

"No one asked me," the Kid said honestly.

"Well, would you like to say something now?"

"Yes," the Kid mumbled. "Very much."

*"Well?"* Dakron pressed.

"You're pinching again," said the Kid.

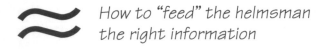 *How to "feed" the helmsman
the right information*

# DON'T LOOK NOW

**D**eep Dakron's head snapped back and forth on a nervous, three-second circuit from spinnaker to compass to *Pigeon Kicker*, close astern. Meanwhile, *Snafu* drew a snake-wake down the reaching leg.

"Are we okay? How's the spinnaker? Is our air clear? Are those guys behind going up on us? Should I head up or down? Where's the mark? Are we okay? How's the spinnaker? Is our air clear? Are those guys behind going up on—"

"Hold it!" said tactician Scratchen Sniff. "I'm going below."

Dakron's head caught for a second then continued on, like one of those battery-powered barking puppies you see outside department stores at Christmas.

Back on the rail, Scratchen Sniff popped a beer for himself and passed one to the Mumbler.

"Mr. M., I hereby appoint you downwind wind watcher," said Sniff in a grave voice.

"Oh! Aaaah!" replied the Mumbler, glad of something to do on what had been a rather dull downwind leg.

Sniff elaborated. "This vital task, while easy to learn, requires supreme dedication and concentration on the part of the downwind wind watcher. But your efforts can save us losing countless boat lengths, possibly even the race itself—." Here Sniff jerked a thumb in Dakron's direction. "Not to mention saving us having to listen to that racket."

The Mumbler nodded and grunted.

"As *Snafu*'s early warning system, your responsibility is to monitor and verbalize the opposition's movements so that we can sail as fast as possible while remaining ready to defend against or attack the other boat or boats. You'll use two techniques; the first is to talk in **boat lengths of clear air**, and the second is to report **bow up—bow down**."

Sniff paused to glare at Deep Dakron, whose head rotation and soundtrack seemed to be faltering.

Sniff went on, "First, the most important aspect of tactical downwind sailing is to know how many boat lengths of clear air (hereafter known as BCA) exist between you and your competition, particularly when they are threatening to cut off your wind from astern. I define BCA as *the number of boat lengths between the spinnaker shadow of the boat behind and the mainsail of the boat ahead.* On a dead run we'll try to figure in the mainsail shadow too, as best we can.

"Spinnakers throw a huge cone of dead and disturbed air in front of them, and the watcher's job is to estimate the position and length of this shadow. One way is to use the angle of the masthead fly of both your boat and that of the competition's as a guide to the spinnaker's blanket, but remember that on a tight reach the shadow will fall slightly farther aft than what the masthead indicator might lead you to believe.

"Another way of estimation is good old trial and error; try judging where the spinnaker's blanket cone will fall on various points of sail and in different wind strengths, and then watch in tight situations how close your estimates actually are. Most of the time you'll find that the spinnaker shadow is quite distinct in its width but much less defined in its length. Also, of course, a shadow that is closer is more potent and easier to judge than one that is farther away. One way to tell if the shadow is reaching you is when your sails relax or start to act funny, or just by feeling the disturbed air on your face."

"Hmmm," said the Mumbler, nodding.

Sniff found himself nodding too. "However, BCA can differ from the boat lengths separating the boats in question, depending on the positioning of the boats and the relative wind direction. For instance, on a pole-on-the-headstay-reach, BCA corresponds pretty closely to the boat lengths between boats; if your competition is one length behind, then their wind shadow will be about one length behind. But on a broad reach or run, where the spinnaker's wind shadow projects forward of the boat, the leading boat will need more BCA to stay clear of the trailing boat.

"Sure, the concept is rather basic, but your real mission as downwind wind watcher is to keep the helmsman constantly informed of his BCA when ahead and defending against an attacker astern, and, when he's behind and attacking the other boat, the BCA left between him and the boat ahead.

"Having a watcher reporting to the helmsman that he/she is three lengths, two lengths, or one and a half lengths safe makes it unnecessary for the skipper to keep turning around and looking. And, of course, this drives the skipper and crew of the other boat crazy; your skipper seems to know exactly what they are doing without ever looking back. No one, not even a good loser, likes to look at the back of someone's head while they sail away."

The Mumbler grunted and nodded.

Sniff nodded and grunted and said, "And the second part of downwind wind watching is keeping your helmsman updated on the **bow up—bow down** interplay between you and your adversary. Remember to talk about *your* boat's course relative to the competition, not about their course. For example, when you are sailing a course higher than that of your opponent, tell the helmsman that he is 'bow up' relative to them. When you are sailing a course lower than your opponent, report 'bow down' to the helmsman. You can also add degrees (such as 'bow up 5 degrees') to your reports; that helps your skipper visualize exactly what the competition is doing. And, of course, when you are sailing a course parallel to your opponent, let your skipper know that he is 'parall—' "

Sniff stopped. Deep Dakron's head rotated and his voice droned, getting slower and slower. Sniff considered the Mumbler for a moment, and said, "Maybe you'd be better off just saying something simple, like 'even' or 'same' when you're sailing parallel to the other boat."

The Mumbler grunted and nodded.

Sniff nodded, but caught himself before he grunted. "After you get good at this you can combine all the BCA and bow up—bow down information that a worried skipper needs to know in one breath: 'Two lengths, bow down 5,' for example. The beauty of this is that not only does it free the helmsman, it focuses a crew member full-time on the crucial job of watching the opponent's movements. What do you think, Mr. M.?"

"I think," said the Mumbler, jerking a thumb in Deep Dakron's direction, "that our skipper needs new batteries."

 PART TWO

# WATER AND WIND

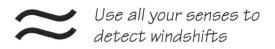 *Use all your senses to detect windshifts*

# SNIFFING OUT THE SHIFTS

Deep Dakron's crew smelled victory—a very, very rare victory—in the air.

As they rigged the sheets they fairly bubbled with excitement: the ultimate guest-star tactician, Scratchen Sniff, would be calling the shots today on *Snafu*, Deep Dakron's Meltdown 34. Scratchen Sniff's mysterious powers, his knack for always going the right way, his gift for sniffing out the shifts were legendary, and his reputation cut a wide swath ahead of him.

"He works a kind of voodoo with the wind," whispered one of the crew reverently.

"He has a sixth sense," agreed another. "Psychic."

"Magic," a third kept repeating. "They say he's the Wizard of Wind."

"It's that mustache," confided someone else, "and those nose hairs. Ultra sensitive. Temperature, moisture, barometric pressure. Nose hairs."

"No," said a crew who seemed to know. "*Ear* hairs."

While Deep Dakron didn't quite subscribe to voodoo, or the magical, mystical, or hairy origins of Sniff's powers, he had observed that whichever boat Sniff guest-starred on tended to look awfully smart. And better, even if Sniff's boat didn't win, the skipper never looked dumb. Oh! what Dakron would give for that! Dakron had scored a coup, luring Scratchen Sniff aboard for the Weekend Warrior Series, and he intended to watch Sniff closely and uncover his mysterious way with the wind.

At nine forty-five Scratchen Sniff bounded down the dock, handlebar mustache flying, and leaped through *Snafu*'s open transom. They were off!

The race went well. Following Dakron's usual mediocre start, Sniff dialed up several shifts and puffs and directed Dakron around the course to a rousing comeback and a stunning second-place finish.

The crew was exultant. Finishing second was, by *Snafu* standards, equivalent to a horizon job. Sniff's voodoo was powerful indeed; the shifts and puffs had seemed to come out of nowhere, and more often than not went their way, like magic. As the crew motored the boat back to the yacht club, Sniff disappeared below. Dakron, burning with questions, followed him down the hatch.

"Care for a tot?" Sniff offered, producing a flask of rum.

"Thanks," said Dakron. "You know, I was watching you all day, and, er, how did you do it? With mirrors? A puff magnet? I mean, those times you said, 'There's a shift coming,' or 'More wind ahead,' how did you know? None of us saw anything to indicate that. What's your secret?"

Sniff's eyes twinkled as he twirled the ends of his mustache. "It hurt your steering, you know, all that staring," he said merrily. "How did I do it? What's my 'secret'?" Sniff lowered his voice and said, "Many years ago, trekking the Himalayas, I took refuge in a snow cave, and met a wizened old guru who lived on nothing but wind, and he taught me—"

"Don't do this to me," Dakron pleaded, squishing his eyes shut. "Do it to my crew, not to me. I'm confused enough already about the mysteries of wind."

Sniff grinned. "All right, but you might find that story easier to believe than the truth I'm about to tell you. Like you, I've always been puzzled about wind, why it did what it did, and I've always thought it curious how little we sailors really know about the wind. Sure, the scientist-types rattle on about inversions, gust cells, and katabatic winds, and all that is useful to a point, but once you're on the water the theory stops and the sailing starts. And wind, that unseen, unpredictable, all-encompassing element of sailboat racing, is what it's all about. Squeeze your boat for that last drop of boat speed, but when that 20-degree shift comes through, boom!, you're either a hero or a has-been. Funny thing is, most sailors are so wrapped up in sailing that they don't notice or respond to the wind's signals."

"Funny, all right," said Deep Dakron.

"So for years now I've made a point of studying the wind. Not in a scientific sense, but in a physically intimate one: how the wind feels on my body. Studying the pressure of the wind on my face, skin, eyes, ears, the back of my neck, the hairs on my arms. I began feeling the different air temperatures in puffs and lulls, the bumpy airflows of puffs that stayed in one place and tumbled, the smooth airflows of puffs that moved across the water and fanned out. I'd notice when the sound in my ears varied, and even the smell of the wind, though I think this thing tends to overfilter that."

Sniff smoothed his mustache, and Dakron thought: Nose hairs. *Ear* hairs.

Sniff went on, "When we sail, the wind is a force that is all around us and pressing directly upon us. We just have to open up and feel that force. Remember *Star Wars*? Obi-Wan-Kenobi kept telling Skywalker, 'Feel the Force, Luke, feel the Force.' Before Luke opened himself up to the Force he was off target, out of phase, and Princess Leia thought he was a drip."

Deep Dakron looked on morosely.

"Right, I know, it all sounds pretty cosmic, but it's really just common sense. Different smells, temperatures, flows and pressures hitting your skin are the truest wind indicators, and at the slightest change in any of them you know instantly that the wind is up to something."

"And here I've been using my shroud telltale all these years," said Dakron. "Tough for a nylon ribbon to sniff out the shifts, I guess."

"Shroud telltales aren't sensitive enough," Sniff said. "No telltale is sensitive enough. I use my whole *body* as a telltale. Remember, when the wind died on the run, and I peeled off my shirt?"

"Man, it got *hot*," Dakron agreed.

"I didn't take my shirt off to cool down; I was putting my antenna out. It's a favorite trick of Buddy Melges. When the wind fizzles, Buddy whips his shirt off so he can feel the gentlest puff on his skin, and it works: Melges is amazing at finding and riding puffs you'd never see on the water. Well, that's what I try to do all the time—to raise my antenna and receive all the wind signals I can."

"Would the shirt trick work if you were wearing sunscreen?" Dakron asked.

Sniff said, "I believe that all top sailors, whether they are cognizant of it or not, depend on the physical signals the wind is giving them for their first signs of a wind change, both in velocity and direction. Ask the winner of the race why he tacked and he'll try to give you a concrete reason, such as the compass, but dig deeper and he might just admit that he responded to 'intuition,' or had a 'gut feeling' that the wind was beginning to change, and reacted to that. I feel that a lot of such 'feelings' are the unconscious rendering of the wind's message on our skins. So, the more receptors you have out, the more signals you receive, the better your interpretation of the wind. But top sailors rarely verbalize this 'secret weapon' of theirs."

"Why?" wondered Dakron. "Wait, I know: so we don't beat them. I *knew* they had a secret weapon."

Sniff shook his head. "Think of the repercussions of an America's Cup tactician telling his skipper, 'Gee, the little breeze that was doing curlicues on the back of my neck isn't tickling me there anymore, so I think we should gybe.' That tactician would be dropped quicker than a financially-challenged major sponsor. Yet the body is a supersensitive instrument. It's just a question of focusing on it and listening to it instead of depending solely on our eyes, or on pushing the usual buttons."

"No buttons?" said Dakron. "Then what would we do with all of our wind instruments and black boxes? I suppose some of it could be converted to car stereos."

Sniff ignored him and said, "You know how some world champs can detect a windshift or new breeze right before the start, when they're in the middle of the popcorn machine of a big fleet? I'm convinced it's their *wind equilibrium*. Even in all that confusion they maintain a connection to the wind, and if something changes, they sense it. Maybe it's the way the sun hits the sails, or something about the color and texture of the wind on the water, but it's that connection that's important. Any time I feel an inkling of change in my wind equilibrium I begin looking for what's coming next, and looking for things first is a big part of finding them before others do. Many times, I've noticed that the wind will ease, sometimes almost imperceptibly, before a windshift—and the hairs on my arms are the first thing to have told me. Amazing, that arm hairs could win a race for you."

"Or nose hairs, or ear hairs," Dakron was about to add, when *Snafu*'s motor raced in reverse and feet began thumping overhead, the crew yelling and throwing dock lines. Dakron knew that his interview with the fabulous Sniff was over; Sniff was equally famous for his quick exits.

Sniff hoisted his duffel and jumped through the open transom onto the dock. Dakron thought his crew, lined up on the deck, were going to salute.

"Sorry team, got to run," Sniff farewelled them. "I've got a feeling I'm in for something very special tonight up at the Rusty Furler happy hour," he said, grinning wolfishly.

"They say it's a kind of voodoo," whispered one of the crew, "and that it works for *everything.*"

When they looked up Sniff was gone, his only trace an air of mystery trailing behind him.

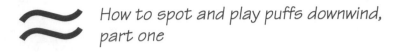 *How to spot and play puffs downwind,*
*part one*

# DON'T LOOK BACK

As *Snafu* rounded the windward mark, Scratchen Sniff dutifully eased the mainsheet till the boom was nearly to the shroud, then he cleated it. The master tactician then moved placidly amid the mark rounding noise and haste—agonized howls from the foredeck, screams from the cockpit, flailing elbows, Deep Dakron barking orders—and settled himself in a quiet spot on the stern.

Judging by his expression, Sniff considered the much-ballyhooed mechanics of mark rounding a necessary but rather distasteful part of yacht racing. During the time it took to get *Snafu* settled—the spinnaker up and pulling, the genoa dragged out of the water, the boat on course—Sniff had been looking aft intently. His handlebar mustache floated on the breeze.

"A word to the wise is sufficient," he said, turning forward to address the back of Deep Dakron's head, "but have you ever considered that clichés are the root of all evil?" Sniff paused, giving Dakron time to register his triple *entendre*.

Hunched over in steering concentration, Dakron grunted, never taking his eyes from their customary spot on the bow pulpit.

Sniff continued, "Take the worn out phrase 'Don't look back, someone may be gaining.' Trite and cutesy, to be sure, but some sailors seem to sail as if they believe it, and they get themselves into trouble that way, especially on downwind legs."

When Dakron made no reply, Sniff cleared his throat and intoned: *"The very type of downwind leg that we are sailing at this very moment."*

"Are you hinting that I'm sailing into trouble?" Deep Dakron said. "But I'm concentrating so hard."

"The only trouble is that since we've started this downwind leg, you haven't looked back once," said Sniff, "and behind us is where all the action is."

"But I have," Dakron protested. "I looked back to see where *Pigeon Kicker* rounded."

"Not good enough," sniffed Sniff. "You haven't been watching the wind behind. It's a simple matter of exercising some new muscles."

Sniff gave a sigh. "During the downwind legs on some boats I end up sounding like an aerobics instructor: *Twist* your neck and shoulders. *All* the way around. Now the other way. *Move* your eyes. Use that peripheral vision. *Watch* the wind. Swing your torso!' But it's a sad fact that most sailors are so used to looking forward that they don't spend nearly enough time watching behind them—crucial when sailing downwind.

"Ever raced a radio-controlled model boat? The best part is the great vantage point. Standing on the edge of the pond is like hovering above a normal race in a helicopter; you can see every approaching puff and lull clearly. Why do you suppose match racing skippers stand up so much when they steer?"

"To look better for the photographers?" ventured Dakron.

Sniff said, "Touché, but it's also a way to improve their vantage point. Standing up in the boat gives you a much wider and deeper perspective on the wind patterns, increasing your ability to see changes farther up the track. It's easier to turn around and look aft when you're standing, too. But if the skipper is uncomfortable watching aft, then a crew member should be assigned the responsibility."

"Perhaps I need a rearview mirror," said Dakron. "Sounds like I'm missing the forest for the trees."

"And meanwhile sailing yourself into a sea of clichés," Sniff noted. "There are four major wind groups worthy of serious neck rotation off the wind: **Streaks**, **lines**, **rollers** and **movers**. Movers are moving puffs that catch up with you as you sail down the course. Rollers are patches of tumbling wind that tend to stay in the same spot or else move very slowly for much of the leg. Lines are sweeping shifts that bring both a new direction and velocity, rearranging the tactics and boat positions of the leg.

"But let's start with my favorite, Numero Uno for off the wind puff watchers, the **streak.** Streaks look like they sound: long, narrow bands of increased velocity running with the direction of the wind. I think of them as rivers of wind flowing at a faster rate through the general flow of air. Streaks vary in width from half a boat length to a dozen boat lengths, but once you hook into a streak, you'll know it. It's as if you've picked up your own private air current, the way you'll start moving out on the boats around you."

"Otherwise known as 'streaking,'" said Dakron. "Or, life in the fast lane."

"Press your luck with another cliché and there'll be hell to pay," Sniff warned. "Streaks are indeed wondrous, but conditions have to be right; the wind has to be, well, *streaky*. Streaks occur naturally in long, narrow lakes and near obstructions which tend to funnel or channel the wind. But streaks can't be relied upon to be found in the same place or at the same strength every time. They come and go, and you've got to watch carefully for 'em. The tipoffs of a good streak are the length of it, the darkness of the catspaws, and the noticeably lighter air on both sides of it. The bigger the velocity difference between the streak and the lulls beside it, the farther and faster the streak's 'river' of wind is likely to flow—and all the more reason you should be riding that streak."

"When do I pay the piper for my ticket to ride?" said Dakron. "Give me the bottom line."

"When opportunity knocks," Sniff parried, "be in like Flynn. Basically, any nearby streak is worth chasing. This means gybing over, heading up, or even sailing by the lee to get into a streak. Once you've reached the streak, the key is to follow it carefully and stay in it. Immediate tactics can become secondary to staying with the streak; picking the closest gybe to the mark isn't as important as picking the gybe that keeps you running down the center of the streak. If despite your best efforts you find that your streak is dying, look for the next one.

"The best example of streak riding it's been my pleasure to witness came during the last race of a dinghy Nationals on a narrow, high-sided lake. The champ rode one streak from the top of the lake all the way to the bottom, while all about him the competition plowed through a series of puffs, lulls and mushy spots. The champ must have made eight gybes following that streak, but he piled up some impressive distance on the fleet."

"Really on a lucky streak," Dakron observed.

"Not by any stretch of the imagination," Sniff said. "Other boats sailed into the same streak, but because they failed to recognize it for what it was, they sailed right out again. Streaks don't always run straight; they can snake and zigzag. This, of course, ties in with the first step of putting your boat into a streak: unglue your eyes from the bow and twist your torso and neck around to see what's going on behind your back."

"I shall stand tall, and look back in anger," vowed Deep Dakron. "But what about lines, rollers and movers? Don't leave me out in the cold."

"Patience is a virtue," said Scratchen Sniff, "and good things come to those who wait. But to put clichés like these out of their misery, permit me the last word: Silence is golden."

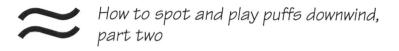 *How to spot and play puffs downwind, part two*

# PUFF PARANOIA

"**I** thought downwind legs were a time to relax," said Deep Dakron, wiping sweat from his brow with his non-tiller hand. "Are you sure we don't have any beer?"

"You *used* to think downwind legs were a time to relax," corrected Scratchen Sniff. "Technically, there is beer aboard, but since I moved it into the keel sump, the lowest part of the boat, underneath the floorboards and the heavy air genoas, we won't be able to get to it until after the race. But try this: open wide!"

Producing a tri-athlete's squeeze bottle, Sniff shot a stream of electrolyte replacement drink across the cockpit and into Deep Dakron's mouth.

"Mmphh!" Dakron gurgled. "I needed that."

"Especially when there's a **mover** coming up fast behind us," agreed Sniff. "What's a mover, you ask? Why, a mover is one of the reasons none of us can afford to relax off the wind. Simply, it's a puff, similar to the ones you play when sailing upwind, but this one is moving down the course from over our stern. Most movers behave the same as your garden variety puff; increased airflow comes down from aloft, hits the water and fans out in a spray pattern of catspaws, then gradually the puff fades as the whole thing moves along. The object, just as it is upwind, is to anticipate the direction of movement of the mover and to try to be in the right place at the right time to ride it."

"Not a problem for those of us exercising our eye, neck, and torso rotational muscles in a rearguard action," said Dakron.

"But, there's a trick," cautioned Sniff. "Most movers create and push a lull in front of themselves, which you will naturally want to avoid. So, it might not pay to take great pains to park yourself in the glide path of an approaching mover, because you may end up sitting too long in Lullsville, waiting. It might be better to try and rendezvous with the front edge of the puff; that way you can avoid as much of the lull as possible. There's also likely to be a lull following the mover; when your puff card has played itself out, head up and away quickly to make sure you aren't caught in the lull coming behind the mover."

"Movers sound tricky," said Dakron. "Like stock-index futures, or politicians."

"They're not half as tricky as **rollers**," promised Sniff. "Rollers look exactly like movers—those same enticing catspaws on the water—except that the darn things don't *move*. I'm no meteorologist, but roller puffs seem to be composed of air that tumbles in place instead of rushing down to the surface and fanning out. While there is increased wind inside a roller, as a whole it is stationary, or else moving too slowly down the course to be useful for any length of time. Rollers are basically not worth chasing, because once the chase is over the fun's over, too. Listen, there's nothing more soul destroying than positioning your boat for a puff that never arrives. It's worse than unrequited love."

Dakron nodded. "Amen. So how does one avoid the heartbreak of rolleriasis?"

"You, or one of the crew, such as myself, your trusty tactician, watch the sucker carefully to see if it moves," said Sniff. "The danger, of course, is that whenever we see a puff of wind on the water, our knee-jerk reaction is to assume that the gust cell is traveling. If it looks like a gust, smells like a gust, and feels like a gust, it has to *move* like a gust, right? Wrong. A roller is the mirage of the puff world. You keep telling yourself that the thing is getting closer and closer—so mouth-watering you can taste it—until you realize that, like for the proverbial man dying of thirst in the desert, the mirage is not getting any nearer."

"Are you sure we couldn't get just one beer out?" Dakron rasped, throat dry.

Sniff squeezed off a shot of electrolyte, hitting Dakron square in the chest, and continued. "I may be more sensitive than most," he allowed, stroking his mustache, "but I'd swear that the wind inside a roller feels different—kind of hot and cold and tumbly and buffety all at once—than the wind inside a mover, which feels clean and brisk and lined up. The game's not over if you sail into a roller, though; you'll sail out again, even gain on your competition who aren't as fortunate to have sailed into it. Just don't get sucked into chasing one, that's all. But the downwind wind phenomenon that sends my personal adiabatic lapse rate really plummeting is the **line**."

Here Scratchen Sniff fell silent, keeping watch astern while chewing nervously on the tube of the squeeze bottle.

"Lines are that devastating, huh?" asked Dakron, unsettled.

"They can be," Sniff said. "Like everything, it depends on what side of the line you're on. If we were to spot a line ahead of us, I wouldn't be too worried. But usually when you spot a line it's behind you, and that's trouble, brother."

"Why couldn't we just sail around it, or gybe away from it?" asked Dakron.

"There is no escape from a line," Sniff declared. "A line affects every boat on the leg, just like those damnable 'wall of death' fishing nets that scoop up every fish in their path. Besides, because there is increased wind in a line, the correct strategy is to sail toward it, not away from it. Visually, lines are unmistakable: a distinct dark band, often approaching at a marked angle to the prevailing wind, which it is about to change. Often there's a dead calm, a 'parking lot' ahead of and sometimes behind the line. Usually lines bring a new wind and a new direction that last the rest of the leg, the rest of the race, or even the rest of the day. The line itself is the *concentrated leading edge of a new wind*. The raw downwind truth is that boats to windward of the line will gain on or even pass those to leeward of it, simply by sailing down with the line. Such is the power and the centuries-old karma of the line."

"What you're saying is that whether you gain or lose comes down to luck," said Dakron.

"Luck," said Sniff scornfully, "is nothing more than the second most popular four-letter word sailors turn to when things go sour. We could explain everything away to 'luck' if we tried, but the concept is a dead-end in life and on the racecourse. At least karma gives us another shot at a white-on-white Mercedes in our reincarnation, assuming we behave ourselves. But—"

"But, you digress," Dakron cut in. "And you've given me a stiff neck, worrying about all these puffs."

"The main thing to worry about when a line appears is being caught out in the cold," Sniff advised. "Almost without exception, when you sail downwind and you see a line coming, you should do all that you can, short of tacking, to get to the nearest part of it as quickly as possible. This means gybing over, putting the pole on the forestay and reaching to get into it, if necessary."

"Why?" asked Deep Dakron.

"Because the boats that reach the line soonest will be enjoying more wind, and they'll be sailing in the *new* wind, which tends to sweep away all the boat positions previously established. You know, the leaders become tailenders, and vice versa."

Sniff paused and looked closely at Dakron. "You know what? You're wound tighter than a syndicate boss at a press conference. You should really try to relax a little."

"At least," Deep Dakron said through gritted teeth, "at least I'm not relaxed on the downwind legs anymore."

Sniff looked concerned. "Another hit of electrolyte?" he offered.

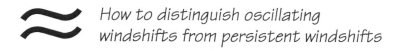 *How to distinguish oscillating
windshifts from persistent windshifts*

# HOT AIR

**"L**ife used to be so simple," sighed Scratchen Sniff, swinging his legs up and parking his yachting sneakers on *Snafu's* cockpit coaming. Deep Dakron glanced nervously at the salty shoes, then back to the jib telltales he was reading, anxious he'd lose his place.

Sniff said, "I mean, when I was young I'd just consult my copy of the 'Racing Sailor's Bible' and all the answers were in Chapter IX, Windshifts. It told me that there are two kinds of windshifts: **oscillating** and **persistent**. Black and white. You had one, or the other. Simple. You know, in a lot of ways the old-time morality was the easiest way to sail your ship through life."

Deep Dakron groaned. *Here we go,* he thought. Here I'm waiting breathlessly for the maestro's call on the windshifts—boats on both sides of us, one group looks good, then the other, then both—and I get an Acsop's fable.

"What do you mean?" asked Dakron, uncorking the genie.

"Well, the 'Racing Sailor's Bible' defines oscillating shifts as ones that go back and forth, and tells us that to be saved we must tack on each header and sail on each lift. Easy. Persistent shifts are defined as ones that keep going in one direction for the duration of the leg. To save yourself from damnation you sail toward the direction of the persistent shift, gladly suffering the penance of a prolonged header to gain the ultimate salvation of the lift."

"So, what's the problem?" Dakron wondered, noticing for the first time that he was sailing a header.

"The problem is, it's just not that simple," said Sniff. "The old morality play doesn't wash. These days, between ozone depletion and mirrored office buildings and all the asphalt in the cities making the hot air rise, we're seeing windshifts that aren't covered in the books. Bizarre, unexplainable stuff. It's the only time I envy the round-the-world racers; their wind may be full of sleet and snow, but at least it's *understandable*. For example, why do you suppose the boats on both sides of us are both sailing lifts around us?"

"Because we're unlucky?" ventured Dakron.

"Because we've got our old-time heads in the sand, that's why!" Sniff snorted. "Let's suppose that the present wind condition is what I call a **ratcheting** shift, one of the ozone-inspired nasties common today. Ratcheting shifts are impossible to predict, difficult to read, and require an iron will to deal with correctly."

"Explain," said Dakron, "before I have a nervous breakdown."

"A ratcheting shift is the sneaky hybrid of an oscillating and a persistent shift," said Sniff. "Neither fish nor fowl, Republican nor Democrat. It's persistent because it is shifting in one direction, but it is also oscillating because it ratchets back and forth as it goes. It's those teaser oscillations that can lure you into simply tacking on the headers, but if you don't eat some headers to get farther over to the side where the shift is going, you'll end up behind those who have. The first step in dealing with a ratcheting shift is in recognizing it.

"The best way is to keep close tabs on the wind's *median direction* (the average direction, the middle point between its swings right and left) and its velocity. In other words, in an oscillating wind pattern you'll normally be sailing to a range, such as tacking every time you're headed 5, 10 or 15 degrees, whatever the size of the shifts that day. So, your subconscious warning buzzer should go off when you are lifted or headed beyond that range: Something funny is going on. Same thing with velocity; if you or other boats start getting more or less wind than the range of velocity you've seen so far, watch out! The ol' ratchet may be waiting to grind you up."

"Wait a minute," said Dakron. "Aren't those the same signs you told me to look for to spot a persistent shift?"

"Yes, they are," admitted Sniff, "and here's the tricky part. When you start getting swings outside of the range of the normal shifts and/or velocity you've been seeing, *and* there are still good shifts to be worked on both to the right and the left, you are suddenly caught in the gray area between the black and white of oscillating and persistent shifts. Where you thought you had things figured out they've turned foggy, and you start getting fuzzy on whether to play the wind as back and forth or as going one way. So, who ya gonna call?"

"ShiftBusters!" said Dakron, revving the genie.

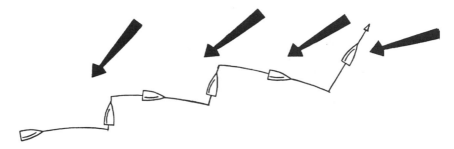

Not every windshift is either oscillating or persistent; the "ratcheting" shift is a hybrid. In this case, the wind is shifting persistently to the right, but oscillating as it goes. On port tack, stretch out the lifts as long as possible to work toward the starboard side of the course—the direction in which the persistent shift is moving. On starboard tack, ride the biggest puffs and lifts for a quick gain, then tack to port and continue toward the right.

"To illustrate, back to the here and now. We've been getting these tasty little starboard tack lifts beyond the range of the oscillating shifts of the first beat—good thing I wrote the high and low compass headings for both tacks on the bulkhead. There seems to be a bit more breeze in the starboard lifts as well, which could be the beginnings of a persistent shift toward the right side. Probably it will assert itself more and more, such as the sea breeze does when it fills in and pulls the breeze around. But—and here's the ratchet effect—we cannot just sail blindly toward the right side, because the left side is still showing signs of life in the form of lifts. If we ignore the port lifts, we lose out to the boats on our left."

"So why are we sailing a port tack header now, instead of a lift?" Dakron wondered.

"We aren't sailing a header," Sniff said grandly. "We're sailing the ratchet. Remember when we tacked onto port? Lifted 10 degrees, right? In order to work our way as adroitly as possible toward the right side, where we sense the persistent shift is moving, we are stretching the port lifts for all they're worth. That's why when we tacked onto port we started out with a lift and good velocity, and we'll keep riding it as far as possible, even to the point of sailing a relative header, until we begin losing *too* much angle and velocity. That's a sign of the starboard side wind's increased lift and velocity coming back into play, and time for us to jump onto starboard and ride *that* for awhile. Then when some of the velocity and angle start going out of starboard tack, we should think about getting back onto port again and heading deeper toward the right, in the direction the playing field is ratcheting."

"Sounds like we're sailing on a winch top," observed Dakron.

"Good analogy," said Sniff. "Port tack is each clockwise turn of the winch, and the 'click' of the pawls and anti-clockwise jog back is starboard tack. When that fresh breeze and lift from the starboard side hit, think of it as a 'click' of the winch, and time to take a jog back on starboard tack."

"But how do we know how much of a header to sail on port tack, and for how long?" asked Dakron.

"We watch the other boats religiously," Sniff explained. "If we see people on the right side getting more velocity and lift than we have been able to find over there, we start sailing more of a relative header on port tack to drag ourselves over there with them; the persistent shift may be taking precedence over the oscillating shift sooner than we had figured. Then, too, if the boats on the left appear to be hanging onto their lifts for longer than we reckoned, we should consider following suit. Why fight what's working? Books and theories are dandy, but I've yet to find any that are waterproof, or wind-proof. Look around carefully. React to what's happening. Leave your preconceptions and local knowledge on the dock. I've a feeling we're going to see everything in this race—and that's not a bad mindset to take into *any* race."

"I'd feel naked without my local knowledge," said Dakron, and thought: Is nothing sacred to Scratchen Sniff? "But at least now I feel like I know how to use the ratchet, that gray area between oscillating and persistent shifts," he added.

"Make sure you use the gray matter between your ears, too," Sniff said.

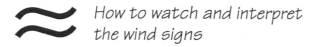 *How to watch and interpret the wind signs*

# RED LIGHT, GREEN LIGHT

**D**eep Dakron's eyes bugged out and sweat popped from his forehead.

"No! Please! Don't make me go in there! I'll do anything, anything but that! Just please, please don't make me go *in there.*"

"We are going in there," said Scratchen Sniff.

Dakron's steering hand began to tremble. "You know what they call this corner? 'Last Gasp Gulch.' The Race Committee sets the mark on the other side just so they can watch boats get sucked into the black hole. No wind! It's flypaper! The last person who cut this headland too close stayed there until the next weekend's race. Can't you *see* there's no wind? We'll lose everything, we'll—"

Sniff cut him off. "Steer the boat," he commanded, "and steer it calmly. The light ahead may be red, but by the time we get there the light will turn green. I've been watching the situation closely, and our timing is about right."

"Red light? Green light?" said Deep Dakron. "Wha—"

"Haven't you ever noticed," Sniff cut in again, "how the wind can make sailboat races resemble the ebb and flow of traffic? When the wind is steady and the course is wide open the race becomes a drag race, a burn down Highway 61. But when the wind is spotty and the course is full of twists and bends—as with this wind-obstructing headland—the race and the driving get trickier, like Manhattan around East 44th Street. Boats bunch up at intersections and lose precious time and distance getting stuck in the slow lane. Tempers and concentration levels become frazzled, and it's all because drivers, I mean sailors, don't correctly anticipate the lights."

"This may come as a surprise, but I do not see these lights of which you speak," said Dakron, eyeing the calm ahead.

Sniff exhaled. "They're figurative, of course. To me, red lights and green lights are those wind signals—catspaws on the water, the direction of smoke and flags, the sail trim of other boats—that tell me how to approach the next 'intersection' of the racecourse, and whether my timing will be right to whizz through the intersection without getting stuck. But because you are blinkered by 'local knowledge,' it is unlikely you'd see these lights even if they were flashing in front of your face. Take 'Last Gasp Gulch,' for example."

"I'd rather not," said Deep Dakron.

"To you, the light is always red because local knowledge tells you that it is 'always' dead, no wind in there. So you aren't watching this intersection anywhere near as carefully as you should; you've already assumed that a wide berth is best. You are seeing only what you expect to see. And trust me: **assuming** and **not watching** are dangerous, even fatal things to do in a sailboat race."

"But there's no wind in there!" Dakron protested. "Even I can see that."

"But you haven't been *watching,*" said Sniff, "and that's the difference. I have been watching, and I've observed that today the gulch has plenty of gasps left in it. This particular geographical combination of headland and bay fills and flushes with wind like a pool in a mountain stream; it fills up slowly with stagnant wind and then periodically overflows with a rush, flushing itself empty, then filling up slowly again. Even if we have to wait a bit, it's likely quicker than sailing a wide berth around it. There's a very good chance the gulch will flush us just as we get there."

Deep Dakron flinched. "What a choice of words."

Sniff reasoned, "Besides, it's too late to turn back. Here we go!"

The genoa backed suddenly against the shrouds and the main boom flew across the centerline as *Snafu* sailed into the windless hole. Deep Dakron yanked on the tiller extension to make *Snafu* fall off, but found Sniff's foot braced firmly against the tiller.

"Keep the tiller in the middle," Sniff whispered. "That's just our momentum making the sails back, not a windshift. Steer straight and preserve your speed. In a few moments the sails will fill again."

After long seconds the sails did refill, but with only very faint air.

"Uh-oh . . ." Dakron groaned.

"Wait for it," whispered Sniff. "*Watch* for it . . . soon it'll be time for the light to change . . . ease the sails out, get the flow reattached . . . most people stay stuck in holes because they keep their sails in too tight . . . the genoa too tight means the main will be overtrimmed, too . . . pretty soon we shut down the airflow over the entire sailplan . . . that's it . . . ease the genoa, more, more, way out, make it luff . . . that's not a luff, that's just the sail bouncing, you're being tricked . . . ease it more . . . there . . . now, bring it back in s-l-o-w-l-y . . . we don't want to stall her . . . now ease again . . . even if *not* in doubt, ease it out . . ."

"I've downshifted all the way to first gear. Should I get out and push?" said Dakron, adding, "I don't like this."

"Of course you don't!" Sniff snapped. "Your local knowledge, your preconceptions have handcuffed your sailing. I say that each day should be seen—*watched*—with fresh eyes. Even when the wind is from the 'same' direction it doesn't blow the same way every time, and this is the trap of local knowledge. Current flow is more predictable than the wind, but think how many times you've been surprised there, too. People get so used to the crutch of local knowledge that they only look for what they expect. You, for example, didn't see any wind in the gulch because you had already *assumed*— even before you left the dock—that there wasn't any. And during the race you aren't watching anyway—your local knowledge has already given you the answer."

"I'm just playing the odds," Dakron retorted. "There's never, I mean, there's hardly ever any wind in here. "

"When you play poker, do you keep track of the cards with your eyes open or closed?" asked Sniff. "I prefer to keep my eyes wide open. I'll use a magnifying glass if it helps me stay ahead of the game. See those boats on the other side of the bay?"

"Those specks?" asked Dakron, squinting. "How can you tell what tack they're on?"

"I use an antiquated technique, lately out of favor with today's high-tech racers, called 'looking through binoculars,'" Sniff said, proudly holding up his binoculars. They were top quality, emblazoned with 'SNIFF ONLY' and a skull and crossbones. "Most valuable, these 'long eyes,' but you must remember to hold them up to your eyes. Anyway, those specks across the bay are sailing in a new wind which will shortly turn our race upside down."

"I see, I see," said Deep Dakron.

"I *watch*, then I see," said Scratchen Sniff.

"But I still don't see any wind in the gulch," said Dakron. "All I see is . . . *a puff.*"

Sniff cackled, "Green light! We're about to be flushed."

As *Snafu* heeled Deep Dakron thumped the deck with his fist. "Second gear! Third gear! Fourth gear! I'm exhausted. What could be more nerve wracking than this?"

"The next leg," said Sniff.

"But isn't that only downwind?" asked Dakron.

"Downwind," agreed Scratchen Sniff, "but never downplayed. You'll see."

Dakron pounced. "No, I'll *watch.*"

"Well, we'll see," Sniff said.

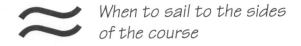 *When to sail to the sides
of the course*

# BEGGAR'S BANQUET

**S**cratchen Sniff's mustache quivered.

Which was peculiar, because although yacht club bars are noted for hot air, there is rarely enough wind to ruffle a handlebar mustache, especially one as luxurious as Sniff's.

"I sense a disturbance in the Force," Sniff muttered. "Somewhere, a racing yachtsman's strategy has come horribly unraveled. Somewhere, a racing yachtsman has tumbled and come face to face with the Dark Side."

"Here!" said Deep Dakron, seated behind a half-empty beer across the bar. "Right here. And I wish it were the Dark Side I faced today. At least it would have only been *one* side. "

"You mean?" Sniff recoiled, his face painted with horror.

"Yes," said Dakron.

"No!" Sniff pleaded.

"Yes," Dakron repeated. "Today I did everything right on the first beat, I sailed according to the Gospel of Sniff. I took no chances, I sailed conservatively, I played the odds in the middle of the racecourse, stayed out of the high-risk corners. I kept my eyes open and worked every shift and puff till they screamed, and can you guess what happened?"

Sniff flinched. "I share your pain."

"What happened," Dakron went on, "is that the boats from the right side *and* the boats from the left side came out of the mists and met in a joyous, backslapping first place at the weather mark while I, drenched in sweat from working every 5-degree shift up the middle, was so far behind I couldn't even read their sail numbers."

Sniff turned his palms up. "You have my complete and utter commiseration."

Dakron glared, then clicked the countdown button on his watch.

"You have ten minutes for an explanation. Nine minutes and fifty-nine seconds. Nine minutes and fifty-eight seconds."

Scratchen Sniff punched his watch. "First, a history lesson," he said.

Dakron said, "It had better be an abbreviated one."

Sniff said, "Ever since Tactical Man stood up on his hind legs and waded out of the primordial ooze of yacht racing ignorance and into the modern era, one thing has continued to annoy the hell out of him: How can the right side and the left side of a racecourse *both* win? One or the other, sure, but both? It boggles the mind."

"Nine minutes, fourteen seconds," said Dakron.

"Eons of yacht racing history have demonstrated that over the length of a series it is the conservative, risk-minimizing middle course that most often adds up to a regatta-winning scoresheet. And common sense, Geometry 101 and the roulette tables at Vegas all tell us that only red or black, only right or left, only one high-risk side or the other can possibly win at one time. So how the devil is it possible that both sides can pay off at once while the middle languishes in limbo?"

"Purgatory," corrected Dakron.

Sniff said, "Let me illustrate with an example from my past. This goes back a ways, back when it was okay to just grab a bunch of friends and go racing. Back before you needed a budget, media campaign, sponsors, a multi-boat testing program, videotaped practice sessions and Gucci crew shirts just to cast off your dock lines."

Dakron said, "This sounds positively Cro-Magnon."

Sniff continued, "In this antediluvian state, my friends and I started a race, hit the first few lifts and found ourselves doing darn well. The fleet soon grouped itself into a bunch to our left and a bunch to our right. The wind was back and forth, back and forth, big shifts, and going up and down quite a lot in velocity as well. Every shift was accompanied by a long-lasting and dramatic jump or drop in the velocity, depending on which way the shift went.

"As usual, we seemed to be picking off boats on both sides, because they would lose in a big way whenever their side crashed, due to the crushing geometry of high-risk high leverage (the farther a boat is out in the corner of the course, the more it loses in an unfavorable shift)."

"The Force was with you," said Dakron.

"It was!" Sniff agreed. "But then we met the Dark Side—or sides. For we began to realize that although the boats on either side of us appeared hugely hammered in their respective headers, they enjoyed extremely harmonious moments in their respective lifts that, in time, delivered them into the sunshine of victory. Meanwhile, I was stuck underneath the banquet table, scrambling for crumbs."

"Crumbs?" said Dakron.

"Crumbs. The measly crumbs of puff and lift that trickled through to the middle. You see, every time the wind shifted to the left, the group of boats to the left got more of a lift than I did, *and* they also got more wind velocity than I did. In effect, because they were above and inside me, they got more of the good stuff. And not only more, they got it *sooner* and it lasted *longer* for them than it did for me."

"The old double whammy," said Deep Dakron. "But what happened to the left side boats when the wind came in from the right?"

Sniff drew a forefinger across his throat. "They fell hard, of course, and looked absolutely terrible. But because they had previously enjoyed *more lift* and *more wind* both *sooner and longer* than poor middle me, they had rolled up a handsome gain that saw them through the bad times. They had leapfrogged, climbed a full ladder rung toward the top mark while I moved up only half a rung."

Dakron said, "So when the lefties' wind shifted to the right they looked bad, but coasting on their newly earned left side dividends, they survived the recession."

Sniff nodded and said, "And meanwhile, the group of boats on the right side enjoyed more wind and more lift, sooner and longer— are we seeing a pattern here?—and climbed a ladder rung past middlish me. Again, I was left with only crumbs. So that's how it went; right, left, right, left, the groups on both sides scooted past my unbelieving eyes like a fast-forwarding video. I was forced to identify the leaders by their spinnaker colors, and also forced to assess my sailing-the-middle strategy."

Dakron asked, "So why did you get only crumbs?"

Sniff shrugged. "Because that was what the wind was parceling out that day. The shifts were coming in from the left and the right in the form of large, slow-moving but potent puffs. It could be that the puffs were shaped more like wind lines than round-type puffs, because the boats farthest 'inside' or to windward in the lifts/puffs got more benefit sooner, better, and longer than did those of us to leeward. In this particular wind condition—streaky, concentrated, hitting the edges of the course first—you had to be where the action was, which was definitely not in the middle, to leeward of the puffs from *both* sides."

"And in hindsight . . . " prompted Dakron.

"In hindsight I should have recognized that something strange was going on when boats I thought I had buried kept coming back to haunt me. Edging forward, getting a rung up, a net gain on me every time it was their turn, and me not getting mine back when it was my turn. My alarm buzzer should have gone off when my astounded eyes spied boats to windward of me, whichever tack I was on, enjoying bigger puffs and bigger lifts—"

"And enjoying them sooner and longer," finished Dakron. "So what should Tactical Man have done?"

"He should have said, 'Okay, I'm sick of crumbs: the edges of the racecourse are where the action is. I must work my way over to whichever edge looks best and take my seat at the banquet. It's time to join the rest of the adults at the big table.'"

Dakron's eyes sparkled. "If a little is good, then more must be better. Why not be first in line and grab a seat in the corner? Extreme right or left corner, that is."

Sniff shook his head. "I'm no glutton. It's enough for me just to be in with a group playing the edge, as long as I'm getting the benefit. If the first beat (or the second, or third, or the run) ended in a two-mile-wide line squared to the average wind, then working from a corner would be less risky. But the problem with the extreme corners is that the windward leg ends in a single point known as the windward mark. Coming into this point, one side will win and the other will lose—usually on the last shift at the last second. So, even in a wind condition that favors the edges it's smart to hedge your bets just a little bit."

"Control the appetite," said Deep Dakron, "or else you'll miss dessert. But I'm a dessert first kind of guy."

"That's the Dark Side in you," said Scratchen Sniff.

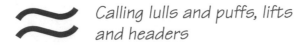 *Calling lulls and puffs, lifts and headers*

# REALLY, TRULY CONNED

"**A**re we lifted or headed?" Deep Dakron asked his tactician, Scratchen Sniff, in a voice woven with anxiety. After all, with *Snafu* this far up in the fleet, every shift was life-or-death.

"We are lifted *and* headed," Sniff reported.

"What?" Dakron said. "Impossible. We've got to be either one or the other."

"Not necessarily," Sniff countered. "Just a moment ago we were headed, but not *really* headed, and before that we were lifted, but not *really* lifted. Right now we are lifted *and* headed, but, in actual fact, we are neither."

Dakron sighed. "Obviously my question was too simple to elicit an answer I could understand," he said, managing to hold a civil tone. "I'll try another tack: What does the compass say?"

"Don't believe the compass," warned Sniff. "The compass is a con. Those blue and white numbers on the almighty rotating dial are not black and white, if you follow me. The compass doesn't tell the whole story. The 'good' numbers (lifts) fill you up with false confidence and the 'bad' numbers (headers) panic you into making a rash decision. In short, the compass does not work."

"It worked *last* weekend," said Dakron. "Don't tell me I need to buy a new one?"

"Oh, the compass still indicates the direction the boat is pointing," Sniff said, "but that's about all. In all other important matters the darn thing remains its blind, mute, inscrutable self. Even, as I have noted, when we are headed but not *really* headed, when we are lifted but not *really* lifted, and when we are both headed and lifted at the same time."

Dakron groaned. "Okay, I give. Uncle."

Sniff rubbed his hands together.

"Tell me why my compass is a con," said Dakron.

"Soon all will be really, truly apparent," promised Sniff. "You see, the compass is unable to differentiate between a *puff* and a *lull*, and as everyone knows, the effect of a puff on how a boat sails is totally opposite to that of a lull."

Dakron nodded. "Sure. We heel in a puff and we straighten up in a lull."

Sniff nodded. "Sure, but more importantly, because increased wind velocity increases the efficiency of our sails and raises our boat speed, and decreased wind velocity decreases the efficiency of our sails and consequently slows our boat speed, which reduces the efficiency of our underwater foils, we must remember that, *when sailing to windward, in a puff we will point higher, and in a lull we will point lower.*

"Thus, even when the wind direction is holding steady we will experience a 'lift' with every puff and a 'header' with every lull. These aren't true lifts and headers, or shifts in the wind direction—that's why I told you we weren't *really* lifted or headed—but they are known as **velocity lifts** and **velocity headers**. The degree of course change you'll experience depends on the amount of increase or decrease in wind velocity and the type of boat you are sailing. The sailing angles of a high-performance catamaran, for example, are extremely sensitive to fluctuations in wind strength, whereas a heavy, low-performance keelboat is much less affected.

"As a general rule when sailing to windward, a solid puff will result in about a 5-degree—could be more, could be less—'lift.' In a major lull you'll get a 5-degree or so 'header.' But definitely, even if it doesn't add up to 5 degrees, the change will be significant enough that your tiller hand won't fail to notice the 'lift' or 'header.' And I'll bet that the first place you'll look to confirm that you are lifted or headed is the compass."

"Of course," said Dakron. "Everybody does. And what's wrong with that?"

Sniff raised a qualifying forefinger. "Nothing, as long as your search for the truth doesn't end there. *Any time you experience a course change, you should look for a possible change in wind strength*, which may be the underlying cause behind it. Most times it won't be too hard to find; look at the wind on the water, your angle of heel, the feel of the helm, the set of your sails. Has this course change been heralded by more wind, or less wind? In other words, do your best to sort out whether you are experiencing a velocity lift or a velocity header, or a true windshift."

"Why?" said Deep Dakron. "A course change is a course change. What difference does it make what caused it?"

Sniff's forefinger went up again. "Plenty, and this is why. Say you are sailing merrily along on starboard tack, when suddenly you hit a lull. The drop in wind velocity results in a velocity header which convinces you to tack on what seems like a 5-degree header. You tack over onto port, but what do you find? Another 5-degree header! Now you've made an unnecessary tack, a slow, costly tack in a lull, and you're still not heading any closer to the mark than you were before the initial 'header.' All you are doing is sailing wider apparent wind angles on both tacks; the true wind direction hasn't shifted, the velocity has just dropped."

"I've done that little gambit," Dakron admitted. "It's called 'tack and die.'"

"We've *all* done it. So, just as tacking on the wider apparent wind sailing angles of a velocity header will not get you to the windward mark any quicker, neither will mistaking the 5-degree 'lift' of a velocity lift for a true shift in the wind direction help your overall windshift strategy. Since the wily ways of wind velocity changes can get confusing, I've written this little note to myself about the puff/lull/sailing angle/true wind relationship."

Sniff produced a rumpled pocket notebook and opened it for Dakron. Keeping one eye on the telltales, Dakron read:

| | | |
|---|---|---|
| Lull with 5° Compass Header | = | NO WINDSHIFT |
| Lull with 10° Compass Header | = | 5° TRUE HEADER |
| Lull with No Compass Change | = | 5° TRUE LIFT |
| Puff with 5° Compass Lift | = | NO WINDSHIFT |
| Puff with 10° Compass Lift | = | 5° TRUE LIFT |
| Puff with No Compass Change | = | 5° TRUE HEADER |

"It's hardly the whole story," said Sniff, snapping the notebook shut, "but I find it helpful to look at now and again so I can remember which combinations of velocity and angle change to consider tacking on, which to carry on through, and which combinations are apt to con me into doing the wrong thing."

Dakron looked dubious. "Very slippery stuff. How am I supposed to think about this while I'm sailing? Don't I have enough on my mind?"

Sniff said, "The easy way to look at it is this: Puffs (velocity increases) *that are accompanied by no compass change or a slight header in the compass heading are likely candidates for tacking on,* because the true wind direction has headed you. Likewise, lulls

(velocity decreases) *that are accompanied by a compass header greater than what you usually get from just the effect of a lull 'heading' your boat mean that a tack may be in order.*

"You can be indecisive and hang fire on all the other combinations of velocity and compass change because they either mean that the true wind is not shifting or else it is lifting, and a tack is not in order. The important thing is not to be lulled into tacking when you are headed but not *really* headed, and not to start thinking you are lifted when you are not *really* lifted."

Now Dakron raised a forefinger. "So when I'm not really headed but truly lifted I'll keep going until I'm not really lifted but truly headed, unless I get really and truly lifted."

"Hmm," Sniff pondered. "Run through that again? I'd better write this down."

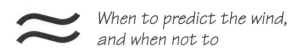 *When to predict the wind, and when not to*

# PREDICTION? REACTION!

"**W**hat's the wind going to hit us with next?" asked Deep Dakron, wrung out at the end of *Snafu*'s tiller extension.

"Dunno," answered tactician Scratchen Sniff.

Dakron tried again. "What do you *think* it's going to do next?"

"Dunno," repeated Sniff. Absentmindedly, it seemed to Dakron.

"If you had to guess," wheedled Dakron, "which way would you say the wind is going to shift next?"

"Dunno," said Sniff.

"If you had to *bet* where the wind is going to come from, which way would you bet?"

"I never bet," said Sniff.

Desperate, Dakron unleashed the bomb: Guilt. "As our esteemed tactician, don't you have *any* kind of a plan for this race?"

"Nope," said Sniff.

Dakron snorted. "You mean you're content not to make *any* predictions about what the wind is going to do? You're willing just to let us sail along without *any* plan? Just exactly what kind of an idle tactician *are* you?"

"A smart one," said Sniff, "and I'm not idle. I'm just rehearsing for the next act."

Dakron said, "Next act? This is real life. A real race! And if we don't connect with the next windshift, our act is history."

Sniff said calmly: "A sailboat race is like theater. We aboard this boat play the part of the protagonist, naturally. Our competitors are cast in roles from villains to bit players, everything but a love interest. And the stage, of course, is the ever-changing wind and water of the racecourse, upon which this drama—or comedy, or mystery—will unfold."

Dakron looked incredulous.

Sniff went on, explaining, "But unlike theater, about half the 'acts' in a yacht race are rehearsed and about half are improvised, according to the way the 'play' takes shape. The way the play evolves depends upon how the players play off each other and—more to my point—what that magnificent stage of wind and water serves up."

"Hark! Do I hear the curtain rising?" cried Dakron.

"Act One, Scene One," Sniff confirmed. "The heroes of this play—that's us, we're the heroes out here—have embarked on a valiant quest to wrest the holy grail of the Weekend Warrior Series from the clutches of the infidels. Our heroes know their lines well, at least those which can be rehearsed: the mechanics of tacks, gybes, spinnaker sets, the positions and rounding order of the marks, how many sandwiches are onboard, etc., etc. But our heroes also know they must be adept at the street theater of improvisation because—"

"Ta-da!" Dakron trumpeted.

"Because the wind and the other players are notorious for ruining best-laid plans. So, our heroes will try to predict what the wind and their competitors will do, which is a noble pursuit, up to a point. But unless their fellow players and the great stage of wind and water actually *are* extremely predictable (such as occurs when everyone scuttles off to one side of the course to reap the benefits of a predictable current flow, or the like-clockwork strengthening and shifting of a sea breeze) our heroes know that deep down in their gut—"

"Ta-dah-da-da-dah!"

"They know that they will be faced with making some very tough choices between using a sailing strategy based on **prediction** and one based on **reaction**. Now, prediction is exactly that: based on past experience and present indicators, our heroes will try to *predict* what is going to happen with the wind and the competition and place themselves in the right place at the right time (which usually means *ahead* of time). Reaction, however, is quite the opposite; our heroes will not attempt to foresee what the wind or their competitors will do, but will endeavor to place themselves in the best possible position—one with the minimum potential for loss—and thus be ready to *react* to whatever the wind and the infidels may do."

"So what will bring home the grail for our heroes?" asked Dakron. "Prediction? Or reaction?"

"Each will have its moment in the spotlight," said Sniff, "though personally I am quite happy practicing reaction, which you have already noted. Prediction is a risk-taking, aggressive style of sailing which, like *Jeopardy!*, is predicated on interpreting tricky clues to guess the tricky answer, all, of course, before you are allowed to see the question.

"Prediction can work very well, *if* you can beat these 'ifs': if you really, *really* know the conditions (as in my tide and sea breeze examples); if you really, really know what your competitors will do; if the high risk is worth taking for the high gain (in other words, you need a top finish to stay alive in the series); and quite simply, if you are really 'on' that day—and you *know* you are on—go for it, because you'll probably make prediction work.

"Reaction, on the other hand, is a risk-minimizing, defensive style of sailing. Reaction will work for you if your situation includes these 'ifs': if you don't know what the wind will do next, or what the current is doing or will do next; if you need a respectable finish but don't *have* to have a winning finish to stay alive in the series; and if you are just plain 'off' in the speed and smarts departments that day, then dig in and curb your losses with reaction."

"What a drama! And what a searing choice for our heroes," Dakron said. "Make the charge to glory and/or annihilation? Or beat a retreat to the sensible but cowardly mediocrity of the trenches?"

Sniff spun the idle windward genoa winch a few times. "You, sir, overdramatize the gulf between prediction and reaction, but each style of sailing does have its adherents. The nonconformist predictite, for example, is usually seen 'sailing his own race,' which more often than not takes him deep into the corners of the course, extra high or low on the reaches, and generally into such places on the course relative to the other boats that he will be a big winner *if* (there's that 'if' again) his predictions come true.

"The predictite believes he is gifted with an above-average 'wind sense' and an intuition that tells him which moves are 'right' and 'wrong.' He leans too heavily on local knowledge and his familiarity with his competitors, is willing to take the long odds on the strength of a hunch, and tries to stretch the art of prediction to desperate levels when he is tail end Charlie. Once in a while, fortune smiles on one of these desperate flyers, but in general the predictite does much better when he is 'on' and has a handle on the wind and current. Then when he wins he looks double-smart."

Sniff proceeded to spin the genoa winch loud and long, much to Dakron's irritation. "By comparison, the reactite is quite a cautious soul. He operates from the premise that he simply doesn't *know* what will happen next, and thus spends his time looking for clues rather than formulating and pursuing predictions. He tries to think of all the possibilities that could happen, and what would happen to him in each case, instead of counting on only one good thing to come true. Instead of sailing his own race he tots up the odds, keeps track of the good players (especially those he has to beat in that race) and tries not to get hurt. But you can believe this of our mild-mannered reactite: he has won plenty of championships sailing this way, because he very rarely bombs out in any one race, ruining the series."

"So who will be the true hero of this drama?" asked Dakron. "The predictite or the reactite? What choice will our protagonist, namely us, make? The suspense is killing me."

"The answer, dear Dakron, lies within. On any chosen day we can sail as either predictites or reactites. We make the choice and we live with the consequences, but the main thing is to remember that we *have* a choice, and to make a conscious decision," said Sniff, spinning the winch and ratcheting it back and forth:

Whir-ring! Ka-chiing! Ka-chiing-ching-ching!

Dakron looked down from the telltales in extreme annoyance. He opened his mouth, then decided not to say anything.

"Oh, don't worry about me," said Scratchen Sniff. "I always get a little nervous right before the curtain goes up."

 *Racing in up and down winds*

# WHEN THE PRESSURE IS ON—AND OFF

**D**eep Dakron stared into the foam of his beer mug. "I believe I am losing my grip," he muttered to no one in particular.

On the next stool, Zig Zag Brooke threw his hands up and nearly fell off. "Hell, man, don't lose your grip! Ever seen a yacht club beer mug explode? Shrapnel city, let me tell you."

Brooke lifted his chin and ran a finger over a faded scar. "See this? Weekend Warrior Series of '78." He pulled a shock of gray hair aside and revealed a line of stitches. "Spring Series of '91. Been through the wars, a combat veteran. Look, if you're going to go down, go down like a yachtsman. Fall off your stool, sure, but never lose your grip."

Dakron looked up wearily. "It's not my beer mug I'm dropping. It's races."

Brooke checked his watch. "Well, another happy hour is history," he said mournfully. "Guess I might as well listen to your story. It's *hell* having the best hindsight in the business. I get *tired* of telling people, 'I told you so.' Sometimes, all the *fun* goes out of explaining to people how stupidly they've sailed."

Brooke took a sip of rum and pulled his back-up into range. "Course, you just might prove to be the exception. What's your problem?"

"My problem is, whatever I do, I can't win," sighed Dakron. "If I try to tack on lifts, then my competition finds puffs and roars by me on boat speed. If I try to sail after the puffs, my competition goes *around* me on the lifts. I can't even get a break on the sail back into the club."

"Mmm," murmured Zig Zag Brooke. "Sounds like when the pressure is on you're into it, but when the pressure is off you're out of it."

"Huh?" said Deep Dakron.

"Pressure, man! Wind strength! Velocity! That's where you're going wrong. You are not giving pressure the proper priority. Always remember Zig Zag's Golden Rule: *When you're sailing below the threshold, make pressure the priority. When you're sailing above the threshold, make windshifts the priority.*"

"Threshold?" blinked Dakron.

Brooke tinkled his ice cubes. "Threshold is just my pet name for the point at which your boat shifts from first and second gear into third and fourth. You know, from being underpowered and crew off the rail in the soft stuff to fully powered up and the crew hiked out in a fresh breeze. Below the threshold is light air; above the threshold is moderate breeze and on up."

"Oh," said Dakron.

"So, in light air, make sailing to the puffs, make finding the most pressure on the course a higher priority than tacking on windshifts. There are lots of reasons for this. In light air, pressure moves down the course very slowly. Consequently you'll spend more time, sometimes most or all of a leg, sailing in one or two hunks of pressure. In light air the wind speed can literally double in the puffs, and your boat speed can jump half again or twice that of competitors who aren't in the pressure. The massive difference between being in pressure and being out of it just obliterates all else. A healthy dose of pressure makes someone else's 10-degree lift look like the booby prize."

"And how am I supposed to *find* this pressure?" Dakron asked.

"Well, that's the hard part. The chronic eye and brain strain of puff location sends many yachtsmen into Puff Rehab. Can't take the pressure. One technique which works for those people who have trouble seeing wind is to work backwards by process of elimination; first look for the areas of *least* wind pressure: *Oh, not looking that good to the left . . . Okay, a definite desert scene in the middle . . . I guess the right isn't so bad after all; most of the pressure is on the right.* Compare area to area, and note the absence of catspaws, the lack of heel in the boats or the limpness of their sails. Then, make your commitment. *In the light stuff, you can't wait for the puff to come to you; you have to sail to the puff.* When you're *almost* there you will probably get a glorious header, tempting you to tack. *Don't.* Remember: you have to get *into* the pressure."

"And then?"

"And then just don't do anything dumb, like sail yourself back out of it. Tack to stay in it, gybe to stay in it, just stay with the pressure and ride it as far as you can, ride it to the next patch of catspaws coming down the track. Don't fret about sailing a small header or going a bit out of your way, as long as you're enjoying pressure that your competition isn't."

"So when the wind is light, head for the piece of real estate with the most breeze," said Dakron.

"Basically," said Brooke. "Though it wouldn't hurt to *peek* at the compass for windshifts. But, yes, follow your nose and dig into the water with the most truffles, I mean ruffles."

Brooke finished his drink and slid the next one into play.

Dakron said, "What about sailing above the threshold, when everyone's hiked out and we're sailing at top speed? Should I forget about the pressure and just tack on the shifts?"

"Well, like most things in sailing, it's neither black nor white; I'd say it's a checkerboard. Nothing in sailing is ever clear cut, is it?"

"No, especially the rules. Lots of gray heads and gray areas," Dakron said cheerfully.

Zig Zag Brooke choked on an ice cube. "Keep it down, would you? The Protest Committee is lurking around here somewhere. Now: when you're sailing in good breeze, above the threshold, you certainly shouldn't ignore puffs, but you have to understand that the run-of-the-mill fresh puff is a different animal than the light air puff. Fresh puffs move down the course and away quickly, so you will spend less time in them, and they may also be of too short a duration to tack or gybe on. Usually the wind speed jumps by a quarter or a third, not half again or twice as much as in light air, so the jump in boat speed and boat lengths gained over those who aren't in the pressure is less dramatic. Therefore, just sailing the lifted tack instead of chasing after pressure areas may get you to the top mark sooner and be less risky. Of course, the exception to this is planing dinghies and catamarans, which take off with a few extra knots of wind. These sailors are on a pressure hunt *all* the time. Speed freaks; just look at the size of their pupils."

Dakron asked, "What about, say, if you are sailing a rather sedate 34-foot keelboat?"

"You are better off to change your priority away from chasing the pressure patches and concentrate on tacking on shifts. For example, it may not pay to commit yourself to sail a long way to a patch of pressure because (A) *it* will come to *you* and (B) it will likely be a shallow puff that will blow through quickly and (C) the header you may have sailed to reach this puff could wind up being distance wasted."

"But couldn't I have it both ways, pressure and shift?" Dakron asked.

"Yes, you can," Brooke said. "The ideal is to sail the pressure *and* the shifts, which on a puffy fresh day comes naturally: like Tarzan swinging through the jungle, sailing from gust to gust, lift to lift. And just as naturally, you'll find the need to make a big, risky commitment to chase after a hunk of pressure usually doesn't arise like it does in light air. So, on reflection, just what has been your problem, anyway?"

Here Brooke made a sour face and took a sip of his drink.

"I was doing it backwards, that's all," Dakron admitted. "Sorry."

Brooke said, "Know what I always say?"

"Don't lose your grip?" Dakron ventured.

"I say, 'Some look at the wind and ask, Why? I look at the wind and ask, Why not?'"

"I'm still working on my grip," Dakron said.

 PART THREE

# STRATEGY AND TACTICS

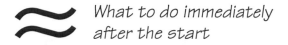 *What to do immediately after the start*

# THE FIRST 300 SECONDS

"Three, two, one! Gun!"

"Go, go go, legs over, everybody! Hike hard!"

"What a start! We're outta here!"

Deep Dakron focused his being into the tiller extension in his fist, willing *Snafu* to go even faster. Suddenly, he looked up.

"What," he wondered, "do we do now?"

"Glad you asked," replied tactician Scratchen Sniff. "The first 300 seconds after the starting gun are the most important part of the race. The boats are close together, commitments are made, wind patterns emerge, tactical battles shape up. For every move we make—or don't make—in this crucial period we will gain twofold from or pay doubly for later in the race—as well as back at the yacht club bar. Let's consider the following four things carefully."

"Only four?" said Dakron. "This is an easy weekend."

"First," said Sniff, "let's **look for velocity**. Nothing will bounce you out of a boat race quicker than your competition picking up more wind velocity than you right out of the starting blocks. We should look for signs of wind on the water, of course, but just as importantly we need to look for more subtle clues that tell us our competitors are enjoying better wind than we are. Their bow waves, the motion of their boats through the water, their angle of heel, the set of their sails, how hard their crews are hiking, all signal whether they have more or less wind than we do.

"If they have less wind, that's great; let's make the most of our good fortune while still keeping an eye on them. But if competitors on one side or the other of us have *more* wind than we do, it's time to pose The Question: Is this just a temporary thing, such as a random puff, or is this the beginning of a wind trend that may have escaped our prerace homework? The question as well as the an-

swer—even if we don't have a definite answer—may make us want
to sail toward the side with increased velocity, to protect ourselves.
At the very least, we'll keep a watchful eye on the velocity reaching
the boats on that side."

"That's your department," Dakron interjected. "I'm only trusted
to steer."

Sniff continued: "Second, we should **look for angle**. From our
prerace homework, where we studiously wrote down the high and
low port and starboard tack compass headings, we have a reasonable idea of whether we are sailing a headed, lifted or average heading coming off the starting line. Are we within the range we found
during our prerace homework? If so, good, because that tells us we
are operating in the same conditions, the same playing field we
researched before the start.

"But how about our competitors? If any of them are showing a lift
or a header beyond what our prerace spade work has unearthed,
beware. Where the wind is concerned we obviously can't know the
whole story, and more, much more may be revealed shortly. Fortu-
nately, our vigilance observing boat angles immediately off the starting line allows us to react and protect ourselves that much sooner.

"Even if we are comfortable with our angle and that of our competitors, we should still be looking for signs of which phase of the
windshift we might be in. Are we all the way lifted, or all the way
headed? Does the velocity seem to be building, or dying? In which
direction is the wind most likely to swing next? The third thing that
we should be doing in these first five minutes is to be careful that
we **don't make a commitment**."

"My specialty," said Dakron. "Or so I've been told."

Ignoring him, Sniff said, "Sometimes—especially if you are claw-
ing your way out of a dirty air, boxed-in start—you may have little
choice but to commit yourself to one side or the other, just to clear
yourself on the fleet. By doing so, of course, you begin to lose strategic options, like going toward the side with the best wind or the
most favorable shift.

"The obvious moral is: Don't get a bad start. But the not-so-obvi-
ous lesson is: Next time you line up for a start, think about how
committed you are getting with the boats around you, with whom
you may be forced to live with for the crucial five minutes after the
gun. By setting yourself up too close to another boat, will you be
pinning—committing—yourself to their game plan? By trying to give
yourself a little more room between your boat and your neighbors,
you maintain the option to tack, duck, foot off and generally make
your own choices.

"But if at all possible—and lots of the time you *do* have a choice—

this early in the race it's most unwise to seal your fate by sailing off to one side, or by letting other boats drive you to one side. For example, if you're on port tack in a close crossing situation just after the start, consider ducking that starboard tacker instead of responding with a knee-jerk lee bow tack. Ducking one, or even a couple of transoms, may be all it takes to pop yourself clear of traffic and into freedom. The same applies if you are on starboard tack; by dipping or waving a port tacker across your bow you lose a half boat length but will gain invaluable maneuverability and strategic options. Once you're in the clear, it's easier to grasp the big picture of how the fleet is spreading out, who is sailing what angle, and who has the most wind on the course.

"If you get locked into a dogfight your sailing becomes restricted to the tunnel vision of beating just one boat, not the fleet. And trust me, sailing the first 300 seconds of a race with tunnel vision may make you want to close your eyes when you exit the tunnel."

"You will have won the battle but lost the war," said Dakron.

"Or lost the battle *and* the war," said Sniff. "The fourth and final post-start priority is to **establish your competitors' positions**. As soon as possible after the start, place the positions of your competitors *relative to your boat and to each other* on a mental grid so you can begin to judge your gains or losses against them, and begin to judge the right and left sides of the course. Put the tailenders as well as the leaders on your grid; from then on it's their relative gains or losses that will tip you off as to what wind strategy you should pursue.

"How many times have you looked up five minutes after the start and gasped, 'How did that boat get *there?*' Well, it got there while you weren't looking. At no other time in the race does it pay more dividends to keep close track of the other boats. After all, how can you beat your competition if you don't know where they are?"

Dakron said, "Well, they've beaten me, and they didn't know where *I* was."

Sniff ignored that and said, "One thing to watch out for: If a particular boat has pulled off an excellent start from the favored end of the line, don't let that mislead you into assuming that side of the course is favored. Just put them on your position grid and use them to read subsequent windshifts and velocity differences. That's why you should do your grid as soon as possible after you cross the start line."

"So, how are we doing in this race?" asked Dakron, hunched over in concentration.

Sniff waffled. "It's still a little early. Give me another hundred seconds."

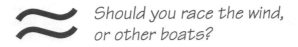 *Should you race the wind, or other boats?*

# STRATEGY? OR TACTICS?

"A 10-degree lift can sure solve a lot of life's problems," Deep Dakron said cheerfully to his crew. Especially when you have a rock star guest tactician like Scratchen Sniff finding them for you, Dakron noted to himself.

Feeling *Snafu* heel to a puff, Dakron let his tiller extension arm relax and follow the lift up. Then, as he was prone to do while sailing a lift, he let his mind wander.

It struck Dakron that he was beginning to feel rather ambivalent about having an expert like Sniff calling the shots. Dakron was learning a lot about wind and tactics, and Sniff's smarts had elevated *Snafu* to second place in the Weekend Warrior Series, but Dakron felt like he didn't know how to sail his own boat anymore. Sniff had this way of posing loaded questions—Should we tack, keep going, sail for the new breeze?—and then gleefully springing the correct answer when Dakron invariably chose the wrong one.

Racing with Scratchen Sniff is like sailing your way through a minefield, Dakron mused, *but winning is worth any ignominy.*

The wind lightened and headed, and Dakron tensed; he'd sailed into the next minefield. He glanced up and saw a patch of light air immediately abeam and to windward, and then a darker, windier patch an enticing 100 yards beyond that.

"Well?" wheedled Sniff, who had been waiting. "Shall we? Shall we tack on over and go get ourselves some of that nice breeze?"

Dakron groaned. "Yes. Let's go for it. If there's one thing I *know* is right, it's that you always sail toward the most wind, especially when it looks as good as *that* does."

Dakron bit his lip, and braced for the fallout.

"Sir, I half-congratulate you," Sniff said from beneath his handlebar mustache. "You are 100% correct, *strategically*, but 100% incorrect *tactically*. Permit me to expound as we continue on this tack."

"Strategy? Tactics? What's the difference?" asked Dakron. "Semantics?"

Sniff said, "**Strategy** is the course you would sail, in the absence of other boats, to reach the mark the fastest. This means taking maximum advantage of the wind and current and paying attention to nothing else—such as boats. Strategy is literally you against the wind, racing the elements, anticipating and outguessing them as best you can to get to the mark as quickly as you can. That's strategy: *racing the wind.*

"**Tactics**, on the other hand, is the course you would sail solely to beat the other boats in the race, regardless of what the wind or current is doing. You know, the way match racers try to sail each other off the course to get to the mark ahead of the other boat, that sort of idea. That's tactics: *racing the other boats.*

"Obviously we must use both strategy and tactics in a sailboat race. We use tactics to place our boat relative to the other boats, such as in a covering or controlling position that gives us the upper hand. We use strategy to pass boats by sailing around them on a windshift or past them with more breeze. How much strategy and how much tactics we use depends on the situation we find ourselves in, but I've always held that it helps to first assess strategy and tactics separately, and then decide which one to give the most emphasis.

"Take our present situation. We see what appears to be a good, solid breeze within our reach, just a tack away, and *strategically* it would be an excellent idea to go after it. But, there are other boats close to us in this race that we have to worry about, and we don't want to risk losing contact with them *tactically*. We may even lose the ones we are ahead of if this wind we go chasing fizzles out, which is always a possibility. Or if, ten minutes later, the boats we left find something even better than what we have found, we'll be kicking ourselves. So in this case the strategic ideal is tempered by the tactical requirement of staying in contact and keeping a loose cover on our competition. In other words, we compromise our wind strategy in favor of boat-to-boat tactics.

"Once you start looking at your racing decision-making in terms of tactics and strategy, you can sort out which might be the best approach to improve your standing at each juncture of the race. And, of course, this can change from the beginning of a particular leg to the end.

"For example, say you start a downwind leg about five boat lengths behind a group of boats that are clustered together. Trying to cover all of them—a tactical ploy—will probably only result in you picking

off only one of them. But if you make a strategic move—like split-ting gybes onto a likely looking puff—your odds of riding past the whole group are better. Then, as you near the mark, you should shift back into a tactical mode, blanketing the nearest boat and jockeying for the inside position at the mark.

"So the whole point of looking at decision making in terms of strategy or tactics, or more likely a combination of both, is to make you cognizant of your options on the racecourse. If you are winning, or ahead of some boats that you really need to beat in the series, you are better advised to think tactically rather than strategically. The fastest route to the next mark is not as important as sticking close to your nearest boats (even turning yourself into a roadblock, if they are faster) and thus reducing the chance that they will sail around you on a windshift."

"When ahead, cover," Deep Dakron said.

"When ahead, act tactically," corrected Scratchen Sniff. "Covering has such a narrow connotation. Real boat-to-boat tactics include covering, controlling, even intimidation and nonverbal threats. You know; the sharp luff or steely-eyed stare that says 'No *way* are you sailing over me on this reach.' Look what a little muscle has done for Arnold Schwarzenegger. If you've got to stop someone, whether it's on the starting line or approaching the finish line, flex some tactical muscle. Separate it out from the more intuitive, right brain, wind strategist side of your sailing repertoire and use tactics when it counts.

"So when I'm behind, I turn on my wind strategy?" asked Deep Dakron.

"Well, more so, but you don't have to be behind to use strategy. In general, the first windward leg of a race goes to the best wind strategists, and subsequent windward legs tend to be more cautious, covering affairs between the handful of boats in the lead; more tactically oriented. Basically, on any leg of the course that you need to pass *groups of boats* you'll need superior strategy to do it. You can't mow 'em down by boat-to-boat tactics if you aren't near them.

"Once you decide to focus your efforts on strategy you'll become less tangled up in those frustrating dogfights that characterize life in the middle of the fleet. If you need to pass fifteen boats, don't get into a match race with the pugnacious individual in 18th, because you'll likely both drop back to around 35th. Sail *around* them with strategy instead. You can still knock 'em off one by one—a shift here, a shift there—and it's preferable if you can do it that way, because that means you're taking fewer risks, such as hitting a desperation corner. And you know how I feel about sailing yourself into 'all or nothing' corners and long-shot laylines."

"Speaking of laylines," Dakron cut in, "shouldn't we have tacked? Our neighbors have all tacked."

"Whoops, so they have," said Sniff, red-faced. "So busy postulating I wasn't watching. Looks like we'll be a little overstood here."

"Let's cut out the chatter," Deep Dakron chided, and put the helm down. "Our tactics are weak, our strategy sloppy," he barked, and as Sniff and the crew scrambled he couldn't keep a grin from sidling onto his face. If a little muscle works for Schwarzenegger . . .

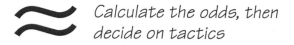 *Calculate the odds, then decide on tactics*

# SNIFFING OUT THE ODDS

"**S**hould we tack, or should we keep going?"

Deep Dakron's voice carried an anxious-going-on-shrill tone as he turned to his tactician, Scratchen Sniff.

All the windward rail crew had felt the header, and now their eyes went to Sniff, that maestro of strategy, that Wizard of Wind, that calculating tactical genius.

Sniff stroked his mustache and said thoughtfully, "Do you feel lucky?"

Dakron groaned. "Lucky? Lucky. I always *feel* lucky, I mean, I never give up *hope*, not completely, but—"

Sniff shrugged. "Then today could be your day," he said. "What do you think?"

"What do I think?" Dakron repeated. "What do I think. Well . . . I think that if this shift keeps going, and we keep sailing this header for another two minutes, we could tack and cross the fleet and find ourselves way out front in first place, that's what I think."

"Think, or hope?" Sniff pressed.

Dakron barely had time to reply, "Uh, both, I guess," when Sniff said, "Thanks for answering my question, and your question. We should tack, of course. Right after this wave. Everybody, ready about!"

When they had settled down on the new tack, Sniff climbed up to the windward rail and perched behind Deep Dakron.

"Now, isn't this just swell," Sniff whispered in Dakron's ear. "Riding an 8-degree lift in good velocity. This puff has a solid look and feel to it. There are no flat spots ahead or to windward of us, and by the look of the wind's paw prints farther up the course there'll be plenty more shifts and puffs to work. Aren't you glad that you decided to tack?"

"Yes," answered Dakron. The sight of boats in less wind below his mainsail was, indeed, most enjoyable. "But what would have happened if we'd kept going for another minute? Or two minutes? We would have been gone! We'd be so far out in front we'd be in a different zip code—"

"*Shhh,*" said Scratchen Sniff. "Remember, always look where you steer. There. That's better. Eyes on telltales. What would have happened? I don't know, but I do know one thing: it would have been a gamble. And I also know that for the foreseeable future we will stay lifted, in good pressure, and with excellent odds of another shift with which to come back at our competition. We are making the smart, odds-on move here, which is why I made that little point about luck before we tacked."

"So you think we may get even luckier?" Dakron asked, brightening.

Sniff shook his head, as if he'd taken a cold unpleasant wave in the face. "I can see that it's time to trot out the Sniff Guide to Odds-On Shiftsmanship," he said, adding, "keep watching that genoa."

Dakron threw his eyes back onto the telltales and pulled the tiller toward him.

"Rule Number One," Sniff began, "is to remember that **today is my unlucky day**. Never forget that today will be the worst day of your life, from the moment you leave the dock until you get back to the yacht club. Why? Because believing anything otherwise, believing that you are somehow going to get 'lucky' is nothing but a thinly disguised excuse to take chances you wouldn't take if you were looking at the race rationally. But by assuming that you're going to be a bit unlucky you'll sail smarter, more defensively, to cover yourself. For example, because you are aware that if you sail yourself into a corner that corner is going to fold up around your ears, you tend to shy away from taking gambles that come with big loss consequences. If you sail defensively you never look dumb, and on those days when you do stumble into some good fortune, you look absolutely brilliant."

"You mean, some days it's your good fortune to have good luck, but most days it's your good luck to have bad luck?" said Dakron.

"You got it," said Sniff. "Which ties in with Odds-On Shiftsmanship Rule Number Two: **Don't give in to greed**. Greed, that unappealing but uniquely human trait which has spawned so many mini-series, can be quantified in boat lengths on the racecourse: for every boat length that you sail yourself away from the other boats, *the higher the probability for gain or loss, and the greater the amount, measured in boat lengths, that gain or loss will be.* Simply, separation and distance magnify the gain/loss effect of shifts and increase the chances of encountering a wind strength different—and, since you are among the chronically unlucky, it will be *less* wind—from that of the fleet. The next time you feel the need to split from the fleet, consider this: Are you that much smarter or more perceptive than all the others in the race, who are also fervently studying the wind and the fastest way to get to the next mark? If you're *sure* you are, then great. Go for it. But if you're not sure, might you just be caving in to greed?"

"I believe that Rule Number Two can be applied to the stock market, too," Dakron noted.

"Now, Odds-On Rule Number Three: **Wind prediction is folly**. No one—and I mean no one—can consistently predict the wind. Yet we all persist in attempting this every time we race. Do we ever learn? *Will* we ever learn? A huge percentage of the time our 'predictions' amount to nothing more than conjecture and wishful thinking and wild hopes, as accurate and well informed as Monday morning quarterbacking on the preceding Friday night. How many times have you sailed a long header out to the layline only to—surprise!—wheel up into a lift right before you were forced to tack for the mark? Instead of predicting, at which history shows we have dismal records, I focus on *reacting* to what we do have and making the most of it. I keep my eyes open all the time, and I don't go streaking off for some good thing I think or hope or have talked myself into believing will happen. I might set myself up a bit *toward* that direction, but I will continue dealing with the here and now. After all, who really knows what the wind will do before we reach the next mark? I don't, you don't, and the rest of the fleet doesn't."

"I know what I hope the wind will do," Dakron said, "but now you've taken my hope away, too. What, I ask, is left?"

"Sniff's Rule Number Four of Odds-On Shiftsmanship is what's left: **Calculate the odds**. Why do I say 'calculate'? When people say, 'I think that the sea breeze is going to fill in pretty soon,' think about how vague that statement is. Soon? *How* soon? Ten minutes? Half an hour? An hour? Will the breeze reach us before we round the next mark, or sometime after that? And are they giving the sea breeze a 100% chance, or is it really more like 70%, or 30%? On the racecourse, that difference is make-or-break. So, try to think in terms of odds instead of using fuzzy words like 'may' or 'probably.' Talking in terms of the odds also gives me a better idea of how much I stand to gain or lose, say, if I decide to tack, or to keep going. For example, considering the wind conditions we've seen so far, what are the odds of the wind going left? Fifty percent? How about the odds of the wind going right? Seventy percent? Makes you assess it more carefully, doesn't it?"

"Are some odds luckier than others?" Deep Dakron wondered. "I know that's the case in Vegas."

Sniff said, "I also calculate my odds for gain or loss based on the number of boats around me. If 80% of the 20-boat fleet is to my right, then my chances for loss in a right-hand shift are high; 16 boats are in a position to gain on me. And of course, if it shifts left, I am in a position to gain on those 16 boats. Obviously, I've gotten myself into a high gain/high loss position, which should lead me back to reconsider my odds on the windshifts. Taking everything into account, am I out on a limb? Or am I reasonably justified, by the odds, in being here? Is it time to get myself into a more conservative position relative to the fleet? Or should I keep running the present risk to get the gain?"

"Those are darn good questions," said Dakron. "But, uh, what's the answer?"

Sniff said, "The answer is Odds-On Rule Number Five: **Play the odds**. Once you've calculated your odds, based on the wind's behavior and your position relative to the fleet, play the odds *sensibly*. Right after the start, when the fleet is clustered and it's easy to lose a lot of boats very quickly, smart money says not to play the high-risk odds. Stay low-risk—don't take early flyers or commit yourself to radical tactics—until you see how the wind and fleet are developing. Once you get a sense of how the race is going—once you get a handle on the various odds—play on from there. Late in a race, if your series scorecard will stand to gain by picking up a few places in the race, go ahead and play some high-risk odds. Whether to play high-risk or low-risk depends on both the stage of the race and the series, and your points relative to boats you can or need to beat. Why take a big risk trying to pass three boats when you might lose six boats, and one place in the overall standings, in the attempt? Play the odds."

Suddenly, the wind headed and *Snafu* straightened up. Deep Dakron yanked the tiller. Everyone felt the freshening air.

"Should we tack, or should we keep going?" Dakron asked anxiously.

Sniff smoothed his mustache. "Do you feel lucky?" he said.

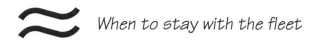 *When to stay with the fleet*

# DO THE BRIGHT THING

"The left side of this racecourse looks soooo good," purred Deep Dakron, salivating at the wind-ruffled, darkening patch of water in the distance ahead of *Snafu*. "This left side looks so good I can taste it, or at least taste the beers those guys on the right, on port tack, are going to owe me."

"Let's tack," Scratchen Sniff said abruptly.

Dakron's face looked as if it would crack. "Tack? Why?" he wailed. "Why should we tack when deliverance lies straight ahead, just waiting for us to sail into it? All I have to do is stay on starboard tack, hold the tiller somewhere close to the middle for two minutes, tack when that glorious header hits, and we'll be heroes. Look at that puff up ahead. Look at that header up ahead."

"I see 'em," said Sniff, "and they do look magnificent. But I am making the most difficult call a tactician has to make, and that is to turn my back on temptation and tack without a header, a puff, or any of the usual reasons. I am uncleating the genoa now, and I hope that you will tack the boat, otherwise the flogging may seriously shorten the racing life of this sail."

"Give me a second!" cried Dakron, putting the helm down as Sniff unpeeled the wraps from the genoa winch. Sniff noted that *Snafu* turned through the eye of the wind much more reluctantly than usual.

"Now, *why* did we do that?" Dakron complained once they were settled down on port tack.

Sniff cleated the sheet. "We have chosen the sure thing, the most basic, underrated tactic there is, the only move that will never get you into trouble, the move we all learned early in our sailing careers and then forgot once we became big-time smarty pants hotshots. This outstanding play of plays from the master playbook, this championship-winner, this time-tested, sure-fire move, this bacon-saver, points getter, smart investment and all-around top performer is known as . . ."

Sniff paused theatrically. "Are you ready to hear what this move is called?"

"I'm ready to use this tiller extension to demonstrate one of my Weekend Ninja Skipper moves," snapped Dakron. "All right already!"

Sniff beamed. "This race saver of a tactical move is called **staying with the fleet**. Because we are not absolutely, positively sure that the wind we see on the left side will still be there when we get there, or that the puff will last the rest of the leg, or that our competition on the right side of the course might not find something even better two or ten minutes from now, I have chosen to *go with the fleet*. Play the safe numbers. Reduce our odds of loss."

"How incredibly dull," said Deep Dakron.

"That's exactly right," agreed Sniff. "Staying with the fleet *is* dull. I suppose that's why so many sailors choose not to do it. There's much more adrenalin, more of a high in throwing your last dollar down on the jackpot of a mega-header or lift. Everybody likes to think they're smarter than the next guy. Everybody wants to beat the system. But if you feel like gambling go to Vegas, or the track, where at least you know the odds."

"But why are all of our competitors sailing toward the right, when the left is so obviously right?" Dakron asked, wishing he'd rephrased things a little.

"I don't know," said Sniff. "The left looks right to me, too, but for reasons unknown to us, *the race is to the right.* This is a perfect example of a curious phenomenon; at different points in any race, and this applies either upwind or downwind, the race—*the movement of the fleet*—can be to the right or to the left.

"In this particular case, maybe our competitors heading toward the right side haven't seen the wind we've spotted on the left. Maybe they see something better on the right, or know (or think they know) of something better on the right. Maybe they're locked into covering or drag-racing each other. Maybe they're just following each other. Maybe they all have overrides on their genoa winches and *can't* tack. Or maybe they're just psychic."

"That's a lot of maybes," noted Dakron.

Sniff nodded. "Sailboat racing is fraught with maybes, and as far as I'm concerned we are taking the most dangerous maybe out of this situation by staying with the fleet. The point is, the more separation we allow them to build up between us and them the more leverage they gain. Even though it does look remarkably similar to grass growing, a sailboat race never remains static; distances between boats grow or shrink, depending on whether they are converging or separating. Armchair pundits have compared sailboat racing to chess, but chess is as fast-moving as moss compared to your weekend regatta."

"Better grass than moss," said Deep Dakron. "That's a little higher up the excitement chain."

"Pawns and rooks don't go zigzagging over a shifting playing field while you contemplate your next move," agreed Sniff. "But back to the here and now. Unlike chess players, we can't afford to dilly-dally. The farther apart boats are, the more they stand to gain or lose from a windshift. Before, when we were on starboard tack, we were moving away from our competition at 90 degrees while they were moving away from us. And with everyone making five knots, we're moving through the water at over 500 feet a minute.

"Boats sailing diverging tacks at five knots pile up a physical separation at the rate of about 720 feet a minute. If we had continued to sail for another three minutes on starboard tack, we'd have put over 2,100 feet between us and our port tack friends. This amount of leverage is substantial; just a 5-degree shift in their favor would put them about 300 feet ahead of us."

Dakron gasped. "Nine boat lengths. Ouch."

"If they were to sail into a nice header, tack and come out riding a 10-degree starboard tack lift—and let's throw a little puff in with that lift— and, of course, we were forced to eat a corresponding port tack header all the way back, they would cross 650 to 750 feet *or more* in front of us."

Dakron gulped. "Twenty-two boat lengths. Double-ouch."

"Now, if we had stayed on starboard tack and sailed away from them for *five* minutes, and they were to pick up a 15-degree lift on their side—with added velocity, naturally—why, we'd be—"

"We'd be buying them beers all the way into next June," said Dakron. "Now that you've given me a healthy paranoia about leverage, I still don't understand: If the wind is obviously doing the left thing, why do we have to follow these guys to the wrong side of the course? Why don't we do the right thing, and go left? Just a little bit? Pretty please?"

"The left does look right," Sniff agreed, "but looks aren't everything. The advantage of staying with the fleet is that if the left side does fold we won't crash that badly, because we haven't allowed much separation to build up between us and them. But if the left side happens to turn golden we'll gain, because we are already to the left of our opponents."

Dakron grumbled, "So even though the best-looking puff I've seen all season is waiting for us, we are practicing safe shift playing. Bor-riiing."

Just then the genoa luffed. Dakron yanked the tiller toward him. "Uh-oh. Feels like a header."

Sniff pointed. "See the left side, where you wanted to go? Going flat rather quickly over there, isn't it? Everyone to leeward of us is headed, too. We'll hang in here, but just."

Dakron whistled. "Maybe I'm glad that instead of doing the left thing, we're doing the right thing."

Sniff said, "More precisely, instead of doing the left thing, or the right thing, we're doing the bright thing."

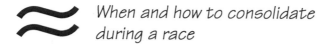 *When and how to consolidate during a race*

# COVER YOUR ASSETS

"**W**hat do we do now?" asked Deep Dakron.

"We do what Napoleon, Donald Trump, and Little Richard should have done," Scratchen Sniff answered.

"Tack?" wondered Dakron.

"We pull the most mundane yet cunning, the most mild-mannered yet ruthless trick in the Sniff strategy playbook."

"And will you deign to reveal this magic strategy sometime soon?"

"We consolidate!" said Sniff grandly.

"Consolidate. You're asking me to attempt something with the tiller that requires four syllables."

"How about, we cover our assets."

"Even more difficult. That's six."

"You're probably wondering, what is this wonderful thing called **consolidation**? Is it related to fluoridation, carbonation, radiation, or local politics? No, my friend, consolidation is the racer's salvation, emancipation, and indeed, his very salivation!"

"Mind keeping your syllables down?" Dakron said. "I'm trying to steer."

"Consolidation is simply a strategy for protecting and quantifying our position in the race. Consolidation is a form of covering without covering, at least not in the sense of blanketing or tacking directly on our competition. Consolidation is a way of checking in, to insure that we don't check out."

"Syllables are to the brain what cholesterol is to the vein," Dakron admonished.

Sniff said, "The conscientious consolidator keeps a weather eye on the weather (Are the conditions stable, or erratic? Will they hold, or change?), on leverage (The more distance between you and your competition, the greater the effect of windshifts), on the position and grouping of the fleet (Are the boats you have to beat on the right, left, or center? Is the mass of the fleet evenly spread, or bunched to one side?). By tacking to cross their bows, or gybing over to place himself between the competition and the goal (be it the next mark, the finish, or the favored side of the course), the consolidator makes a positive move to solidify his position."

"He keeps his eyes open," summed up Dakron, "closing off access behind him, like drawing a velvet rope across the entrance to a nightclub."

"Of course, consolidation doesn't necessarily mean crossing from one side of the course to the other just to place yourself in front of the other boats—though it could involve that. But that tactic is really nothing more than good old-fashioned covering. With consolidation, the idea is to cover *yourself.*"

"Like underwriting your own insurance policy."

"Exactly. You insure yourself against the favored side, or against your close competition getting excessive leverage on you, or against letting groups go around you, or all of the above. Consolidation is *using what you've got, strengthening your defenses, setting yourself up for future gain.*"

"Sounds wonderful, like Soma. Only $19.95, and available in powder, tablet, or injection," said Deep Dakron.

Sniff ignored him and kept on. "But when, you ask, is the right time to consolidate? Is the first beat too early? Is the last beat too late?"

"I'd say sometime after the start, and before the finish."

"You're not far wrong. You should consolidate any time you are either satisfied with or worried about your position. If you've made a gain, or if you're doing well in the race, then a move toward consolidation—as long as you don't move too radically and end up losing the plot—is a good investment. And too, if you're worried about your position, or if you've suffered a loss, then cutting your losses (and the potential for further damage) is smart strategy. Digging back in from an overleveraged position, working toward the new favored side and the boats that have gained may be the first step in turning your falling fortunes around. It's amazing how our perspective on the race can change as we alter our physical location on the course. Those world-beating lifts we were pursuing on the left side, for example, may pale compared to the fresh fingers of pressure that are sneaking through over on the right. Consolidation can tip you off to any funny business a lot sooner than pursing a single-minded vision will."

Dakron noted, "Single-minded has twice the syllables of good old stubborn, and four times the stressed accents of boring old blind."

"Another time to consolidate is when you find yourself with absolutely no idea of what will come next, in terms of windshifts and velocity. This happens more frequently than most of us will admit. At times like this, the object is not to sail yourself out of the game, because you don't know what the game *is*. Rather, you need to hang in there and stay poised for further developments.

"And it may never be too early to consolidate. After the start in a big fleet, when it's common to find yourself being herded off to one side or the other, an early slice back to the middle or toward the largest or best-looking group can save a lot of heartache later."

"In other words, engage brain before sinking teeth into mainsheet, sinking mainsheet into cleat, and super-gluing the tiller extension to your left hand," Dakron said.

"Or, opening your mouth," Sniff added. "Possibly the easiest and most natural time to consolidate is when you've dug up a little bit of buried treasure on the racecourse: a secret eddy of tide, private puffs coming off the cliffs. Once you've made your gain, go back and cross their bows, get between them and the good stuff."

Dakron said, "Question: If we're doing so well, why do we need to consolidate?"

"Answer: We consolidate *because* we're doing so well. We've struck gold; we don't need to go on digging, getting in over our head, searching for the mother lode. We've got some nuggets, let's cash them in, tuck the money away and start collecting some interest."

"But if we've hit it big and they haven't, why worry about them?" Dakron wondered.

"Because in sailboat racing, what is gained can be even more quickly lost, and usually in a most spectacular and crowd-pleasing fashion. One tremor and our gold mine may come crashing down on our greedy little heads. In sailboat racing you're never *really* ahead of another boat until you round a mark or cross the finish line in front. Until then you are merely occupying a square on a treacherous, shifting playing field. Your spot may look good at the moment, but it's subject to earthquake, fire, flood, water skiers, ferry boats, and all manner of blackest voodoo and unexplainable occurrences."

"Oh," said Deep Dakron.

"So, we consolidate."

"That's still three syllables too many. You've got to make this simple. Pitch it on a ten-year-old's level, like the news. I want consolidation reduced to a single sound bite. One syllable."

Sniff frowned. "Consolidation is . . . "

"And no fair using smart, safe or sane," Dakron told him. "Consolidation is . . ."

Sniff struggled, and Dakron looked on smugly.

Sniff brightened. "Consolidation is supercalifragilisticexpial-idocious!" he cried. "And it's fun, too."

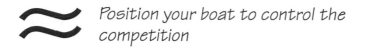 *Position your boat to control the competition*

# HOW TO BE A NUISANCE

**"W**ake up, everyone!" Scratchen Sniff hollered at the crew spread over the deck of *Snafu*. While waiting for the Race Committee to start the second race just about everyone, including helmsman Deep Dakron, had dozed off.

"This is a quiz!" cried Sniff. "Can anyone tell me why the Race Committee—"

"The Race Committee is waiting for the arrival of a new case of tonic before they'll start the race," said Dakron, rolling over.

"The Race Committee is waiting for the wind to shift back and square their start line," offered the Kid, yawning.

"They're waiting for lunch," mumbled the Mumbler.

"They're waiting for dinner," moaned Lisa Quick-Cam.

"They're waiting and waiting because they know it drives us absolutely bonkers," said a knowing Zig Zag Brooke. "Plus, they don't want us in the yacht club bar before four-thirty."

Scratchen Sniff wore a sour look under his handlebar mustache. "Wrong, wrong, and wrong," he said testily. "You didn't wait for my real quiz question, which is this: Who is the biggest nuisance in the fleet?"

"That's easy," answered Deep Dakron. "That guy on *Dust Nuisance*. Everybody hates him!"

"Of course they do," said Sniff. "But *why* does everybody hate him?"

"Well," said Dakron, "he's kind of always right *there* every time you need to cross the starting line, or tack, or gybe, or round a mark, and he's forever screaming irritating things like 'Starboard!' or 'Don't tack!' or 'Inside overlap!' or 'Leeward boat!' The man is basically an all-around nuisance on the racecourse."

"He's more than a nuisance," said Sniff. "He's a *control freak.*"

"Uh-oh," said Dakron, wishing he'd stayed asleep. "And now you want me to become a nuisance, a control freak, right?"

"Like it or not," said Sniff, "whenever boats sail in close proximity to each other, especially at starts and mark roundings, the boat in the **controlling position** dictates to the boat or boats in the **controlled position**. In match racing, for example, the dirty tricks of being *in control* of the opponent have been enshrined into legend. Like the skipper of *Dust Nuisance*, world-class match racers are true nuisances—control freaks—and proud of it."

"Oh!" said Deep Dakron, blinking as the sun poked from behind the mainsail and caught him in the eyes.

"And being a nuisance—a *controlling* nuisance—can work for us fleet racers, too. The first step is to recognize that in each stage of a race there are controlling, right-of-way positions waiting for occupancy. The second step is to install ourselves in these positions at important points in the race. Would anyone like to name a few key points and controlling positions?"

No one stirred.

"Uh," said Dakron after a lengthy silence, "why don't you go ahead. We're not very well positioned for deep thinking."

"Yes, I've noted your positions," said Sniff. "First, there's the prestart. In the prestart, which I'll boldly shorten and define as the final starboard tack approach to the starting line, establishing yourself *to leeward with luffing rights* of opponents is, obviously, the controlling position, especially if you wish to continue out to the left side of the course. You can spoil more opponents' starts (and use their boats to open up a hole for yourself the size of the national debt) by being that *!#@*¡`!@!!* boat to leeward, so don't you ever, ever find yourself on the dues-paying side of someone with leeward luffing rights in the prestart."

A few eyelids fluttered weakly.

"On the windward leg, in most people's minds the 'safe leeward' position is seen as the supreme position of control, but unless you are ahead enough to be able to slam a 'killer lee bow' on your opponent, being to leeward has some real drawbacks. If you can't pinch the windward boat off in time to tack when you wish, you are pinned; you, in turn, can be lee-bowed by another boat, and become the dead meat in a fatal sandwich; and finally, you run the risk of being rolled by the boat or boats to windward, with nowhere to go but out the back door. But by hanging out in a 'safe windward,' which I boldly define as being *to windward, safe from backwind but near enough to discourage leeward boats from tacking*, you can control other boats even without being ahead of them. This positioning can be used to good advantage when converging with a crowd of oppo-site-tack boats (your 'blocker' to leeward takes the heat) and ap-proaching the windward mark (where you can hold boats out until you're ready to make your next-to-last or last approach tack)."

Zig Zag Brooke rolled his body slowly into the shade, exposing the freshly imprinted non-skid pattern on his backside.

Sniff continued. "Next, when we come to *rounding the gybe and leeward marks, the controlling position is to be on the inside, with room,* and the only reason I mention something so obvious to you hot dogs is that most of us don't phone in our reservations far enough in advance and too often find that the best seats are taken. Halfway down the first reach, for example, is not too early to begin jockeying yourself into an overlapped-to-leeward, room-at-the-mark position. Same goes for the second reach (and remember, as added incentive, that the boat inside at the gybe mark is already in the high lane to snatch the inside position at the leeward mark, too). For those times when you are unsure whether to sail the reach high or low, getting yourself into the nuisance position—to leeward on the first reach, to windward on the second one—at least gives you clout at the mark."

"Mmm," said the Mumbler, in what could have passed for a con-tented snore.

"There's plenty of nuisance pressure to be applied on the run, too," said Scratchen Sniff, and the crew stirred restlessly. *"On runs, the controlling position is on your opponents' port side,* for two rea-sons: you can always gybe and come steaming back at them on the right-of-way starboard gybe, and you are on the inside track going into the mark (given the usual marks-to-port rounding). The star-board gybe is a much underrated downwind weapon; you can herd pesky port gybe boats over to the layline, shut them out, and gybe for the mark when you're laying comfortably. Plus, unlike sailing to windward, where a 90-degree course change and major loss of boat speed are required to tack, on the run a gybe can be made with very little loss of boat speed, and, if there's enough breeze to run square, with hardly any course alteration.

"As with the reaching legs, it pays to claim the space to the left of your opponents early on, even right when rounding the windward mark, especially if you round close behind a group of boats. Instead of arcing up while the chute is being set, a steep and deep bear away from the mark (don't try this in light air or you'll think you've sailed onto a sheet of flypaper) can establish some valuable *gauge,* or sideways separation, to the left of your competition. Then, when the spinnaker-raising smoke clears and everyone discovers that you're already on the inside track, itching to drop a starboard tack gybe on them like the Queen of Spades, they'll say, 'There he is again, that—' "

"Nuisance," said Dakron from the shade of the mainsail.

"That hated nuisance, that evil, wicked, mean and nasty and not at all nice *control freak,*" finished Sniff.

"Actually, it sounds rather amusing, making yourself a nuisance," said Deep Dakron, putting in an all-out effort to overcome inertia and arriving at a sitting position.

"It is fun, at least for the nuisance," agreed Sniff. "That's why I'm surprised more people aren't nuisances. It doesn't require super crew work, blazing boat speed, or a sixth sense about windshifts. It only requires that you recognize and snatch the right-of-way *before* you need it and make sure your opponents hear plenty about the grave straits they're in. Anyone can and should be a nuisance."

"Hmm," pondered Dakron. "But the prospect of being detested doesn't exactly appeal to me."

"Would you rather be a well-liked loser or a well-hated winner?" Sniff asked.

Dakron considered. "I guess I could stand being despised a little," he said.

"Did anyone hear a gun!" cried the Kid, springing to his feet.

Sniff smashed the binoculars to his face. "The Race Committee has a million flags up. . . . It looks they've started the sequence. . . . It looks like they've started the *race.*"

"That's a bit of a nuisance," said Deep Dakron.

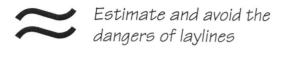 *Estimate and avoid the dangers of laylines*

# THE HEARTBREAK OF LAYLINE-ITIS

"You arc doing it again," warned tactician Scratchen Sniff, drumming his fingers on *Snafu's* cabintop.

"Huh?" said Deep Dakron, moving his tiller extension back and forth gingerly, as if he were roasting marshmallows over a campfire.

"You, sir," said Sniff, aiming an accusing forefinger, "are once again sailing yourself straight into the heartbreak of **layline-itis**."

"Huh?" said Dakron again.

Sniff uncrossed his hiked-out legs and recrossed them, right over left. "Laylines!" he hissed. "Beware! They're as seductive as credit cards. Yes, all of us are guilty of sleep-sailing blithely along, lulled into charging up a few debits here and there, ignoring those 'minor' windshifts, stretching our credit line, prolonging our time spent on one tack, all the while thinking there's plenty of time left before payment is due. . . then, suddenly, *wham*, we are *on the layline*. We've run up a bigger windshift debt than we'd realized, been sailing on borrowed time, and now it's payback time—with interest— and we are feeling the squeeze. Can we scrape together a last minute windshift and bail ourselves out? Or, like that country and western ditty, is there 'Too Much Month Left at the End of the Money?'"

"Huh?" said Deep Dakron a third time.

"In other words: Will there be too much race left at the end of the layline?"

Dakron blinked. "Personally, laylines have been very, very good to me. There's nothing to it: sail to the layline, tack, and *bingo*, you've aced the fleet with yet another perfect layline."

Sniff let loose a most unpleasant raspberry. "The perfect layline!" he smirked. "That's a mug's game. Occasionally a 'layliner' will look like a hero when a wind line hits his side of the course first, but in actuality he's merely been rescued from the dangers of the layline. Have you forgotten that *any* windshift, no matter how small, no matter if it's a lift or a header, works against you once you've reached your 'perfect' layline? And you don't have to be a geometry whiz to figure out that the farther away from the mark you are, and the bigger the shift is, the more you will lose.

"For example, a lift on the layline (either starboard or port, up-wind or downwind) means that you've overstood the mark, making every boat length you sailed on the previous tack or gybe to reach the 'layline' a waste of time and distance. A header on the layline is even worse, because there's nowhere to go; you can continue to eat the header, losing to every boat to leeward as well as those ahead of you, or you can tack out and go further into oblivion, way out to the 'new' layline. From there it's almost guaranteed you'll either overstand or lose even more in subsequent headers."

"Trouble in Layline-land," said Dakron. "But what's so bad about the layline if the wind is steady?"

"That's one huge 'if,'" Sniff pointed out. "But laylines are danger-ous even without a shift. Near the windward mark you are vulner-able to competitors lee-bowing you or tacking on your wind when you're on the starboard tack layline. On the port tack layline, you're defenseless against starboard tackers—you *have* to dip them, no matter how much you may lose doing it—and the wind shadow of boats spinnakering away from the mark can cost you plenty. The other danger is the way you *sail* once you are on the layline."

"What do you mean?" asked Dakron.

"This is why I call it 'layline-itis,'" said Sniff. "Picture this: Our valiant skipper is on the layline, but he's over a mile from the mark. In the back of his mind he is haunted by the fact that even the slightest current or header or lift or puff or lull in the next twelve minutes will put him either under or over the mark, so he tries to compensate, sometimes unconsciously. In headers he pinches to 'make' the mark, and the boat goes slow. In lifts he's tempted to sail freely instead of staying on the wind, and loses distance to wind-ward. The more rattled he gets about 'making the mark' the worse he sails; pinching harder, going slower, sailing lower, slipping fur-ther and further out of the groove.

"By now his sail trimmers don't know what to do with the sails. 'Do we take this mark to port or starboard?' our skipper barks, determined at least to squirrel away one extra boat width and pull it out at the mark, 6000 feet later. Through every header, lift, puff, and lull he's worrying about that one boat width, not about making the boat go fast during the next mile. It's nice to sail with your head out of the boat, but 6000 feet out of the boat is really stretching it."

"That's sticking your neck out," said Dakron.

"The game of calling a perfect layline has become a personal obsession for our skipper, who tells himself: 'If I make it, they'll call me lucky. If I don't, I lose face. Either way, I'm doomed, at the mercy of the wind. C'mon, baby, we've *got* to make it.' Funny, how some people seem to think they've gained something when they reach the layline first, when actually they've lost something. I recommend the use of the **Sniff layline tensionmeter** to prevent layline heartbreak."

"How much does this tensionmeter cost?" asked Dakron. "Is it worth spending another $49.95 on my boat to forestall such pain?"

"The layline tensionmeter is absolutely free," Sniff said. "The 'something' that layliners have lost is their strategic and tactical options. By committing themselves too early to the layline they've reduced the number of choices they can make. Here's how I read my tensionmeter, from wherever I happen to be on the racecourse, whether I'm sailing on a windward leg or downwind, whether I am referring to the port or starboard layline. The scale is read in terms of the *remaining distance to the layline as measured from the center of the course.*

"**One-quarter** (of the way) **to layline:** No problem. I am near the center of the course with a good visual perspective on both the port and starboard sides and the position of the competition on each side. I am maintaining good strategic access to both sides of the course as well as, of course, the middle. I am enjoying the luxury of oodles of time and distance in which to choose my shifts and decide which of my competition I should stay with or harass.

"**Halfway to layline**: I am starting to become concerned as I watch my available options fade. I have made a moderate-to-serious commitment to one side of the course, which means now is the time for review, before it's too late. First and most importantly, where is the bulk of the fleet located with respect to me, and with respect to the center of the course? By being positioned halfway to layline, have I committed myself to one side or the other of the fleet? (Remember, it is quite common for the bulk of the fleet to be grouped to one side of the center of the course. If you are still in contact with them, you may not be getting as far out on a limb as you feared.)

"**Three-quarters to layline**: With this degree of major league commitment comes major league worry. I have now closed off an entire side of the course to my own access. Should a favorable shift or wind line or current advantage appear 'over there' I can't get to it from 'here.' Time is of the essence; the longer I continue toward the layline the deeper I get, for better or worse. It will be a long, long way to the mark on the next tack or gybe. Should I bail out right now, for safety's sake, and get some of that long board over with? Isn't it time to go *toward* the mark? Which way is my competition going? Do I really need to go any farther? What am I waiting for? The clock is ticking: tick . . . tick . . . tick . . .

   **On the layline**: How did I get here? Complete panic, followed by resignation: *Que sera, sera.* What will be, will be. C'mon, baby. *Make it.* C'mon, wind! Oh, it's a loo-oooong way to the mark, isn't it. Try not to pinch, or to foot, try to stay in the groove. C'mon, baby! *Come on.*"

   Dakron shifted uncomfortably at the helm. "Sounds like me trying to start my car on a cold morning."

   "This is a different kind of choke," said Sniff. "A layline choke."

   Dakron noticed that the back of his tiller hand was damp. "And how are *we* doing on the Sniff layline tensionmeter?" he asked.

   Sniff got his head back in the race and put it 6000 feet up the course. Then he leaped to the low side, and frantically uncleated the genoa for a tack. "Actually, it seems we are right on the layline," he reported.

   "Perfect," said Deep Dakron.

 *When, why, and how to cut your losses*

# TAKE YOUR MEDICINE

**"I** feel ill," said Deep Dakron, mock-slumping over *Snafu's* tiller extension. "Doc, can you help me?"

Scratchen Sniff cradled his chin in sailing-gloved hands, surveying the long line of boats in front of them. Only recently, all those boats had been behind them.

"The diagnosis is terminal," Sniff pronounced, "or even worse."

"Is this the end? Are we goners? Is there no cure? Doc, I gotta know the truth," Dakron pleaded.

"Terminal, cubed," Sniff amended, watching the boats ahead sail away, heeling to twice the amount of wind in *Snafu's* sails.

Dakron choked. "So this *is* it. The Final Curtain. It's all happening so quickly. A lifetime of Weekend Warrior scoresheets flashing before my eyes. All those bets I'll never collect on, those stories I'll never have an opportunity to embroider, those—"

Suddenly, Sniff snapped out of his gloom and assumed a detached, professional air. "In light of the diagnosis, there *are* three last-ditch remedies we can try: (1) Motor back to the yacht club, (2) continue with our present gameplan, or (3) take our medicine."

Dakron winced. "Does this involve Dr. Kevorkian? Does the good doctor make water calls?"

Sniff remained stiff-lipped, wide-mustached. "Choice number one—better known as quitting—is odious. You never learn anything by quitting a race, except what a poor sport and a loser you are. It's like leaving the classroom because you don't understand the lesson; you'll never progress in yacht racing by quitting. Even when we find ourselves dismally behind—and sometimes that's the *best* time—we can learn more about our favorite sport, *even if it kills us.*"

"Why do we persist in racing sailboats, if not to kill ourselves?" agreed Dakron.

"The second choice, continuing with the gameplan, carries little logic. Think: something big has just happened on the racecourse, big enough so that we're in the tank, and to carry on doing the same thing is likely to tank us deeper. But changing our plan means admitting that we were wrong in the first place, and also requires overcoming the built-in inertia of our plan, which is even tougher than getting up from the sofa to change channels. Changing our race plan takes an open, inquiring mind. What we thought was going to happen with the wind strategy or the tactics between boats hasn't. *Why*, we must ask. And what positive action can we take now, in lieu of griping? However, the third choice, **taking your medicine**, is my favorite."

"I knew it," said Dakron.

"And, surprisingly, it's the least painful of the three. The first medicine to swallow is attitude: Don't listen to that prideful, stubborn voice inside telling you not to admit that you've flopped. Acknowledging that your chauvinist, insensitive, gloating, catcalling, and all-around boorish competitors have done things a bit better than you today is not a defeat, it's a victory."

"Huh?" said Deep Dakron.

"Taking your medicine is a victory because it shows your fighting spirit, your unkillable determination. Cutting your losses is the first step in getting yourself back into the race. Your competition can only smirk momentarily, because here you come, you're on the mend, watch out world!"

Dakron said, "And how do we know when it's time to take our medicine?"

Sniff jabbed a finger into Dakron's solar plexus. "Usually you'll feel like a snowball has lodged itself here, in the top of your rib cage, but there are empirical observations that you can make, too. Remember, these observations apply to the reach and the run as well as the windward beat.

"First, whenever a **new wind** appears which puts you into the penalty box *for the duration of the leg*, then it's medicine time. But the new wind must be a definite quantity, not an on-again, off-again thing. When the seabreeze finally overpowers a weakening land breeze, when the clouds of an approaching frontal system herald that a big, lasting change is definitely in the wind, those qualify as a new wind of the solid, head-for-the-infirmary variety. However, if there's a reasonable chance that the wind will come back in your favor before the leg is over, it may not be medicine time, yet."

Dakron, distracted, appeared to be taking his pulse with his stopwatch.

Sniff continued: "Another time to take your medicine is when a **shift outside of the range** or a **persistent shift** occurs. Whenever the wind shifts well beyond what you've seen so far in the race, either to the right or the left, and shows signs of staying that way for the duration of the leg, it's—"

"Spoonful of sugar time," said Dakron.

"And, when a persistent shift turns your world inside out, it's also time to take your medicine. Because if you find yourself hurting at the onset of a persistent shift, then, like a bug that goes from being a head cold to a stomach flu to bronchitis and finally pneumonia, things are only going to get worse.

"The final scenario for taking your medicine is a **strategic blunder**. This is when nothing major (like a new wind or a persistent shift) has happened, but rather it's been your hand on the tiller that has, shall we say, compromised your good standing in the race. For example, suppose a bad start buries you back in the pack, but you somehow manage to wrangle a corridor of clear air for the first quarter of the beat, only to discover you've gone the wrong way. It's medicine time; cross behind those transoms and start going the *right* way."

"Get on the road to rehabilitation," said Dakron.

"And suppose you split from the fleet to play a daring corner game, but halfway through the leg you are in sad shape—then the time has probably come to take your medicine."

Here, Sniff coughed loudly, drummed his fingers, cracked his knuckles, and looked expectantly at his helmsman.

"Doc, you mean," Deep Dakron gulped, "that this is it? Tack?"

"Yes," said Sniff. "The time has come to put us out of our misery."

 *How to judge and deal with current*

# CURRENT AFFAIRS

Deep Dakron eased open the back door of McBatten Sailmakers and crept up the stairs.

He'd often wondered how Kent McBatten finished any products; the loft floor was perpetually covered with more bits and scraps of sails than sails. At the top of the stairs, Dakron peeked around the corner. McBatten sat in his sewing pit amid a sea of scraps, his machine silent.

"A-ha!" Dakron cried. "So this is what you call working late."

McBatten was so intent on his scraps that he didn't hear. He was carefully pulling a square of sailcloth over the plywood floor, stopping to arrange something on it, and pulling it again. Dakron stepped carefully through the debris and cleared a place for himself beside McBatten's pit.

The sailmaker had driven awls into the floor in a triangle configuration, within which he was slowly moving his scrap of sailcloth. On it were two cutouts of sailboats, one red, the other green; port tack and starboard tack. Every few seconds he advanced the boats across the cloth as if they were sailing, and then pulled the cloth with both the boats on it.

"What the—" said Dakron.

"Current," McBatten explained without looking up. "We are sailing in current, and we are gaining like mad on the weather mark. I'm the green boat, you're the red boat, and the awls are the marks. You're sailing behind me on port tack. Tell me when you think you're laying the mark."

McBatten continued moving the sheet, giving both closehauled boats a push from behind, against the direction of the wind.

Dakron groaned. "I hate current. It's so *sneaky*. Whenever I race in current, it pulls the rug out from under me."

"Good analogy," said McBatten. "Seeing as how we are sailing on a moving rug of water."

McBatten advanced each boat a few boat lengths on the cloth. Dakron looked to be about five boat lengths astern of McBatten, the green boat, who was also on port tack. Then the cloth—the current—began to move again.

"Tell me when you're laying the mark," prompted McBatten.

"Are *you* laying?" asked Dakron.

McBatten squinted, lining up his moving boat with the fixed mark and something on the other side of the room. "Now!" he said, and tacked his boat to starboard.

"Okay—I'll just tack on your line," Dakron said.

McBatten kept moving the cloth, and "sailing" the boats over the cloth, until Dakron said, "Now." He tacked Dakron to starboard and chuckled. "Sucker! You've overlaid the mark by a mile!"

"Stop moving the cloth!" Dakron protested.

McBatten wore a huge grin. "I told you we were sailing in current. You're on the moving rug, same as me. When you thought you'd tacked on my line you had actually tacked *above* my line. Because you reached my line *later*, the favorable current had moved the true layline down three boat lengths. I warned you we were gaining like mad on the mark."

Dakron wore a sour face. "Damn. Current is so *underhanded*."

McBatten brought his scrap down to the bottom of the racecourse, set the boats up on opposite tacks, and began moving the cloth from right to left.

"Why so freaked out about current?" he said. "It's more predictable and more measurable than wind. All you have to do is look into three areas before the race: **Research**, **gaining or losing**, and **fixed objects**."

"Sounds like the fine print of an investment prospectus, not a boat race, but go on," said Dakron, yielding to the inevitable.

McBatten continued pulling his scrap westward, moving the boats at a weird angle to the mark. "First, do your **research**," he said. "Know the tide tables, sure, but also arrive early out on the course and prowl around for yourself. Your mission is to find out the current strength and direction and, most importantly, *whether the current is constant in strength and direction across the entire course*. If the current flow varies over the course then it will make one side of the course advantageous, often depending on whether you are beating or running. For example, an adverse current on the left side of the windward leg becomes a favorable current on the downwind leg. Anyway, check both sides of the course, the windward mark and the leeward mark. All this takes time, so—"

"So don't leave the dock so damn late," said Dakron, "and between races, cut your lunch break a little short."

"Right," said McBatten. "Check the current against buoys by tossing in a banana peel or something biodegradable, and time how long it takes to drift one boat length from the buoy. Get a compass bearing on the direction. Anchor your own buoys if there are none around. Make a fancy current stick. I don't care how you do it, just get that information so you don't have the rug pulled out from under you. Why go into a race ignorant of the state of the playing field? The current is out there, and it's measurable; why not go get it?"

"And then?"

"Then go sailing before the race, and hammer it into your head, upwind and down, whether you are **gaining or losing**. When you're on that moving rug that we call current you are either gaining or losing on the next mark. It's either pushing you toward it or dragging you back, sliding you above the layline or pulling you below.

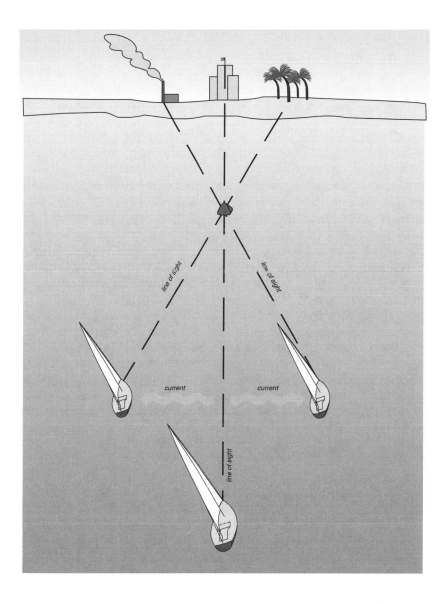

To establish a range, line up an object you are sailing toward
or away from, like a mark, against a feature of the background. If the background changes, you're sailing in current.
Make sure you allow for leeway if necessary.

You ask, how do you tell if you are gaining or losing? By watching the scenery."

"Huh?" said Deep Dakron.

"Get a range going. Line up the mark, or a nearby buoy, with the shoreline behind it and see which way you're being carried, and how fast. Probably one tack or gybe will be more radically affected than the other; you may not even notice the current on one tack, while on the other—"

"Yikes!" said Dakron, watching McBatten's patch of sailcloth skid across the plywood.

"Make sure you observe the current's effect on both tacks upwind, and on both gybes downwind. The object is to get comfortable with what the current is doing to you on all points of sail. Then, you can compensate and steer the shortest, most direct course to the mark. On a reaching leg, for example, using your range of buoy-against-the-shoreline, steer so that the mark doesn't move against the shoreline. If it moves, you are either gaining or losing, and otherwise not moving over the bottom like you thought you were.

"The other way that current contributes to gaining or losing is the length, in time and distance, of a leg of the course. Adverse current lengthens the leg; favorable current shortens it. This can take you by surprise, giving you less or more time than you thought to put your strategic or tactical plans into effect. Then there's the wind strength; the lighter the wind, the more significant, even overpowering, the current effect becomes. If you think the wind will drop before the leg is over, you should stay *up current,* because you'll lose on the mark rapidly when the wind dies."

Dakron's eyes were glued on the red and green boats, which were losing on the windward mark, but gaining on the reaching mark.

McBatten paused to realign the boats so they were heading downwind. "The last area of current cognostication is that of **fixed objects**. Now that your prerace research has told you where the current is strongest or weakest and what direction it is going, and your work in gaining or losing has gotten you comfortable with your true movement over the bottom, you should approach those things anchored to the sea bed that you must not hit or miss during the race, namely the starting line and the marks of the course.

"On current-wracked starting lines, even the hot dogs get into trouble if they don't make a few practice starts. The objective is to uncover the true time/distance relationship to the line, and the layline to the starboard end or port end, whichever you wish to start near. Give yourself a countdown and make a few runs at it.

Try to pin down the approach angle and distance to the line that makes for a successful position and boat speed at the gun. Most people tend to underestimate the current on the start line, and forget that they'll be sitting luffing or stalled during the last thirty to sixty seconds before the gun. Remember your research; while you're loafing along, the current will still be carrying you two boat lengths every sixty seconds, or whatever it is. The idea is to make your mistakes before the *real* start, when they don't count.

"Same goes for the windward mark and the leeward mark. Take a couple of practice runs at a nearby mark, if the current is similar. Are we laying? How about now? Try it—try to learn your laylines *before* the race. Do a practice spinnaker drop and rounding—probably you'll be too late, or too early. Not a problem—before the race. Now you *know*. And you'll realize that it's best to make your final approach on the layline a short one. Trying to lay a mark from 20 to 30 boat lengths out, in current, you'll likely overlay by a couple lengths. Or even more humiliating, you'll have to make an extra, last second tack or gybe in rush-hour traffic."

"I told you current was sneaky," said Dakron. "What are you doing with it now?"

McBatten was intent, moving the scrap from left to right. On it the boats were arranged closehauled, and McBatten was making wind arrows with his hands. The true wind! The current wind! The apparent wind! The true wind plus the current wind *plus* the apparent wind. Or is it minus? McBatten was unlocking the most mystifying, most bitterly argued phenomenon of yacht racing.

"A-ha!" said Deep Dakron. "The old lee-bow-the-current theory. Well? *Is* there a lee-bow effect?"

"Yes," said Kent McBatten.

He shifted the boats around and began dragging the scrap from right to left, making more wind arrows with his hands.

"No," said McBatten.

He was so absorbed that he didn't hear Dakron going down the stairs. He'll be there for hours, thought Dakron. He has the scraps for it.

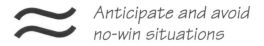 *Anticipate and avoid
no-win situations*

# IF A, THEN B—AND C, D, E, AND F

"**I** don't like this," muttered Deep Dakron. "This is too good to last."

Dakron and his team on *Snafu* were right up in the top handful of boats, sailing up the first beat in clean air and water. They were even on a decent shift.

"*Shhhh,*" warned tactician Scratchen Sniff. "If you're nursing a case of dreadlock, keep it to yourself. We're not going to do anything stupid. We're not going to pull out the bottom can."

"The what?" said Deep Dakron.

"The bottom can. You know, the lowest can in the supermarket pyramid. Dislodging the pebble that starts the avalanche. Digging for those low tide, pre-tsunami clams."

"How reassuring," said Dakron.

"We are keeping the words of the world's greatest mind-surfers and racing tacticians, the Talking Heads, firmly in mind."

"The Talking Heads?" said Dakron.

Sniff sniffed. "You know: *Well, how did I get here?* If you keep asking yourself the Talking Heads question, it keeps you looking both ways, astern and ahead. Particularly ahead. Keeps you antici- pating, thinking two or three moves ahead instead of just one. Case in point: here comes a starboard tacker. We can't quite cross this guy."

"What do we do?" said Dakron.

"First, we resist the knee-jerk reflex. We think a couple moves ahead," answered Sniff. "Most of all, we don't put ourselves **in the sandwich**. We don't put ourselves into a situation that locks us in, or brings a rain of negative tactical ions down on our heads. For instance, we have two options with this starboard tacker: we can dip him, or we can lee bow him. But before we lee bow *any* starboard tacker, what's the first thing we check?"

"That the spinnaker pole isn't over the genoa sheets?"

"Yes, but no. The first thing we scope out is the port tack boats riding along on our hip. We try to estimate if we're ahead, behind, or even with them, and we ask ourselves some hard questions: If we tack, will we cross them? Or will they cross us? If they can't cross us, are they likely to slam a lee bow tack on us? And how many of them can get to us? That's thinking more than one jump ahead. It's no good clamping a lee bow on a starboard tacker if you set yourself up to be crucified thirty seconds later."

Dakron said, "A happy thought. But I can't always estimate port/ starboard crossings so exactly. And the wind may change before we converge, anyway."

"Well, the point is, we think ahead, we weigh the pros and cons, we try to protect ourselves against the nasty people who'd like to do us dirty. We may decide that the half boat length we'll lose in dipping the starboard tacker is made up by keeping our freedom and not becoming the 'meat' in a lee bow sandwich.

"It also helps to know the players: Is Boat A an in-your-face hammer slammer? Is Boat B a live-and-let-live kind of guy? Is Boat C a leave-me-aloner, or a mix-it-upper? Is Boat D a back-of-the-pack chronic dogfighter? It's as bad an idea to try to lee bow the fleet rocket-ship as it is to try to squeak across the starboard tack bow of the local sea lawyer."

"So what do we do?" Dakron asked anxiously.

"The starboard tacker is headed; it looks like we can cross now, barely. But there's another starboard tacker just beyond him that we *won't* cross. Let's think ahead. We have to be careful if we tack under the second boat, because then we'll end up on the hip of the boat we barely crossed. By tacking between them we may be putting ourselves into a **do or die**."

"A what?" said Deep Dakron.

"A do or die is any situation where you insert yourself between boats, and a bad tack or gybe, a significant header or lift, or going slow or pointing poorly for a short period will blow you out the back. You try to never put the *onus of survival* on yourself. You try to never make yourself vulnerable from both sides, with nowhere to go but backwards."

"Why don't we tack short of both starboard boats, and avoid entanglements?" said Dakron, growing more tense as the boats converged.

Sniff looked over his shoulder, eyeing the port tack boats on their hip. "We could, as long as we make darn sure that if those port tack guys can't quite cross us they don't cement a deadly lee bow on us. We don't want to be **dead right**."

"Dead right?" said Dakron.

"You know, converge while screaming, 'Starboard! STARBOARD! STARBOARD TACK!' and make them lee bow us out of sheer peevishness. We'll be right, but we'll be *dead*. Instead, we'll dip a little and give them the full-arm windmill, the friendly after-you wave: 'Nice day, neighbor! Please—we insist—pass ahead. We don't want you to go to all the trouble of *tacking.'* Then we can continue on our merry way in clean air and water."

Dakron said, between gritted teeth, "Got it. Now what are we going to do with this starboard tacker? If you haven't noticed, he's getting closer and closer."

Sniff said, "Course, the same kind of anticipation works downwind as well. Say we're on port gybe, converging with a boat on starboard gybe. He's got rights, but we want to keep ourselves **in the driver's seat**. What do we do? If we wait till we're close to him to gybe to starboard, then we've pinned ourselves, and we can't gybe back or sail by the lee if we wish. All of a sudden he's the one in the driver's seat. We've situated ourselves at his whim, at the mercy of his judgment. The problem is, he may be fond of sailing all the way to the port gybe layline while he's still light-years from the mark. He may make us overlay, or sail us into a hole, or right off the edge of the western world.

"To keep ourselves in the driver's seat we can gybe to starboard while still short of him, giving us the option of gybing again later or soaking down to leeward, as we wish. Or, if we like the gybe we're on and the side we're heading for, we can luff up and cross behind him. If we do it smoothly and with an element of surprise, he'll be hard put to stop us. We keep our freedom, with the bonus of coming back at him on starboard tack before the mark. Once again it's simply anticipation; we decide *before* we get locked in. It's thinking two or three moves ahead, instead of one, that pays off. Why do you think the Italians did so well at the 1992 America's Cup?"

Dakron said, "I've got a starboard tacker bearing down and —"

"C'mon," Sniff said, "take a guess."

Dakron threw up his hands, losing the tiller extension momentarily. "Because they threw more money at the problem?"

Sniff's handlebar mustache curved upward. "Because they *anticipated*. They excelled at talking with their hands."

Sniff made two port tack boats out of his hands and excitedly tacked one to starboard. The other followed, the first tacked back, the other retaliated, then both hands went into a flurry of tacks.

"What do I do with this starboard tacker?" Dakron howled.

"Uh, uh, uh—" said Scratchen Sniff.

It was now or never, or a collision.

*"Tacking,"* Dakron screamed.

The genoa sheet was underneath the spinnaker pole: a bad tack. The starboard tack boat rolled over the top of *Snafu.*

Dakron said, *"Well, how did I get here?"*

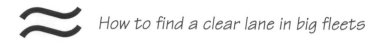 *How to find a clear lane in big fleets*

# LIFE IN THE PASSED LANE

$S$till reeling from their prolonged martyrdom on the starting line, the crew of *Snafu* crash-tacked to port, whereupon everyone took a moment to sum up life with the same four-letter word.

Grim.

Helmsman Deep Dakron groaned.

Tactician Scratchen Sniff groaned.

The Mumbler and the Kid, riding the rail, groaned.

Even members of the Race Committee groaned.

"Welcome to life in the passed lane," said Sniff.

"Guilty," said Dakron, weeping into his non-tiller hand. "Guilty by reason of insanity. I tried for the all-time drop dead start, and I dropped dead. But please, please, please, Mr. Tactician: supply now, flay later."

"I *was* supplying," said Sniff.

"You were?" said Dakron.

Sniff snuffled. "Just you watch Kid Comeback wend his wily way out of this weed patch! Our mode to recovery is simple: Locate a lane where we can live, and proceed in the direction we think best."

Deep Dakron plowed into a piece of chop, and the boat stopped. "Well, I can't live here. *Sea Cup* is dead in front of us, and besides, two other boats to windward are gassing me. I'm feeling about as solid as a bowl of oatmeal."

"Bear up man, and bear down!" Sniff commanded. "Let's power up the sails to get through this blankety-blank slop, because we *have* to live here for a few more boat lengths."

"Why?" wailed Dakron.

"Two reasons. We want to go toward the right side because it's favored, and because there's a starboard tacker coming. See him?"

Dakron peered under the boom. "Yup. He'll cross ahead. So what?"

Sniff grinned a you're-so-dense grin. "Sure, but *Sea Cup* and the other two boats to windward won't be able to cross him. I'll wager

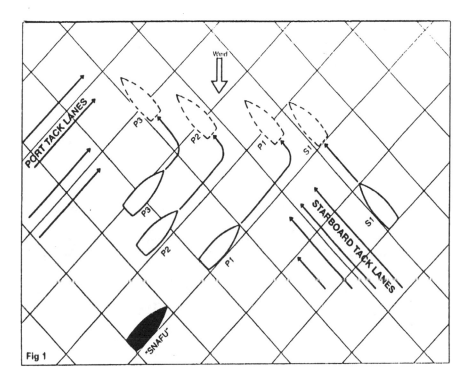

*Figure 1* In open water, choose your lane by anticipating the actions of boats and groups of boats as they converge. Blanketed by boats P1, P2, and P3, *Snafu* chooses to continue on port tack until S1, a starboard tack boat, flops the port tackers and clears *Snafu*'s lane and air.

that *Sea Cup* will roll into a knee-jerk lee bow tack under the starboard tacker, which will force the other two boats onto starboard tack as well. Stand by for some lane changes!"

Sure enough, the whole mess flopped over onto the starboard tack lanes, leaving *Snafu* with clear air and water on port tack, heading in the direction Sniff wanted to go (Figure 1).

"Now that we've got a clear lane and some straightaway, put the pedal to the metal," said Sniff.

"Aye, yi-yi," said Dakron, and he did.

After a while, Sniff reported, "Captain, I've detected a 10-degree header. Now I'll scan for a starboard lane, clear of Klingons and space junk, where we can take this shift across."

Dakron peered under the boom. "Here comes *Germinator* on starboard tack. I can lee bow him."

Sniff made the call. "We'll dip, and then tack to starboard when we're up a safe, clear margin on his hip. Ready?"

After the dip and the tack were over, Sniff felt eyes on the back of his neck. He began explaining before Dakron could ask.

"When you start a race in the cheap seats like we did, you need to capture four things in order to survive: **Clear wind**, **clean water**, **freedom**, and **protection**. We've got the first two. Since we want to be riding this starboard tack lift for a long time, we now need freedom and protection. By tacking on *Germinator's* weather hip instead of his lee bow, we've maintained the freedom to tack back whenever we want. And the best part is that not only are we now controlling *him*, we are also using him as a 'blocker' against port tack invaders. He's our protection."

Sure enough, shortly a stack of port tackers came across. The first of them, seeing he'd have a tough time crossing two starboard tack boats sailing a lift, lee-bowed *Germinator*, the first starboard tacker. Like dominoes, the pack then lee-bowed each other, bang, bang, bang, bang. You could almost hear the groan from *Germinator's* skipper when he looked over his shoulder and saw that Dakron, a length and a half safely to windward, had him pinned.

"We do look pretty smart!" Dakron crooned.

"Well, we are," Sniff agreed, "but now comes the trickiest part—reserving ourselves a lane into the weather mark."

"Isn't it a little early?" said Dakron. "We've still got a third of the beat to go."

"Working from the cheap seats in big fleets requires a lot more advance planning than does sailing merrily along at the head of the pack. Ideally, I'd like to originate from a long port lane with about 10 to 15 boat lengths of gauge, and make our final approach to the mark on a short starboard lane with a fat layline."

"Uh?" said Deep Dakron.

Sniff grinned a and-you-thought-you-were-so-smart grin. "Don't worry, you can lane on me. Let's get down to the nitty-gritty of the four-lane facts of life at the windward mark. First, on both port and starboard, there's the **length of the lane**, on either port or starboard. This is simply the number of boat lengths required to sail straight ahead and reach either the mark or the layline of the opposite tack (Figure 2).

"Then, again on both port and starboard, there's the **gauge of the lane**. This is the number of boat lengths below the layline your lane is situated.

"Then—usually this applies only to starboard tack, fairly close to the mark—there's a **thin layline**, which is a marginally underlaid,

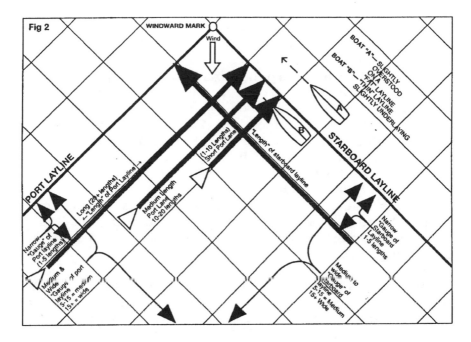

*Figure 2* When choosing a lane in which to approach the windward mark, assess the wind and sea conditions, the crowd factor, and the risk factor. For example, in big fleets a long lane with narrow gauge is high risk; choose a shorter, wider lane to lower the risk.

I-think-we'll-lay-the-mark-but-don't-raise-the-pole-yet kind of layline. Finally, there's the **fat layline**, which is a marginally over-laid lane to the mark."

"Long? Fat? Thin? Short? Sounds like a sausage commercial," said Dakron.

Sniff said, "Remember, relative lane lengths and gauge widths will vary according to the conditions. For example, a lane length of 20 lengths that will be quite long to sail in light air, time-wise, will only be of medium length in moderate wind.

"Here are some combos *not* to order when you're scrambling to get out of the big-fleet skillet. *A long lane with narrow gauge* is always high risk and low gain, especially when you're back in the stack. On the port lane there's the blanket from spinnakers going down the reach; on the starboard lane there's an early buildup on the layline, where every boat ahead wants to tack on you or give you a facial or bad breath or otherwise terminate your cabin pressure."

"Huh?" said Deep Dakron.

"Dirty air," explained Sniff. "More precisely, a suffocating absence of air, so bad that oxygen masks will drop from the boom, but they won't have any oxygen in them.

"So, if due to windshifts or boat traffic you are approaching the mark area from a long lane, either port or starboard, make sure to pick that lane with a gauge wide enough to skirt the blanketing from the spinnakers and the stack of boats packing the layline. Then, as you get closer, you can choose when to take the last tack in and make your final approach."

"How do I know when that time has come?" asked Dakron.

"You'll see," Sniff promised.

Later, as *Snafu* neared the windward mark, approaching on a long starboard lane with ten boat lengths of gauge, Dakron did see. Above them, on the layline, the dogfighting pack slowed down and an opening appeared.

"Should I tack now?" Dakron asked.

"Now," said Sniff, who noted that the boat was already turning. "Dip the first starboard boat; he's on a thin-bordering-on-suicidal layline. When we've got ourselves a fat layline we'll tack back onto starboard for the final approach. Ready about?"

After Dakron completed the tack he moaned, "We've overlaid it!"

But Sniff, who had been thinking ahead, had seen this mini-series before. *"Do not* give anything away. Here come three port tack Klingons at ten o'clock. Crossing us now. Here they go: wham! wham! wham! Tacked right in our face. Gee, what a surprise. Still think you're overlaying?"

"Air!" Dakron gasped. "Somebody give me some air. Are we making the mark still?"

Sniff grinned an I'm-so-smart grin. "Yes, thanks to my perfect gauging of long and short lanes and thin and fat laylines."

Dakron grinned a maybe-you're-not-as-smart-as-you-think grin. "And thank goodness the tide hasn't turned yet."

"Tide?" said Scratchen Sniff. "Tide hadn't even entered my brain."

"Guilty," said Deep Dakron. "I've been listening to a lane brain."

# CLIMB OUT OF THE PASSED TENSE

"**P**ersonally, I rather enjoy being behind," said Scratchen Sniff. "The way I look at it, it just makes this sailing game that much more challenging."

"Hmm," Deep Dakron said, trying to steer and watch for puffs coming down. "I'd rather be ahead. Way ahead, like that red boat, and be a lot less challenged."

Sniff said, "Well, anybody can win a race once they're out in front. It's making a comeback that separates the champions from the chaff."

"Darn. Darn it!" Dakron said, as a puff skittered away from him.

"There, that's exactly what I mean," Sniff said. "To make a comeback you've got to keep your cool. In fact, you should make **damage control** your first priority. Get back in control: get the swear words over with, settle down, get back in the hunt. Calm yourself and your crew. Don't blow your mind, don't mope, don't slit your wrists, don't pound the deck, don't let your steering go to hell and don't trim your sails any differently. Remind yourself that your opponents are likely to find themselves in straits just as dire sometime during the series. You're not a martyr, you're not excommunicated, you're just behind."

"I know I'm behind," Dakron snapped.

"Next, assess the damage. When you're behind, before you make any comeback moves, ask these questions: How bad is it, really? Am I mortally wounded, or just injured? If I finish the race in this position, at this point in the series, what's the bottom line? Will I be history in this regatta? Or can I stay alive with just a modest comeback, or even with no comeback? Get specific: what place do I need to finish to keep my series going? A reasoned assessment helps you get away from the emotionally charged *got to catch up with the leaders right now* form of risk-taking that can land you in even worse trouble.

"A cool assessment helps you set a goal, a realistic goal, for the race. For instance, if you round the first mark midway down or worse in a big fleet, the top ten boats are usually out of reach, so you should cease fretting about them and concentrate on those grouped just ahead of you. When making a comeback, resist the temptation to go for the Big One, to get it all back in one swoop, because in most races there isn't a private Big One to be found. In small fleets, chip away boat by boat. In big fleets, don't aim at passing individual boats; target them as clusters. And if it's early on in the race or series, remind yourself that you have some racetrack, some time available to you, so your comeback moves can be more conservative, less risky. You can wait for your opportunity, your moment."

Dakron glanced up, worried. "Good theory, except there's not much time left in this race, not for catching that red boat."

"Right. So much for theory, time for a **comeback**. When, where do we stage this valiant rescue of our race? Let's look at windward legs. Especially on the second and third beats, crews ahead tend to sail through minor shifts and work out to the side they thought was favored on the previous beat. Often, they wind up loosely covering each other, unconsciously guarding their position, thinking and moving as a herd. Maybe they get focused on trying to cross that one boat they want, or they get involved in a duel. It's very common that as the race progresses, people's heads move further and further inside the boat and they tend to miss the big picture. After one beat, some sailors close their eyes and their minds, simply because they reckon they know everything that's happening with the wind and tide. Maybe the crews ahead have grown a bit lazy, not working the small shifts as hard or looking for the big changes as diligently as they did early on.

"'Course, there are always the boats in the extreme corners you can pick off, one side or the other, and sometimes both. Same goes for the people who have hung themselves out to dry on the laylines. Boats ahead leave themselves open in many ways to being caught or passed on the windward legs."

"So what's the magic formula to catching that red boat? The guy never seems to put a foot wrong," Dakron said.

Sniff chuckled. "There's no magic formula to a comeback. Boat speed, sure, there's a lot of magic in that black art, and it sure makes a comeback easier, but, as you can see, in this particular race we are moving at identical speeds."

"Yeah," said Dakron. "Damn."

"Comebacks on reaching legs are usually measured in distance gained rather than boats rolled, unless you can motor by with magic trimming, wave riding or kinetics. If at all possible, avoid being sucked into a group, because groups almost always do the wrong thing: they sail too high, they dogfight, they slow each other down, and meanwhile the boats ahead and behind gain on them. If you see a potential for a gain on or a breakaway from a group, establish your plan early and stick with it. Breaking low of a group that rounds ahead of you, or working low initially if the reach is broad, can pay dividends at the next mark. If the reach is tight, or if a group threatens from astern, holding high is safer.

"Look at the fleet ahead, particularly the leaders, who are farthest down the reach, to locate the mark and the best course to it, before you start the leg. Lots of crews get so preoccupied with getting the spinnaker up, or gybed, or with defending their position, or with getting the sandwiches out, that they don't realize where the next mark is. You do, because you've already checked, and made your plan, and you can gain on them or break away from them while they're snoozing."

"I see the mark," Dakron said.

"Now, the run. If ever a leg favored those behind, this is it. Everyone knows that puffs come from behind, bringing the boats astern up on those ahead, so that's one built-in advantage right there. Watch the boats ahead to see where and when they go light, but make sure you look *behind* you and check out who is bringing down the next puff, and from where. Watch the boats behind to make a comeback on those ahead."

"There's no one behind me," Dakron said.

"Then you've got no worries," Sniff said. "On runs, the boats ahead tend to leave themselves open the same way they do on the second and third beats: moving and thinking as a herd, or else heading for a side and not working every shift and puff. If possible, keep yourself clear of groups; they curtail your movements, disrupt the air and tend to cost their members during the approach and rounding of the leeward mark."

"Damnit," Dakron snorted. "I've tried, but I can't take being this far behind. I hate it. This is absolutely no fun."

"Don't take it so hard," Sniff said. "Remember, sailing is only a game."

Deep Dakron threw his hands up. "I've had it. I'd rather play golf, and I *hate* golf."

Suddenly, GAME OVER flashed on the screen, and the red and blue sailboats cruised back and forth in a soup of electronic squawks.

"Got any more coins?" Scratchen Sniff asked. "You can be the red boat this time."

 *When and how to take a flyer*

# GO FOR THE, UH, GOLD?

"**D**ark, dank, dismal, and, no, let me enlarge on that," said tactician Scratchen Sniff. "Our situation is dark, dank, dismal and depressing, *but...*"

"But?" said Deep Dakron, on the tiller. He looked astern at the empty seascape: no danger of being passed. He looked ahead: funny, when boats got a certain distance way out in front, how the ones with spinnakers became dandelions, the ones under main and jib, party hats.

Sniff continued, "But there's hope, a light at the end of the tunnel, gold in them thar hills, a rainbow around the bend—"

"You mean it's time to go for the, uh, gold?" Dakron said.

"That's my boy!" Sniff cried. "I promise I won't tell anyone at the club it was your idea to take a flyer. Unless, of course, we bomb."

"When you're in our kind of shape, isn't it *always* time to go for the gold?" Dakron wondered.

"Depends on the conditions," said Sniff, "and the fleet, and the stage of the regatta, and your scorecard, and the mental health of your crew."

"Mental health?" said Dakron.

"First, let's define flyer. *A flyer means doing what your competition isn't, and, usually, taking it to an extreme*, like betting all your chips on black 13."

"What if you're out of chips, like us?"

"That's why you have to be a little crazy. If your idea is so smart, why isn't your competition, who is ahead of you, doing it? But we'll touch on mental health later."

"I'll be here," said Dakron.

Sniff said, "Let's start with conditions. In unstable weather systems, such as when two winds are fighting each other, or when there are thunderstorms, squalls, or a front passing through, a flyer can almost make sense, or at least be justified afterward. No one really can predict how the wind will change, which way, how much and how rapidly, so a flyer is a wild guess, but in these conditions, *everyone* is guessing. And the same can apply to lake and harbor sailing at its wackiest; when the smoke goes straight up and begins to corkscrew anything can happen, increasing the slim odds of a flyer working."

"Very clever, how we've set ourselves up for this flyer," Dakron said.

"We are definitely in the slingshot position," Sniff confirmed. "But even world champs and Olympic medalists have found themselves in deep doo-doo, staring a flyer in the face. That's the beauty of sailboat racing."

"It is?" said Deep Dakron.

"Of course, in more normal conditions, such as a seabreeze day or a gusty, tack-on-the-headers day, a flyer is almost certainly a loser. You'll end up sailing headers out to the wrong side, and then you'll sail headers all the way back in, getting even farther behind."

"That's why they're called flyers," Dakron said.

"And early on in a series, especially a championship, avoid taking a flyer; you probably don't have a feel for the venue, your competition, or your chances, and you could hurt your series irreparably with an early rash move. And anytime during the regatta when you're in trouble, before doing anything radical, consider your scorecard: am I out of the regatta if I bomb this race? Or can this be my drop race? Can I conceivably come back from this debacle and get near my regatta goal? You know, especially in big fleets, things can feel a lot worse at the time than they turn out to be in the final tally. You're so far behind, so discouraged, and so many boats are in front that you just give up counting. If you're not careful it can push you into taking a major flyer."

"So what should you do?" Dakron asked.

"Summon up some mental toughness," Sniff said. "You never thought you'd get over your first love at sixteen, right? Glad you didn't step off the pier with those sandbags, right? Life goes on, and it's usually not that bad. We've all heard this one: 'Hey, I finished ninth in the Mucky-Muck World Championships, and I was really depressed because I thought I'd do a lot better, but ninth was enough to get me funding for next year, and qualify me for the Interstellars in Rio, and guess what: I did it counting a 47th in the first race! If I'd taken a flyer like Ferd Fearless I'd have come in 78th, and would have wound up 17th overall.'"

"Point taken," Dakron said. "But Interstellars? Ferd Fearless? And Rio?"

"Of course, there are two types of flyers. I have a soft spot for the good old **speculative foray**."

"Sounds like a first date, or a corporate takeover."

"The speculative foray is the thinking man's flyer. You don't have to be in deep yogurt to go to it, but the setup should be right. The best time is usually well into the race, when the boats are spread, and you've got a bit of a cushion between you and the boats astern. Say there are a few boats ahead you'd like to knock off, but you're not getting to them by chipping away, and conditions are shifty, puffy, or unstable enough so that a little speculation just might turn your situation into gold."

"There's that word again," said Dakron.

"A speculative foray means going maverick: punching out from the group and what the group is pursuing, whether it means gybing away toward the other side or sidling low or high on the reach, wherever you see a possibility for gain, or even maverick speculation, an opportunity the leaders may have left open. You set yourself up in that opening with the biggest, widest grin on your face, imagining the stress you're putting on those guys."

Dakron said, "Playing your 'what if' trump for all it's worth."

"But the glory of the speculative foray is, if you do it right, you're not putting your whole race at risk, and you're not guaranteed to lose the boats behind you if it backfires. In a speculative foray, we're not going for the gold. A little silver, maybe, but we don't sail off the edge of the planet; it's a calculated risk. We estimate what we'll need to pass the group ahead, and, if it backfires, what it would take not to be passed by the jokers behind, and then we give it a calculated shot: The worst we can do is lose distance on the boats ahead, but not places in the race. That's why it's better to wait till later in the race, when the boats are spread out and there's not much racetrack left."

"I take it we're not in speculative shape here?"

"We are in full-on, **go for the gold**, tunnel till we hit daylight or China kind of shape," said Sniff. "But still, there's a right and a wrong way to pull off a go-for-the-golder."

"You mean should we drop our sails, get a little further behind, pile up some truly impressive leverage?"

"I mean we should ask ourselves, what are we trying to gain with this flyer? Boats, right? We want to pass as many boats as outrageous fortune and an ironic, sadistic wind god will permit, but *how* many boats? Do we need to pass a mere 15, or do we need 25, or 45, or the whole fleet? So, where are most of the boats? Are they on the right, or the left? Where are the nearest big bunches we could hope to get? And we plan our flyer accordingly.

"The second thing we ask concerns the wind: what's the stupid-est thing the wind could possibly do between now and the finish? We take that into account. The third thing we ask is, what's the stupidest thing *we* could possibly do between now and the finish? We factor these three things in, reach into the hat and pull out a flat-out fabulous flyer."

"You make it sound like a master tactic," Deep Dakron said. "I didn't realize we had so much choice in our situation."

"Well, we don't have a lot of chips to work with, that's why we're taking a flyer, and the three questions usually boil down to the same conclusion: we have to do the stupidest possible thing, hope the wind goes stupid, and that everyone else in the fleet is stupid. But, hey, once in a great while, a flyer works."

"Such is the beauty of yacht racing," Dakron said.

Sniff went on, "Now, just because we're being stupid doesn't guar-antee it'll work. Where do you think most people go wrong in a go for the gold flyer?"

"They go too far?" said Dakron.

"Wrong. *They don't go far enough.* You've decided to go for a new wind, killer leverage, an all-out miracle? *Go for it.* Halfway won't cut it; you have to make it memorable. Get over there into that breeze, get *solidly* into that new breeze—if there turns out to be any."

"All right. I'm going for it. Tacking, everybody," Dakron said, and the winches spun, though not with their usual enthusiasm.

"Finally, this brings us to **mental health**," Sniff said on the new tack. "The devastating aftermath of a failed flyer is well documented, but what I want to touch on are the lingering effects on crew psyche. *We* know we're doing something stupid, but our competitors, eager to grind us down, will tell us we *are* stupid. And if we start resorting to flyers every time we're in rotten shape, we undermine ourselves: *We took another flyer and got our butts handed to us again.* Our id will grumble, and pretty soon we'll start believing that negative voice in our head. Every flyer you take sends little shock waves of nega-tivity through your racing. Sometimes it's better to keep your self-respect and tough it out, take your lumps, swallow that bad race. Then you can say: *We had an all-time bad day, but at least we didn't stoop to taking a flyer.* At the end of it all, you might just emerge with something resembling a grin on your face."

"Now you tell me," Deep Dakron said, *"after* I've tacked."

Scratchen Sniff headed below. "Anybody want a beer?" he called out.

"Beer?" Dakron cried. "Look, we're still racing up here."

"I'm still racing," said Sniff. "I'm just putting a grin on my face."

 PART FOUR

# Sails and Sail Trim

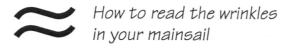 *How to read the wrinkles in your mainsail*

# SAILS TALK

"**W**hy are my—I mean *your*—sails so ugly?" Deep Dakron complained. "A wrinkle here, a wrinkle there, wrinkles everywhere."

Sailmaker Kent McBatten, playing the backstay like a Stradivarius, seemed not to hear. He focused on the leech of the mainsail as he tensioned the backstay. As the mast bend increased, the sail flattened, and the top batten responded by twisting off to leeward more and more. Then, as McBatten slowly released the backstay, the sail deepened, the leech tightened and the top batten angled itself back up to windward again.

"That's my baby," purred McBatten, cleating the backstay at the perfect spot.

"It's a mainsail only a mother could love," Dakron put in. "Can't you *do* something about all these wrinkles?"

McBatten seemed to hear for the first time. "Wrinkles? I prefer to think of them as creases of character, lines of distinction, folds of fastness."

Dakron sighed. "To me they're worry wrinkles. Why, for instance, must we put up with these corrugations running from the clew to the spreader area?"

"Every pucker tells a story," McBatten said. "First, understand that, even in this age of high-tech, low-stretch materials, a sail is but a thin membrane. In the case of this mainsail, we are subjecting the membrane to a wide variety of stresses in the form of different wind pressures, mast bend, and loadings from the outhaul, cunningham and mainsheet.

"So while we are mercilessly tweaking every corner of this membrane in our quest for the perfect shape, it's almost unavoidable that a few wrinkles will result. But instead of worrying about them, I like to use specific wrinkles as indicators of how the sail is reacting to my trimming."

Dakron furrowed his brow. "I don't mind a *few*. But so many! And they're so deep!"

Using the tips of his fingers, McBatten pulled lightly on his crow's feet until they disappeared. "All right, let's read this mainsail line by line. First, the clew-to-spreader corrugations, which reflect the relationship between mast bend and the luff curve of the sail. At present they are deep, indicating 'overbend,' because I am flattening the sail to a depth that is shallower than what I cut it to. In effect, you are getting two mainsails here—a flat one with overbend wrinkles, and a normal one without overbend wrinkles. Two mainsails for the price of one!"

"Do I get a discount on the ugly one?" wondered Dakron.

"Ugly is fast," replied McBatten, "and fast sails aren't cheap. But let's move on to the next line, the cunningham. Here the cunningham wrinkles have become inextricably mingled with the overbend wrinkles. I have purposely left the cunningham loose to let the point of maximum draft migrate aft.

"This gives us a flat shape in front with a rounded 'kick' to the leech; perfect for this flat water and moderate wind condition. But by straightening the mast and applying cunningham tension—which would eliminate these wrinkles which irritate you so—we can change the membrane to a full, draft-forward shape for choppy water. Two, two, two sails in one."

Dakron wrinkled his nose. "Maybe fast, but definitely not easy on the eyes. And what about these other major league crinkles? I trust you won't sidestep the fissure, Senator."

"Your crease is my command," smiled McBatten. "We'll go between the lines."

Dakron pointed, and moved his arm diagonally. "This wrinkle from the clew to the inboard end of the lower batten particularly annoys me."

McBatten offered, "I can eliminate it, recut the sail and take it out, but then the sail wouldn't be as fast."

"Why not?" said Deep Dakron.

McBatten explained: "This is a high load area, where direct stress from the clew combines with torsion from the batten. To get rid of that wrinkle I'd have to cut off some leech roach, thus losing sail area, and I'd have to dramatically flatten the broadseam adjacent to the batten, which would reduce the sail's power in choppy water. Cosmetically it'd look great, except that you'd be slow in conditions where you used to have power."

"Hmm," said Dakron. "Guess that one can stay. But how about

the crease running from the headboard to the inboard end of the top batten?"

McBatten said, "The top third of a mainsail is a very busy, highly stressed area of crisscrossing load lines. As you may have noticed, this crease comes and goes depending on mast bend and wind strength. It appears in very light or very heavy air, when there is either too little or too much mast bend for the built-in luff curve of the sail. This creates a corresponding dearth or surplus of fabric in the head area, which leads to the crease. When the mast bend is matched to the sail, the crease goes away. I could eliminate this by sewing light- and heavy-air zippers onto the luff, but at today's labor rates . . . "

"Hmm," said Dakron, visualizing a stuck zipper. "But what about those little vertical wrinkles that go from batten to batten? They *never* go away."

"That's right," admitted McBatten. "Full-length battens just about eliminate those little ripples, which shows the tremendous support—and problems—that battens transfer to the membrane. Conventional-length battens tend to concentrate leech loads in a small area, which magnifies the tiniest, most infinitesimal sewing error in the batten section. I could take a few seams apart and resew them to try and smooth out the area, but I'd probably do more harm than good. Unless there is a major problem, a sail's most sensitive areas are best left undisturbed, I've found. Like a marriage."

"Hmm," said Dakron. "All right. We've progressed from Egyptian cotton to Orlon to Rayon to Dacron to Mylar, Kevlar, and Spectra, but can you please tell me why we still get leech hook? Don't you find it embarrassing in this age of enlightenment?"

"Not at all," said McBatten. "After all, countless smart sailmakers the world over have attacked the problem of leech hook, and all of them have sighed trying. It's just what happens when you hoist fabric in the wind: the very edge will either flutter or curl. Besides, a slight leech hook has never proven slow in actual sail testing. But if you do happen upon a solution to leech hook and flutter, I suggest we patent it, quick."

Dakron waved his non-tiller hand. "I admit, I'm impressed. You've got an answer for everything. But there must be some way, some magic membrane that will get rid of these wrinkles."

McBatten stroked his chin thoughtfully, then said, "There is *one* membrane . . . "

"I knew it!" said Dakron.

McBatten ticked off the attributes on his fingers. "This membrane is super-light, and paper-thin. It has absolutely zero stretch, yet it's very flexible, and it folds and stuffs easily. Amazingly, it performs just as well when it's old and creased as when it's brand new and crispy. And best of all, it will never become obsolete."

"What is this wonder material?" cried Deep Dakron.

"Money," said Kent McBatten.

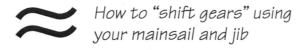 *How to "shift gears" using your mainsail and jib*

# SPEED À LA MODE

**D**eep Dakron trudged through the front door of McBatten Sailmakers and flopped onto the office couch. Dakron sighed, closed his eyes, and sank back slowly. When he opened his eyes, Kent McBatten had pulled up a chair.

"Tell me about it," said McBatten.

Dakron sighed. "They went by us on both sides this weekend. Not around us, like on a shift, but *by* us. Right *next* to us. We had no speed, and we couldn't point. We were the bologna in the bologna sandwich."

"I see," said McBatten, crossing his padded knees. He cocked his head, a doctor listening to familiar symptoms. "Precisely where on the racecourse did this occur?"

Dakron thought back, painfully. "At both starts. Each time, we had a nice hole to leeward of us at the gun, but less than a minute later we were ground up, pinched off by the boat underneath. After that, we had no option but to tack off and take all those sterns. Then, near the windward mark, a small windshift put us overstanding the mark. We eased the genoa, but the boat abeam and to windward of us just rocketed forward and over the top, and we were history. Like I said, we had no speed, and we couldn't point," Dakron finished up miserably.

Deep Dakron discovered he had laid back on the couch while telling his story. He looked up to see McBatten leaning forward, fingertips supporting his temples, no doubt contemplating an expensive cure: a new sail, a new keel, a new boat. Dakron straightened up; in McBatten's office, psychoanalysis could get expensive.

"Your problem, though humiliating, is actually a very common one," said McBatten. "Many racers suffer from it, and don't realize it. Quite simply, you have been sailing in the wrong mode."

Dakron's forehead wrinkled. "Huh?" he said.

But now it was Dakron who leaned forward; McBatten's rise through the dinghy and Olympic class ranks some years earlier made him a man to listen to.

"Once you realize that you can sail your boat to windward in several different modes—much like driving your car in different gears—you can work at matching your mode to your tactical needs on the racecourse. Of course, there are specialized methods of sail trim and steering for light, moderate, and heavy air, for smooth and for rough water, but to keep this simple let's assume that there are three basic modes for whatever conditions you are sailing in at the moment.

"First, there's **normal mode**. That's how you trim and sail in open water, when you're free of other boats and the requirements of marks and start lines. Normal mode is a roughly equal trade-off of pointing and footing, which requires trimming the sails, well, normally. During the course of a race, you'll sail in normal mode most of the time. But—and here we come to your particular dysfunction—if the situation calls for it you have to be able to shift gears into two alternate modes: **Point mode** and **drive mode**.

"Point mode means trimming the sails to gain pointing, or height, at the expense of some forward speed. It's the gear to shift down to when the competition to leeward is threatening to work up and squeeze you off. Protecting yourself off the starting line, against boats tacking on your lee bow, and anytime you round directly astern of a boat at the leeward mark, that should ring your alarm bells: time to shift into point mode."

"Sounds like heaven on water," Dakron said. "But how do I get into point mode? Press down and pop the clutch?"

McBatten ignored him and said, "Point mode means grunting up the mainsail for power. Let some backstay off (less mast bend creates a fuller sail and a tighter leech), ease the cunningham and outhaul, bring the traveler car farther up to windward. And most important: *tighten the mainsheet*. We are trying to add a dose of fullness and close off the mainsail leech here. In other words, we are removing much if not most of the leech's twist. Observe the leech telltales on the end of the top two battens; one or both may be stalled while trimmed for point mode. That's a good indicator that you have closed the leech down and put the mainsail into point mode.

"You'll feel all this in your helm, the best indicator. The increased weather helm, the added 'bite' will help you crab to windward. The jib or genoa leech can also be de-twisted for point mode. Jib lead

cars that are adjustable under load are the best bet; pull them forward to shift into point mode. Before the start, some crews routinely move their headsail leads forward to get more power and height out of the confused chop and bad air of the starting area.

"This is subtle stuff we're talking about here; usually it's only a few inches on the mainsheet or a degree or two of pointing angle. A lot of times you may not point higher, but you'll *hang* higher; lulls and powerboat wakes won't cause you to have to fall off to keep the boat moving, and compared to your neighbors you won't sag off to leeward nearly as much. The beauty of point mode is that it saves you from becoming a marshmallow on the racecourse; coming off the start line, for example, that leeward boat may truck forward on you a little, but he won't come up *into* you, and thus he won't have forced you to tack away into oblivion. Then, once you're safe and sailing in open water, you can shift back into normal mode and get on with the race."

Deep Dakron, flat on his back on the couch, looked relieved. "I feel more at peace already. Hang 'em higher, sheet it down, pull the lead forward, farewell to oblivion," he said. "Now, how do I shift up to drive mode?"

McBatten stretched his long legs and pulled up his kneepads. "The object of drive mode, or fifth gear, is to gain forward speed at the expense of height. When you need to roll over the top of a boat to leeward, or foot down to a mark that you shouldn't have overlaid in the first place, put it in drive mode.

"Basically, the sail trim techniques are the opposite of point mode; move toward flattening the mainsail via increased backstay, outhaul, and cunningham tension. The main point, though, is to *twist both main and headsail leeches by easing the sheets*. You need to free up the feeling on the helm, try to get it as neutral as possible so you can fall off and let the boat scoot. This seems like a basic concept, but it's amazing how often our sail trim on the racecourse gets 'locked in,' and those times that we do try to change it, we realize that we haven't experimented with it beforehand and don't know how to change our trim.

"Again, use the feel of the helm as an indicator of proper trim. If you find that weather helm is holding you up from driving as much as you need to, then ease more mainsheet, ease the traveler down until the bite goes out of the helm. Even if you don't need to make a radical course change—say you only want to fall off a few degrees— you can substantially increase your forward speed by freeing up the sails and letting the boat romp in drive mode."

"I feel so much better," Deep Dakron said dreamily, and his head lolled back on the cushion. He seemed to float off the couch, visualizing next weekend. "Outmoded no more. Higher and slower, faster and lower, power shifting, meshing the gears: eat my spray, you weekend warriors."

"Well, don't overdo it," said McBatten. "Anything that's worth doing can be—and usually is—overdone. When you start pulling on those important sail trim strings, pull them tenderly. Before you try shifting gears in a race, try it in practice. Sail alongside another boat before the start, or go sparring with a buddy. And the best way to go higher and faster is to order a new genoa. I've got this new warp-oriented, super-scrim material that—"

Deep Dakron shot off the couch. He was across the room and down the stairs before he realized his feet were in motion, and not even the words "radial clew" could catch him before the front door slammed.

Kent McBatten was impressed. "Now *that,*" he said, "was a mode shift."

 *How to improve your pointing*

# WHY JOHNNY CAN'T POINT

"**Y**ou're wearing an awfully wide smile for a man who spends his days in the pits," observed Deep Dakron, standing in the middle of the loft floor of McBatten Sailmakers.

Kent McBatten looked up, grinned even wider, and went back to sewing his seam. "It's these evening yacht club lectures I'm doing. Comic relief, except I'm not sure who's the straight man. Right after I finish my hour-long explanation of aerodynamic theory, lift and drag coefficients, and the intricacies of sail design, sail shape, and cloth stretch, I ask for questions from the audience."

"And some scientist type in the back row nails you about the interrelationship between upwash, backwash, and car wash," guessed Dakron.

McBatten's sail bunched at the machine and he swerved off the seam. "No, there's always dead silence for at least thirty seconds. Then, somebody in the back row asks the vaguest but most eloquent and all-encompassing question in the world of yacht racing. But I'm ready for it, because I get this question every time."

"I can't imagine!" said Dakron.

"They say, 'How come I can't point?'"

"Gee," said Dakron, "that's something I've always wanted to know, but was afraid to ask."

McBatten gave a burst at the end of the seam, lifted the pressure foot and clipped his thread. "Nothing is worse than the other guy outpointing you. It's like he's getting something for nothing! The first thing I do with this question is to explain that there are two aspects to pointing: **Angle** and **height**. Then I diagnose whether their poor pointing is a height problem or an angle problem. Angle, of course, is simply the angle your boat is pointing relative to the wind and, more importantly, to the competition. And the easiest way to improve your angle is to push the tiller to leeward."

"Why didn't I think of that," Dakron said. "Simple."

McBatten rolled his sail up to the next panel and started a new seam. "It's true. Many sailors, even the hotshots, forget that successful pointing is like a first date: you've got to cajole, squeeze, beg, pinch and use all your powers of concentration to get anywhere. So, pushing that tiller more to leeward more often, creeping up to windward in the puffs and stretches of flat water, sneaking your bow up to get that stolen half boat length when no one's looking, *working* at pointing really works. It's vastly underestimated, like flowers."

"Yeah, but what *kind* of flowers?" Dakron wondered. "Roses, or white carnations? And what if that doesn't do it?"

"Then, I go down the sail trim checklist. Simple stuff, no magic or mystery. First, more mainsheet tension, enough to make the batten section of the mainsail stand up and start pushing the stern to leeward. Enough to load up the helm a bit. But if this only hurts your helm and doesn't help your angle, try pulling the jibsheet in a few clicks and/or moving the lead forward to close off the upper leech for more 'bite.'"

"What about tightening the backstay to flatten the jib?" asked Dakron.

McBatten shrugged. "Sure, maybe that'll help, but the leeches of the main and the jib influence pointing a heck of a lot more than do the luffs. Any good jib is cut with the right amount of hollow in the luff to match a given boat's normal amount of forestay sag and backstay tension, so if your rig tension is in the ballpark there's little to be gained from overtensioning the backstay. And remember, too much backstay tension in light air will overflatten and depower the headsail, and actually hurt your pointing. So, a little tiller pushing and some simple sail trim changes should up your angle, but that's the easy part."

"It is?" said Deep Dakron.

Kent McBatten jiggled along merrily in his chair, in time to the zigzagging of the machine. "Yep. Anyone can get angle. But the Catch-22 is that the tighter you trim your sails, the more sideforce the sails generate, and the higher you point into the wind, the less boat speed your boat generates. Now, put this deadly duo together; not only are your sails pushing you harder sideways, but your reduced speed through the water means that the lifting surfaces of your underwater foils, namely the keel and rudder, are working less efficiently. Do you get my drift?"

Dakron nodded. "Humongous leeway, super side-slippage, an absolutely appalling inability to hang in there."

"Let's just call it lack of height," said McBatten. "Some have it, some aspire to it. And the moral of height is memorable: *It's not where you point, it's where you end up.* Height is all that matters over the long haul, such as on a long tack. If your boat speed and pointing angle are equal to that of your neighbor, but you seem to be slowly slip-sliding away to leeward—"

"Sayonara, baby," Dakron filled in.

"Height is invaluable in the short term, too; the ability to gain or maintain height in close-quarters situations, such as coming off the start line or rounding the leeward mark in a crowd, or whenever another boat tacks close on your lee bow, surviving and turning those encounters to your advantage can win regattas for you. Especially in big fleets, height is a lifesaver."

"Sold. Where do I pick up a one-year supply?" said Dakron.

McBatten's thread broke just as he reached the end of the seam. "Damn!" he said, rethreading his needle. "Picking up height isn't so easy. The first thing to understand, like I hinted at earlier, is that closehauled boats do not go where you point them."

"They don't?" said Deep Dakron.

"Because of the awesome sideforce exerted by sails when they're trimmed in closely, your boat does not go straight: it crabs sideways a little. Next time you're sailing closehauled, look over your shoulder; your wake will be angling away to windward. That is the shocking degree of leeway you are making, the amount of precious height you are losing. Toss a banana peel into your wake and give it one minute; now visualize that peel as a boat that started out in your wake but has now worked up on your hip."

"I'm not sure a banana peel would float for a whole minute," Dakron said. "How about a chocolate chip cookie?"

McBatten ignored him and continued. "Once you witness this loathsome leeway with your own eyes, you'll never forget it. Of the four major things contributing to height loss, the easiest to diagnose is **excessive heel**. Simply, boats that are sailed too heeled or pressed too hard tend to slide to leeward more. Remember the dinghy sailors battlecry, 'Flat is Fast!' They could have added, 'and High.' Sail your boat as flat as possible, and your foils will resist the leeway gremlins better.

"Another bogey is having your **sails too full in flat water**. The truism 'flat water, flat sails' is sailmakers' shorthand for the deadly stall and sideforce that too-full sails develop in flat water. An airplane will fall from the sky if its wings go into a stall; don't let the same thing happen to you on the racecourse."

Dakron said, "I *knew* sailing was safer than flying."

"And of course the opposite, keeping the **sails too flat in choppy**

**water** is equally disastrous to height. Sails that are trimmed too flat have little power, and lack of raw power in chop results in faltering, on/off boat speed, which translates into less efficient underwater foils and the need to plead."

"Huh?" said Deep Dakron.

"The need to plead," McBatten repeated. "You know, continually falling off, hunting for power but getting stopped and bounced sideways when the chop hammers you."

"Oh."

"Finally, there's keeping the sails **sheeted too hard** for the conditions, which contributes negatively to both heel and sideforce. Almost always, it's a leech problem; the main leech is *too* tight, or the jib leech is too closed in heavy air. You know, the usual culprits."

Dakron frowned. "But didn't you just tell me to tighten both my main and jib leeches to point better?"

McBatten grinned his end-of-the-question-period grin as he gunned his sewing machine. "I did, to improve angle. Experiment, but don't overdo it or you'll kill your height. Now, one last question."

Dakron said, "How come you're sewing that seam without any thread?"

McBatten frowned. "Good question."

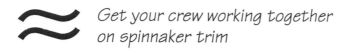 *Get your crew working together on spinnaker trim*

# CHUTE TO THE TOP

"**A**aarrgghh!" bawled Deep Dakron, swerving at the helm of *Snafu.* "If that damn spinnaker collapses *one more time,* I'll, I'll—"

"You'll, you'll, *play it yourself,*" finished sailmaker Kent McBatten, "and then you'll find out how hard it is to play in these tough conditions."

"Well, I guess it can collapse two more times," Dakron fudged.

The Kid, who was trimming the spinnaker sheet, took a second to wipe off a faceful of sweat before riveting his eyes back onto the spinnaker luff.

"Tough conditions?" Dakron came back. "A beautiful sunny Saturday, five to eight knots of wind, a little bit of chop, a little exhaust from a gang of waterbikers, you call that tough?"

"I wasn't referring to the weather," McBatten said dryly. "I was speaking of our human condition."

"Not that again," groaned Dakron.

McBatten said, "Once the spinnaker's up, you can either chute yourself to the top or spin yourself to the bottom. Choose one."

"Top," said Dakron.

McBatten said, "You see, we have to pull together with the Kid on this *spinnaker thing,* and then we'll have a kinder, gentler, *faster* downwind run. And that means getting these other points of light— Zig Zag Brooke, that's him asleep on the afterguy, and the Mumbler, currently snoozing on the topping lift, and Lisa Quick-Cam, bored silly with the foreguy—working, too."

"You mean, everyone thinking about the same thing at the same time?" said Dakron.

"Yes. Yoo-hoo! Everybody, listen up," McBatten said.

The crew stirred, then muttered.

"Welcome," said McBatten, "to the *New Leeward Order.* First,

**helmsman** Dakron: your job is to steer the fastest, most tactically advantageous course to the next mark. Easy, I know, but when the spinnaker is up, you must—except for dire tactical necessities—*sail a course within the parameters set by the sheet trimmer*, namely, the Kid. And remember, as you're trying to maintain a constant, fresh flow of apparent wind over the spinnaker, a straight line will not do. When you find yourself too low and slow, *head up quickly* to rebuild your apparent wind. If you find yourself sailing too high and hot, *head off slowly* so you don't burn off your apparent wind and boat speed suddenly, and lose it. Up quick; off slow. *Up quick; off slow.*"

"Got it," said Deep Dakron. "I sail up and down, up in the lulls, down in the puffs, whatever course it takes to keep my apparent wind flowing and fresh in velocity."

McBatten turned to the Kid and said, "Now, Kid, your responsibility as **sheet trimmer** is to judge your spinnaker's happiness via the behavior of the sail, *judging it mainly by the sheet pressure in your hands,* and to verbalize the spinnaker's health to the helmsman. Is the spinnaker fully pressurized, is it lifting and stable? Or does it look like a sack of potatoes, lumpy and bumpy and ready to collapse for lack of moving air? Feel the spinnaker's pulse with your spinnaker hand. Feel it in your gut. Your stomach will flutter when you have to keep sheeting in and in and in to keep it full; tell the helmsman that the sheet pressure is too light, and he needs to head up, needs to heat up the apparent wind flow.

"But if the spinnaker is pulling *too* hard, if the boat is aimed too high and going too fast, burning up VMGs when it could head lower with a happily pulling spinnaker, verbalize that as well. You are the first to feel it, the most hands-on, the most directly connected to the chute. Only you know how low your spinnaker can go and still be kept pulling properly, and only you know how high is *too* high. You've got to get the helmsman into your groove."

The Kid rolled his eyes. *Groove.* McBatten was *ancient.*

McBatten addressed Zig Zag Brooke next and said, "Zig Zag, as our main man on the **afterguy**, you should follow the lead set by the helmsman and the sheet trimmer. To properly place your pole, tune in to the trimmer's vocals and the line laid down by the person steering. Watch the changing angle and strength of the apparent wind via the telltales, the wind on the water, the wind pressure on the nape of your neck. Keep moving the pole to maintain a consistent angle to the apparent wind. What's the best angle? Watch the telltale spinnaker signs. *What* telltale spinnaker signs, you ask?

There's the aforementioned pressurization, consisting of either happy firmness or unhappy lumps and bumps, and there's the shape of the spinnaker foot.

"If the pole is too far aft the foot gets too tight, making the groove too narrow and critical for trimmer and helmsman. If the pole is too far forward the foot gets too rounded, making the chute too deep and rolly and reducing its projected area and exposure to the breeze. On a good day, the pole is moving forward and back in smooth increments, a nanosecond after the sheet trimmer trims or speaks, or the helmsman steers up or down. But you knew all that, right?"

"I knew all that," grumbled Brooke.

McBatten said, "And no less significant is Mr. Mumbler, poised on the **topping lift**. Your pole height affects the shape of the luff of the spinnaker, as well as the lift and stability of the entire sail. Get the pole up too high and the luff sags away from the end of the pole, the head area gets all twitchy, and the sail grows unstable, collapsing easily. Get the pole too low and the luff gets too tight, too knuckled, and inhibits the rest of the sail from lifting and projecting up and out into clear air. Those are your parameters; apparent wind strength is your guide. If the wind goes up, the pole comes aft (via the afterguy) and up (via the topping lift). If the wind goes down, the pole goes forward (via the afterguy) and down (via the topping lift). And the topping lift is always adjusted *smoothly."*

"Ahhhh," mumbled the Mumbler.

"And lovely, logical Lisa Quick-Cam, keeper of the **foreguy**, your job is twofold; to yield quickly, and then to hold firm. With your close attention to your job, no afterguy or topping lift peon can ever curl their lip and sneer, 'Foreguy?' Because you are so on top of it, you've aced their winch click or sheet squeal with the releasing 'click' or timely tug of your foreguy. Yes, you will open avenues of adjustment previously closed, and here's the best part: you encourage freedom and experimentation, but you are always firm."

Quick-Cam looked skeptical, but McBatten went on: "You know that if the end of the pole bobbles around even slightly it upsets the spinnaker, and that's why you are famed for never letting the pole *budge*, unless, of course, the afterguy or topping lift person deign to adjust it. You are so tireless (some days you hand-hold the foreguy with perfect pressure) and inventive (other days you cleat the foreguy with slack, and push sideways on the line with your Nikes) that you are the sparkplug of our downwind charge."

Quick-Cam snapped her gum and said, "All right, but don't stick me with the foreguy every time. I really should be steering this tub!"

"Shouldn't we all," McBatten commiserated. "But alas, our Skipper simply isn't qualified to do anything else. He can't even make sandwiches."

"Here comes a puff," Dakron cut in.

McBatten orchestrated the crew. "Pressure building," he said, focusing everyone.

"Pressure on the sheet," reported the Kid. "Too much pressure."

"Carving down," replied Deep Dakron.

"Pole coming aft," grunted Zig Zag Brooke.

Before the words left his lips, everyone heard the click of Quick-Cam's foreguy being released.

"Mmnpph!" said the Mumbler as he raised the pole.

"Way to go, team," said McBatten. "But now the puff is dying."

"Losing pressure," warned the Kid, letting his wraps slip on the winch. "The chute's looking soft. We're sailing too deep. Heat it up."

"Going up for air," answered Dakron. "Heading up 10 degrees."

"Pole going forward," said Brooke, and the Mumbler made sure that he eased his topping lift before Brooke had finished easing, so Brooke wouldn't have to crank back what he'd just let out.

Quick-Cam gave a funny little grunt as she snapped the foreguy down tight.

"Perfect!" said McBatten. "And now it's quiz time. Helmsman, what are your responsibilities?"

"Uh," said Dakron. "I, uh, steer for the mark."

"What else?" McBatten prompted.

"Um, I listen to the Kid."

"And?"

Dakron frowned. "I, uh, go *up slow* and *off quick?* No. I go *quick slow*, and *off up?* Wait, I got it: I go *quick off*, then I *slow up.*"

McBatten frowned. "Maybe we'll give you another chance with the sandwiches."

 *How—and how not—to use telltales*

# THAT FLUTTERY FEELING

Deep Dakron's head was swimming. A surf of words, sailmaker Kent McBatten's words, echoed off the walls of McBatten Sailmakers and splashed between Dakron's tympanic membrane and his medulla.

"Telltales are the downfall of Yachting Man, the crutch of the club sailor," McBatten was saying. "They're even more hypnotic than those electronic boxes, those fluorescent numbers clicking, clicking, clicking, those digital readouts chattering, chattering, chattering: *head up, fall off, head up, fall off.*"

Deep Dakron pressed his fingers to his temples.

McBatten crawled over the plywood floor, plowing on with his hotknife, a smoke trail snaking up his arm, and declared, "We're hooked on them. Mesmerized! Our eyes glued, our brains in neutral, our ears, noses, inner ears, the hairs on our arms going unconsulted, our gut feelings put on hold, our brains awash with the white noise of nothingness, with *flutter, flutter, flutter.*"

"Hooked on hypnotic black boxes?" Dakron said.

"No, telltales! Of course, telltales do have their place, as long as you don't let them turn you into a ribbon junkie."

"A ribbon junkie?" said Dakron.

"You know, a wooly head. Strung out on streamers. Tippled, pickled by ticklers! Start mainlining cassette tape—*metal* cassette tape. Become a yarn yayhoo, a telltale daytripper, a threadhead."

"A threadhead?" said Dakron.

"Some turn to thread. Thin black thread, for secrecy."

"Oh. What about us normal, boring types who use dull old wool?"

McBatten said, "You may be boring, but you may still have a problem. Which telltales do you find yourself ogling, jib or shroud?"

"Jib," Dakron admitted.

"And you follow your jib telltales, and what happens?"

"I find the luff of my life?" Dakron guessed.

McBatten's hotknife flared and released a gust of synthetic smoke. "Wrong. You follow your telltales and you lose sight of the waves, the competition, the next mark. Your Big Picture is narrowed to a fluttering ribbon."

"Big Picture first, telltales second," Dakron said. "Right."

McBatten said, "And so we must ask, are *any* telltales worth watching? Take the case of the NASA scientist who covered his jib and main, top to bottom, luff to leech, with telltales. Turned his sails into a wriggling can of worms! No matter what he did, he couldn't keep them happy; some stalled, some twirled, some tangled, a handful flowed, none of them agreed with each other. He went into therapy, claimed his telltales were holding hands and singing the theme song from *Mr. Ed.*"

"Moral: don't *over*telltale yourself," said Dakron.

"For a while, the sailing world was all aflutter over jib ticklers. How many, top to bottom? How close to the luff? What about sequential? Two, three, four in a row?"

"And the outcome of all this flutter?" Dakron asked.

"The answer is, the simpler the better. Less flutter equals more concentration. Three jib telltales, evenly spaced top to bottom, close to the luff but not *too* close, or they get oversensitive and unsteerable. And nix the sequential gimmick."

"Three telltales, to set the jib leads so the sail breaks evenly," said Dakron.

"Not so fast. That's one of those general rules, a one-condition setting, usually medium wind and water, which brings up another danger of slavishly following telltales, or rules about telltales: don't let your telltales tell you what to do. *You* tell *them.*"

"You mean, I should talk to my telltales?" Dakron said.

McBatten said: "Example: in light air, the three-telltale rule can fizzle. The top one may stall no matter where you put the lead or how you sheet the sail. This is probably due to the cut of the sail, especially if it is designed to cover a wide wind range. Then, in heavy air, when you should be depowering by twisting off the top third of the jib, the three-telltale rule is deadly, luring you into judging sheet tension and jib lead position by the wrong end: the luff, instead of the leech."

"Um," said Dakron. "The horse before the cart."

"Telltales don't tell you a thing about the sea conditions, or the power or pointing you need for a given situation. The shape of the leech, the feel of the boat, the trade-off between pointing and forward speed, your boat's performance versus the other boats, all those things tell you how you need to trim and steer, not the tell-tales. In heavy air, twist the main and jib leeches, open them up. For flat water pointing, straighten both leeches, sheet them hard. Go for moderate twist in choppy conditions, to avoid stall. Use soft sheeting in light air to encourage flow. In other words, experiment and work to get the speed, the pointing, the power you need for the conditions, and *then* check the telltales and use them as a reference.

"Take jib reaching," McBatten continued. "All jibs, especially low-clewed genoas, twist off too much at the top when you ease them out for reaching, so you may need to sail your favorite eye-level telltale stalled to get the best flow over the biggest percentage of the headsail. Simple, right?"

"Consider the sail's totality, not merely one pipsqueak strand of colored fluff," said Dakron. "Nail the boat speed and trim first, consult the woolies second, or third."

"Our telltales are slaves to us, not we to them," McBatten stressed.

Dakron said, "I *am* superior to a six-inch tuft of wool. It's always seemed the other way around."

"Let's get back to your case. Do you presently use, or have you ever used a telltale on your mainsail's top batten?"

"Yes."

"If so, what do you do with it, and why?"

Deep Dakron said, "I try to keep it flowing, to keep my mainsheet from getting too tight. I am a compulsive mainsheet tightener."

"I knew it. Another telltale leading you astray, telling *you* what to do. It's only a scrap of ripstop! It cannot think, or reason, but you can."

"I can?" said Dakron.

"You must to tell *it* what to do," McBatten insisted.

"Such as?"

"Such as, constant fluttering is not always the fastest way to the windward mark. For example, in flat water and medium air, a 50% stalled, 50% flowing telltale may indicate the fastest trim. Or stalled 80% of the time, or more, for maximum pointing. Or in sloppy, choppy stuff, the telltale might be flowing 100% of the time, in which case you have to begin judging your top batten angle relative to the boom, because once that telltale is flowing all the time it's giving you the same signal, regardless of what else is happening up there."

"Hmm," said Dakron.

"And don't forget to spot-check your competition's top batten telltale. It's a way to snoop on their sail trim, and it's even ethical."

"What if they're using stealth thread?" Dakron asked.

McBatten said, "And the top batten telltale downwind: I bet you're turning a blind eye."

Dakron said, "The only time I don't watch it, and I should be watching it?"

"You should be using your top batten telltale to judge your vang tension. One can either be a 'flowhead' or a 'plywoodhead.'"

"Flowhead? Plywoodhead?" said Dakron.

"Vang tension affects airflow across the mainsail," McBatten explained. "Most times, you *want* some mainsail flow off the wind, even on a dead run. You want that top batten tickler to come alive with refreshed, vibrant air molecules hopping off the leech."

"Wouldn't that just be spilling wind?" Dakron wondered.

"Stagnant air, stopped flow can lead to a stopped boat. Cat-rigged, single-sailed sailors know the subtleties of the vang; sloop-rigged sailors, fixated on the spinnaker, tend to gloss over it. When you ease the vang you open up the leech, and the top batten telltale confirms this by perking up. This is fast, especially when running by the lee. It's especially good with mainsails with full-length top battens, where the top of the sail gets too deep downwind, and on rigs with swept-back spreaders, where the boom can't go out far enough due to the shroud. Ease the vang, open up the leech, get some flow, and flow ahead of the plywoodheads."

"Plywoodheads," Dakron said. "Who, what are they? A grunge band?"

"That's when one shifts into 'plywood mode,' and the airflow over the mainsail goes from dynamic to static. You stop looking for the telltale because it's *gone*, stalled behind the mainsail leech. This is because you've put the vang on so hard the main is effectively a sheet of plywood."

"Uh, why?" asked Deep Dakron.

"This is a specialty trim. Good for dinghies. It gives you that extra *oomph* for pumping in marginal wave-catching conditions, when you're rowing your way down the course."

"I didn't hear that," said Dakron.

"Air-rowing, within legal limits, of course. An air-shattering, wave-catching, plywood bashing—"

"I think I'm more of a flowhead," said Dakron. "What about spinnaker telltales?"

"Those went out with the blooper," McBatten said. "The apparent wind changes are too radical, and spinnaker luffs too nervous. Besides, if spinnaker telltales 'worked' we'd use them the same way as any other telltale: trim the sail so the boat goes fast, *then* see if the telltales can tell us anything. We'd use them as indicators, which is how telltales started out before we got so hooked on them."

"At least telltales are a cheap thrill," said Dakron.

McBatten switched off his hotknife and said, confidentially, "Hate to tell you, but the price has gone up."

Dakron said, "Oh? What now? Programmable telltales? Climate sensitive? Low flutter? Cling-free? Static swept? Set 'n' forget? Or therapeutic on the eyes: reduces redness and swelling. No, I know: Kevlar telltales!"

McBatten turned hush-hush and eased a pair of black ribbons out of his pocket. "Hard-twist carbon," he whispered, glancing around. "Uncut. Pure. Guaranteed. The flutter, the sensitivity is unbelievable."

"One more addiction," said Deep Dakron.

"Once you've tried a pair of these," Kent McBatten promised, "you can never go back to dull old wool."

 PART FIVE

# STARTS, MARKS, AND RULES

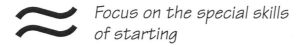 *Focus on the special skills of starting*

# START GETTING IT RIGHT

"**I**'m really, really nervous about this start," squeaked Deep Dakron, as the starting line of luffing sails cracked and shook around him.

"You're only nervous? We're terrified," said Scratchen Sniff, *Snafu's* tactician. "Research has revealed that crews suffer more neck whiplash, pinched fingers, squished toes, and, due to skippers screaming to winch in 65 feet of genoa sheet in 3.2 seconds, damage to eardrums on the starting line than anywhere on the racecourse. In fact, one recent study has shown that—"

Dakron didn't seem to be listening. "I mean, do I go for the Numero Uno position at the buoy, or do I play it safe? Do I luff the dickens out of my neighbors, or just mind my own business? Do I chase the first shift off the line, or wait and see what happens? Do I try to get my bow exactly on the line at the gun, or not push my luck? Do I tack away immediately, or carry on forever? I know! How about I set up early? Come in late. Port tack 'em! *Starboard* tack 'em. Gybe out of there, tack out of there, scream and yell and throw my protest flag!"

Sniff sighed. "Besides being wound 3,000 revolutions too tight, you're planning everything but nothing, your focus is everywhere but nowhere. You're looking for spaces in all the wrong places, you can't see the forest for the trees, the slots for the sails, the holes for the hulls. Listen: It's time to start getting it right."

Dakron gulped, desert-dry. "What do you suggest?"

Sniff spun a winch, the drum roll to an imminent dissertation. "First of all, to get consistently successful starts, forget all the razzmatazz. Don't get fancy, get back to basics."

"But I *like* razzmatazz," whined Dakron.

"I know, but you're no *good* at it."

"I'm not?"

"No."

"Oh!"

"Few people are," Sniff said reassuringly. "When approaching any start, instead of thinking about everything at once, most of which may not even be necessary to getting a good start, we should **focus on the one or two things vital in these circumstances**. Make a simple basic plan and then stick to the plan. Don't get sidetracked or spun out by all the hurly-burly during the countdown."

"Example?" prompted Dakron.

"Let's assume an average size fleet of 10 to 20 boats, ranging in skill level from darn good to merely okay. Given this, *wind velocity—whether it's light, medium or heavy—becomes the major determinant of your approach to the start*. In light air, your priorities should be **all-out speed across the starting line**, and **starting in and sailing toward the area of most wind**.

"Flat-out boat speed is the key to light air starts, much more important than positioning relative to your neighbors at the gun. The boats moving the fastest off the line quickly leave the slow-pokes behind. You should know your top speed in the prevailing conditions and practice getting your boat up to that speed, noting the time and distance required, and you should also get a feel for the wind's ups and downs, puffs and holes, so that your '30 seconds to the line' doesn't stretch into 45 or 60 seconds when the wind drops."

"So, in light air I focus mainly on boat speed, and on starting in and heading toward the most wind," said Dakron.

"Make sure you're up to top, top, *top* speed," Sniff stressed. "Really, really rolling, a steamroller across that starting line."

"Done," said Dakron. "And medium air?"

"In medium air we go for **positioning**, primo *positioning relative to our starting line neighbors, and the favored end or the area of the line that functions as the gateway to the favored side of the course*. In medium air, boat speed between yachts is much more equalized than in light or heavy air, and the wind is likely to be steadier. Thus we need to train our focus on boat-to-boat tactics. Positions on the starting line transfer farther up into the racecourse; the classic example of this is the lone starboard tack boat to windward that prevents a whole string of boats to leeward from tacking. In light air or heavy air you don't often see that, because usually *something happens*; either the wind dies or shifts drastically or comes blasting in, and some of the boats scoot away while others topple over dead by the wayside. But in medium air, getting a good position on the starting line—a safe leeward, a controlling windward, or being among the privileged few to step out for the favored side of the course right off the bat—is where it's at."

"And so?" said Dakron.

"And so we make our plan. For a port pin start or to get to the left side of the course: Know our starboard tack layline, make a port approach, tack under the first or best-timed starboard boat, luff him up, make our hole, protect our hole, get our road cleared ahead and to leeward, luff the windward boat or boats into a compromising position. For a start at the Race Committee boat or to get to the starboard side of the course: Know our layline to the Race Committee boat, establish our territory (Verbally, with gusto! 'Don't go in there, don't you dare go in there!'), control the boat or boats to windward, protect yourself from approaching port-tackers and starboard tack opportunists coming in from astern, don't sacrifice position against boats for position at the Race Committee boat (unless you are willing to take an immediate one- to two-length loss and tack off right after the gun)."

"I thought you said just to focus on one or two vital things," Dakron complained.

Sniff said, "I did, and I am. Except that in medium air it's three, the same three any real estate salesman will tell you: position, position, and position."

"I think you're trying to tell me something."

"Trying to," said Sniff. "Now: heavy air. The big problem in heavy air is that the air is so *heavy*. It takes a lot longer to winch the sails in, and it's more difficult for the helmsman and crew to tack, gybe, luff, and build speed in the starting line chop and confusion, and sometimes it's tough to even hear each other. Ask the skipper and crew of a 470 sitting luffing on an 80-boat starting line; they have to nearly scream at each other just to be heard above the ragging of 160 yarn-tempered mains and jibs and the screams of other crews. So, if you give it half a chance, confusion will reign on your boat during a heavy air start."

"Tell me about it," said Dakron.

"So our focus in heavy air starts is on **boat handling**. You must know how long it takes to tack and get back up to full speed; make some test tacks with stopwatch in hand. And work out the special techniques the helmsman and crew need to adopt to make it easier on each other before the start. For example, by tacking and gybing slowly, you give the trimmers more time to sheet in. With the crew making sure that the mainsail is vang-off and eased out well ahead of time, the helmsman can bear off without a coronary—or a collision. Get your communication terms established and maneuvers communicated and everyone prepared well ahead of time.

"Coming into the start itself, give your crew a chance. Avoid last second tacks or gybes that open up the bomb bay doors of disaster, and lead to winch overrides and fouled sheets. Talk out a simple starting plan, give yourself a reasonable run that allows time for everyone to get hiked out, the sails trimmed in, and the helmsman slotted into the groove right off the line. A rules situation, a luffing duel, or close contact with other boats is best avoided. Make sure your trim is fast, and tested, before the start—the luff tensions and outhaul and backstay are right, the jib leads and main traveler right, and go to your premarked vang-sheeting *before* the starting gun (as soon as you're sure you won't be doing any panic ducks). Be all set to blast off that line."

"Like a rocket to Mars," said Dakron, "or the first mark, at least."

"As I promised, this is basic stuff, but winning stuff," said Sniff. "The final way to start getting it right for all your starts, light, medium and heavy air, is to *practice*. Everyone practices fancy spinnaker sets and flavor-of-the-week spinnaker drops, but do they ever practice starts?"

"Uh, no."

"Why not? It's the most important part of the race! Before each real start, make a practice start. The hot match racers do. They research their laylines, the time and distance it takes them to go from dead in the water to full speed, how long it takes to tack, gybe, run the line, grind the genoa in to closehauled. They give the crew a two-minute countdown, they go through a practice start and try to hit the buoy or the Race Committee boat bang on."

"They hit the Committee boat?"

"Some are infamous for it," said Sniff. "Ever try to get insurance for a Race Committee boat? Now you know why flagmen are jumpy and entry fees are sky high. Don't do your practice start using the warning signal, though; you should be alongside the Race Committee then, punching your watch and looking for sneaky signal flags going up or down. If you do a practice start before every race, I guarantee that you'll discover some important things you didn't know. At the very least you'll burn off some nervous energy."

"I may have been nervous, but now I'm *excited.* Really excited," Deep Dakron piped.

Scratchen Sniff sighed. "I don't know which is worse."

Sniff tamped in his ear plugs, tightened his neck brace, and made sure his fingers and toes were well inboard.

Then he cried, "Let's get 'em!"

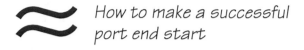 *How to make a successful
port end start*

# LINE CALL

By the time sailmaker Kent McBatten located his dropped bobbin amid the debris of his sewing pit, he'd gotten his fingers oily, which annoyed him. Then, after he'd painstakingly rethreaded his sewing machine and horsed the mainsail back into position under the needle and got sewing again, his cellular phone began to shrill.

Tweeeet! Tweeeet! Tweeeet!

McBatten's gummed-up needle overheated, his thread broke, and he veered off the seam. Damn!

Tweeeet! Tweeeet! Tweeeet!

Irritating chirp! But at least a cell phone in his pit saved the mad dash to the office. "McBatten Sailmakers," he answered with a lack of enthusiasm.

Deep Dakron's voice came through the line against a backdrop of heavy static. "Hope you're not busy, but I could use your input right now."

"Me? Busy?" McBatten didn't hide his irritation. "No, I always work late repairing mainsails that have been Chinese-gybed through Tiananmen Square. I love it when a customer manages to explode his full-length battens into a million pieces. Took all afternoon to get the fiberglass shards out, and of course he wants it Friday so he can do it again. And what do you want?"

"Since you're not busy, can I have you for the next six minutes?" asked Dakron.

McBatten was about to let loose another volley when a shotgun blast reverberated over the line.

"Got it!" cried Dakron. "Make that the next five minutes."

"Are you where I think you are?" McBatten asked, for the static was beginning to sound more like wind and waves and luffing sails.

"Where else?" said Dakron. "It's Wednesday night, the Frothy Lager

Series. Class B just got off, and we've got four minutes and fifty seconds till our start. Since you're always too busy to come out sailing with me, I thought I'd call and get some advice on this start. Aren't cell phones great?"

McBatten sighed. Damn these cell phones! No place was safe.

He shot a few quick questions at Dakron. "Sniff's not onboard? Right. Uh-huh. He's on *Dirty Heir*. Okay, what's the situation?"

There was a flutter in Dakron's voice. "We have eight knots of sea breeze, and it's pretty steady as far as windshifts go. There're 11 boats in our class, and it's quite a long line. We sailed down it and got the compass heading, and we've been checking the squareness of the line by taking head-to-wind readings every few minutes. The port end is favored by 10 degrees, and my crew is hounding me to go for a pin end start. Hang on a second, tacking!"

McBatten held the receiver away from his ear as the winches and sails clattered. In the background a crewman yelled, "Four minutes, 20 seconds!"

McBatten's pulse quickened. "Dakron: hurry down to that port end," he barked, "and take the first step to getting a good port end start, which is to **stake out your territory.**"

"We're in the vicinity now," Dakron reported.

"Good. Any company? Anyone exhibiting territorial behavior?"

"*Dirty Heir* is cruising back and forth by the buoy," said Dakron.

"Figures," said McBatten, "leave it to Sniff. You'll need to use match racing tactics to drive him out of there. But for now just assert your presence in the area so they'll know that you want that port end bad, badder than they do, and they'll have to fight for it. Often that's enough to give the opposition second thoughts or convince them to go for a less risky start farther up the line, away from you. Plus, you'll start to feel more comfortable about the area yourself. You may even find that there's less wind down at the port end than at the starboard end, and you may change your mind. Always keep your eyes and wind receptors on alert when dealing with a long starting line."

Dakron's voice crackled over the phone. "We're sailing by the buoy on starboard tack now, and tacking back to port to pass it again."

McBatten strained to make himself heard over the sails. "Be sure to get a close look at the buoy and make sure there isn't a floating anchor line that can snag your keel or rudder. Then check for signs of current, and get everyone on the boat to note the strength and direction. Toss an apple core or something biodegradeable into the water next to the buoy, then study the direction and speed the current takes it. Have a crew member watch it for 60 seconds to give

you the best possible estimate of how much drift you'll need to allow for during your final approach."

Dakron said, "Arming #1 forward banana peel . . . *fire*. Three minutes, 40 seconds."

"Good. The next step is to take a couple of practice runs at the pin on starboard tack to **determine your layline**. This is crucial. To start successfully at the port end you have to know exactly where the starboard tack closehauled layline is at all times, because once you fall below the layline the game is over. You have to allow for current and the drift you'll make when you're luffing, and also how much you'll sideslip initially when you sheet in. You have to allow for the possibility of a last second header or a lull, as well as possible blanketing by other boats, disturbed water and air from other boats, and the amount you'll need to bear away to get your boat up to speed for the gun."

"We're taking a run at it now," Dakron shouted into the phone.

"Good. While you're at it you should **quantify the approach factors**. First, watch your watch and see how many seconds it takes to sail five boat lengths while going full speed on a close reach. Next, luff the sails enough to completely stop the boat, and then only enough to keep it just barely jogging along, like you'd do if you had to kill time, then sheet in and see how many boat lengths and seconds it takes to get up to full speed again. Got it?"

"Got it," said Deep Dakron. "I'm putting you on hold while we do all of this."

McBatten cursed the dead receiver, and busied himself changing needles. How could Dakron put him on hold at a time like this?

"McBatten?" Dakron was back on the line.

"How much time is left?" McBatten said, anxious.

"Two minutes, 15 seconds. It took longer and farther to accelerate up to full speed than we thought. From a jog it took us 18 seconds and three and a half boat lengths, and from a dead stop it took a full 40 seconds and seven lengths to get her really moving. We also ended up below the layline and had to pinch to lay the mark, so we'll make our final approach from higher up the line."

"Good," said McBatten. "Remember, anytime you fall below even the close reach layline to the pin, you're hampering your speed and slipping into the danger zone. Now it's time to begin **herding your rival(s)** for the port end start out of contention. Scratchen Sniff, whither art thou?"

Dakron reported: *"Dirty Heir* is reaching along on starboard past the buoy, and we're a little behind them. Now they're going into a slow tack onto port just outside the end of the line. I imagine they'll head back toward the middle of the line on port, then tack onto starboard for their final approach to the pin."

McBatten's voice rose. "Dakron, I want you to tack around onto port right behind them and follow them in on port tack. Get on their case! Get your bow as close as possible on their stern, so that you're 'herding' them and able to dictate their movements, just like match racers do to each other."

"TACKING," bellowed Dakron, and after his sails filled: "Okay, we're on port tack now, right on *Dirty Heir*'s transom."

"Perfect," said McBatten, ears ringing. "Stay on his tail and keep driving him away from the port end. Do not, whatever you do, get yourself overlapped either to windward or to leeward of him, because then you lose your freedom to tack or gybe. If he tries to tack, you should head up to prevent him, and if he tries to gybe, head down to discourage him. He can't do either without fouling you, and be sure you let him know that. Keep herding him until you've opened up plenty of room between yourself and the buoy for your final starboard approach."

"There's a line of starboard tackers coming," Deep Dakron said, worry in his voice.

"Okay, when Sniff calls for room to tack you give it to him, but

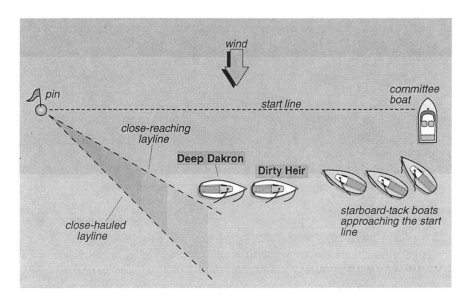

wind

pin

start line

committee
boat

close-reaching
layline

**Deep Dakron**

**Dirty Heir**

starboard-tack boats
approaching the start
line

close-hauled
layline

On the port tack approach, Dakron stays close astern to
herd *Dirty Heir* into the starboard tackers. When both tack,
Dakron will be to leeward, in a controlling position.

not one millimeter extra. I want you to tack close underneath *Dirty Heir* and pin them up against the starboard boats."

"YOU'VE GOT ROOM," yelled Dakron across the water, and hollered "TACKING," to his crew.

McBatten brought the phone back to his ear after Dakron had filled away onto starboard. "What you've got to do now is **control the approach**. Use *Dirty Heir* as a blocker to hold everyone else back and slow the whole procession down. They'll try to push you into arriving at the port end too early, and it's your job to hold them up with some luffs and feints. How much time?"

"Fifty-five seconds," Dakron squeaked. "Coming up! Keep it up! COMING UP."

Even with the receiver at arm's length McBatten could hear the threats, reprisals, and luffing genoas. "That's it, keep stalling them. Keep judging the time and distance versus the amount of wind, chop and sailing angle you've got. When you're *sure* you've got a safe cushion of time and distance to the line—you never, ever want to arrive at the buoy too early, because there's nowhere to go—then peel off and go for it.

"But, Dakron, make sure you've left yourself enough boat lengths and time so that you're going fast at the gun. It's not nearly as important to be right at the buoy as it is to be up to full speed across the line. If you're going slow, the boats to windward will march over you."

"BUILD SPEED," Dakron screamed to his crew.

"Are you *sure* of your distance to the pin?" McBatten pressed.

"I think we'll be a little late to the buoy, but we'll be up to speed," said Dakron.

"Don't worry about the buoy," McBatten told him. "Just stick your nose over the line with the gun, and you'll be fine."

"GUN!" Dakron yelled, and then he was drowned out by squealing blocks and grinding winches. "We're clean and moving and we've got a little speed on *Dirty Heir*. What should I do now?"

"Now you should hang up and start sailing," said McBatten, "and I should start sewing."

McBatten hung up, thought for a few moments, and then a huge grin spread across his face. He picked up the phone and dialed Dakron's number.

"I'm busy!" Dakron snapped.

"No, you're disqualified," McBatten corrected. "It's illegal to receive outside assistance during the preparatory period."

"Hmm," said Dakron. "At least I got a good start."

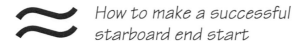 *How to make a successful
starboard end start*

# WHITHER END?

$S$ailmaker Kent McBatten had just turned the key to his shop door, locking up for the day, when the chirping of the cellular phone reached him.

Do not, he told himself, break your fundamental rule: Never pick up the phone after closing time. It's guaranteed to be either a customer with an emergency, the local kindergarten wanting a guided tour, or someone asking if he makes kites.

But McBatten couldn't resist it—breaking a rule, that is. Taking the stairs three at a time he skidded into his sewing pit and speared the cell phone off its hook. "McBatten Sailmakers."

"Yahoo!" yelled Deep Dakron amid the sound of rattling sails and winches, one hand on the tiller extension and one hand on *Snafu's* cell phone. "Twenty-three Frothy Lager Wednesday night warriors on the starting line tonight, and I say the windward, weather, that is to say the Race Committee boat end is the call! What do you say?"

McBatten pressed MUTE, and cursed. See what happens when you break a fundamental rule? He sighed, pressed TALK and asked, "How much time?"

"Nine minutes," hollered Dakron. "Thought I'd call well before the five-minute gun, so I wouldn't get disqualified for outside assistance. The starboard end is favored 15 degrees, and the right side of the course seems to be dealing out the major puff cards. Besides, everyone else is going to start at the Committee boat."

"Impeccable herd instinct," McBatten agreed. "Look, since you're committed to this, I can prep you on what to look out for, but I can't talk you through it. Not even L.L. Cool J., Fresh Prince and Ice Cube could rap heavy enough to pull *that* off."

"What was that?" asked Dakron. "Lots of static out here."

"I said that starboard end starts can be a bad rap, mostly because of the way the starboard end twists reasonable sailors into shameless schemers and prevaricators. Maybe it's the aura of risk surrounding the Race Committee boat, or all the luffing and bluffing and barging, but those bad vibes around the starboard end get *heavy*.

"The first thing to remember is that it's more important to get a good start in relation to the mini-fleet of boats around you—to have a clean, free position and good boat speed relative to them—than it is to start at a particular spot. If your approach is, 'I'm going to start *right next* to the Race Committee boat,' then the odds are you *will* end up right next to the boat—dead in the water."

"Roger," said Dakron. "I'll shy away from the Committee boat. That shotgun makes my ears ring, anyway."

"All right," said McBatten. "With starboard end starts, the best-laid plans are meant to be adapted to the way the other boats are lining up. Focus on them and exploit their weaknesses, and don't let them push you around. The first step toward this is understanding the psychology and *modus operandi* of starboard end starters. I classify them into four groups: **Luffers**, **bargers**, **layliners** and **chronic cases**.

"Let's start with that nasty bunch of spoilers known as the **luffers**. You know the type; veins on their red necks standing out in bas relief, they come screaming and shouting their way up from an incredible distance to leeward. Their special joy is scraping boats off on the Committee boat and protesting any who escape. But because they are so intent on spoiling others' starts, they rarely get a decent start themselves.

"How to defend yourself against a luffer? First, recognize him *early* and take steps to break his potential for an overlap on you by either slowing down or speeding up, thus directing him toward another target. Other tactics are to immobilize him through blanketing, which works particularly well in light air, or to slip a 'blocker' boat in between you to slow him up.

"However, if you wait too long—say he's alongside, screaming at you—your only choice is to stoop to mudslinging and stalling tactics. Via your spokesman (the biggest, most intimidating, most vocal member of your crew), cast aspersions on your opponent's credibility and motives while promising him that everything that *can* be done about the problem *is* being done. Buy time, and never, never bump hulls with him. If you do, it's a protest flag and The Room for sure."

"Seven minutes, 50 seconds," Dakron cut in.

"Now, should you find yourself playing the role of luffer," McBatten continued, "have your spokesman do the screaming and threatening while you concentrate on the positioning and speed of the boats. Don't work against yourself by locking into an overlap underneath someone who just will not respond. You can bump rails all day with some skippers and they'll never get it up. Separate the sheep—those boats that will scatter at your approach—from the bulls, against which you'll come up against with a thud, ruining your start.

"Next, the **bargers**. The classic barger is a furtive type, usually a junk bond salesman or a corporate tax consultant, and his forte is getting away with something he knows he shouldn't. Your defense is largely one of early verbal intimidation. Have your spokesman point a finger directly at the barger and unmistakably inform him: He is barging. He has no rights. He should bail out *now*, and avoid the pain of exclusion from the starting line and disqualification from the race. Then, ostensibly to gather witnesses for your impending protest, have your spokesman repeatedly call out the barger's sail number. Most bargers will find this last gambit intimidating enough to steer clear of you.

"Now, should you find yourself in the indefensible position of *being* the barger, your spokesman should swing into placation mode. While he's soothing them, you focus on judging the position and speed of the threatening boat to leeward. Can he close the distance to windward in the time left? Can he speed up enough to go forward and get an overlap underneath your stern and gain control of you? Can you speed up enough to get across his bow and underneath him? If you act immediately, can you dip his transom? Remember, as the boats converge, your options run out. Act early, when you still have time and distance to work with."

Dakron's voice came over the phone tinny and tight. "Act early, act early. Oh! be still, my heart! Only two minutes till the five-minute gun!"

McBatten pressed MUTE, strolled to the loft fridge, and extracted a can of beer. After several swallows he pressed TALK and resumed his spiel right over the top of Deep Dakron, who was muttering.

"Now we've come to that self-righteous bunch of hardliners known as the **layliners**. Adherents to this cult—and a lot more of us sleepwalk ourselves into this approach than we'll admit—put their faith into coming in 'on the layline,' which they feel will somehow protect them from both luffers and bargers."

"It won't?" said Dakron.

"Trouble is, as the seconds tick down, the starboard end layline becomes about as clear as a mud puddle, and by attempting to hold to this theoretical line the layliner eliminates all his other options.

Your defense against him is simple: luff him up, or barge over the top of him. Don't line up parallel with him or you'll be taken for a ride. Attack him at an angle, that's the best way to put a kink in his inflexibility."

"What's my offensive tactic if I'm the layliner?" Dakron asked, but the line remained silent.

On the other end, McBatten pondered his MUTE button.

"Okay, dumb question," said Deep Dakron. "There's not too much you can *do* when you're on the layline. What's the last type of starboard end starter? Only six minutes, 30 seconds left, I've got to make a decision here."

McBatten set his beer down. "Just remember to keep the starboard end layline in the same box as Christmas: a nice once-a-year present. Now, type four: the **chronic cases**. Once upon a Wednesday night, ages ago, the archetypal chronic case lucked into a big hole at the starboard end, tacked immediately, went all the way to the starboard tack layline, stumbled into a big lift, and led by two minutes at the windward mark.

"Ever since, these types of sailors *always* start at the starboard end of the starting line, which they mistakenly call the 'windward end' or the 'weather end,' regardless of whether it is actually to windward or to leeward of the port end. Chronic cases exhibit classic insecurity symptoms; they need to start 'above' everyone to feel like they've got an advantage. In reality, they're trying to shield themselves from any nasty infighting or boat speed duels, during which their squishy confidence levels might let them down. The rationale goes: *If I get a bad start I can always tack off, and then everything will be fine."*

"Doesn't sound so bad," said Dakron, switching tiller extension and cell phone hands. "How about if I just come in late, right at the Committee boat, and tack off? That's one of my favorites."

"What a wonderful idea," said McBatten, "especially since your awesome boat speed and the shift you're guaranteed to luck into will make up those three to five boat lengths you've thrown away at the most crucial part of the race, the start. But what will your competitors think of your *chutzpah*, waiting till everyone else has cleared the line to try your start?"

"Uh," said Deep Dakron. "Listen, thanks for the advice, but I've got to hang up. Only 40 seconds till the five-minute gun, and I've still got to choose my starboard end starting method. Wish me—"

"Luck!" said McBatten, hanging up.

After McBatten finished his beer, he turned off the lights and went downstairs. Just as he was locking the front door, the cell phone went off. Instinctively, he checked his watch; twelve seconds to the preparatory. It might be too late already for Dakron! What if he's locked in, locked out, or generally in a heap of trouble? McBatten bolted up the stairs and lunged at the phone.

"McStartem here!" he said breathlessly.

"Do you make kites?" a voice asked.

McBatten sighed. See what happens when you go and break your own fundamental rule?

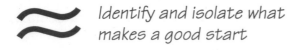
*Identify and isolate what makes a good start*

# TROUBLESTARTING

The dot-matrix whine of the computer printer reached Deep Dakron before he got to the top step of McBatten Sailmakers. Inventory time again, thought Dakron. Or printing out bills, or maybe a breakthrough sail design.

"This is a new go-fast sheet for my customers," Kent McBatten explained. "I have a whole series of sail trim tips, called McTrimTips, but this one I'm calling 'Troublestarting.'"

"Troublestarting?" said Dakron. "Don't you mean, trouble*shooting?*"

McBatten said, "I've got customers that phone in every Monday and complain, 'That new sail you sold me? No speed off the line' or 'I couldn't make my boat point. The boats below ate me up.'"

McBatten continued, "The thing is, I know my sails aren't the problem. My best software went into those keelboat sails, and my choicest yarn-tempered cloth went into the dinghy sails, hot off my hottest patterns. But on the water, something wasn't clicking."

"And your sails weren't winning," said Dakron. "Cause for concern."

"Clicking, I thought, that's it. I took my camera out in the rubber ducky to get shots of everyone's sails and isolate the trim problems. I knew the trouble wouldn't be with my sails, but with how they were being trimmed."

"Spoken like a sailmaker," said Dakron.

"Well, my poor sails never had a chance! My customers in the keelboat fleet couldn't get off the start line. I buzzed over to the dinghy course and found the same story. The boats wearing my product were finished before they even started."

The back of McBatten's neck and the tops of his ears were sunburned. It had been a long frustrating weekend, photographing his handiwork going down the drain.

"So I got a shot of every start, in light, medium, and heavy conditions, and the pictures all added up to one thing," he said.

"Troublestarting," said Dakron, picking up a freshly printed page. "Dinghy and keelboat starts in three basic wind conditions, this seems simple enough."

A spreadsheet format with categories and boxes with terse, cryptic advice, McBatten's Troublestarting Tips carried the unmistakable tone of a long-suffering parent.

"My customers, like many sailors, seem to get distracted by all the wrong things at the start," McBatten complained. "If they'd just learn to focus on the elements vital to their type of boat in the existing wind conditions, they'd find themselves with a halfway decent start."

Dakron read the first box: "*Light Air, Keelboat Start: Make sure your boat is up to full speed.* That's it? That's the whole tip?" he said.

"That's the essence," said McBatten. "Observe the typical keelboat start in light air. At the gun, maybe half the fleet—at best—will be moving at full speed. Those that aren't, regardless of how well they're positioned at the gun, will be quickly left behind—those are my customers. They need to do a dummy run to see just how long it takes to bring their boat up to full speed from a luffing or slowed state. That means finding out how long in *time* and in *boat lengths*, and they also need to realize how far they'll need to bear off to build up to full speed. And when I say full speed I mean *full* speed. In light air, boat speed can double when you go from glued to really romping. My customers, sadly, leave their charge way too late."

Dakron said, "The next box is, *Light Air, Dinghy Start: Don't get bunched.* Bunched?"

"Munched, marshmallowed, gassed, gagged, stifled, suffocated, sandwiched," Mcbatten explained. "In light air, one end of the line will often be favored, and you can bet my customers will be jammed in there like sardines. Bunched, in other words. Only one or two boats are going to survive, so my guys are better off starting a bit down or up from the stack in clearer, fresher air, with their water and their options open. They may not win the start, but they won't lose it, either."

Dakron moved on: "*Medium Air, Keelboat Start: Be able to tack/keep going as per game plan.*"

"Medium air, the great equalizer," said McBatten. "Most people have enough crew work and timing to hit the line near the gun with a good head of steam, and boat speeds tend to even out in the moderate stuff, and the wind is usually steadier, so your position off the starting line relative to the boats around you means that what you start with, you'll live with. The first step is to come up with a basic game plan by asking, am I looking for freedom to tack relatively soon after the start, or do I want freedom to keep going for a stretch? Then, on the final run to the line, position yourself relative to other boats so that you can carry out your game plan. Don't set up below a stack of boats if you'd like to tack soon after the start; protect the hole below you at all costs if you want to continue on starboard tack. It's tough to pass boats in medium air, and it's easy to find yourself being herded one way or the other right off the start line, so put your focus on prestart positioning."

Dakron continued to the next box: "*Medium Air, Dinghy Start: Set up for height.*"

"The medium air equalizer principle applies to dinghies, too, but a little differently," McBatten said. "Because forward speeds are very even, it's often pointing—I prefer to use the term *height*, because it's one thing to point high but it's another to *hang* high, to separate up from the boats below you and squeeze off the boats on your hip—that saves you from an ignominious slide into the cheap seats. So, in medium air, set your tuning for maximum height off the start line. This means sheeting hard, using lots of leech tension on the main and jib, sailing your boat dead flat, even heeled to windward, and steering for height, at least till you're clear of the starting hubbub."

"Hang 'em high," said Dakron. "Next: *Heavy Air, Keelboat Start: Mechanics.*" Dakron looked puzzled. "What does that mean? Strip the winches and grease them?"

McBatten threw him a look of pity. "It means, if you're anything like my customers, during those make-or-break last ten seconds before the starting gun, things turn to chaos—people screaming, too many crew members to leeward, the mainsheet strapped in prematurely, the helm overloaded, crew blocking the helmsman's view, no one can hear the time or anything else—you get the picture. Your carefully planned start becomes a shambles, all because the sail trimming and the choreography of the bodies aren't coordinated. For this there's no excuse, but there is prevention: go through a dummy run at the line, reaching along it and trimming in as a unit. Work out which bodies will go where and when, which commands you'll use for the final winch-in, when and how quickly the mainsail should come on, who should be hiking, who should be advising you of what, who should be keeping quiet."

"In other words, get everyone's act together," said Deep Dakron.

"Right. Trimming in for the start is a simple thing but it's important, and something few bother to rehearse. It's harder on the trimmers than tacking, because they have to winch in a lot of fully loaded sheet, and in the midst of all the other noise they get conflicting signals from the skipper as to what exactly he or she wants. A dummy trim-in run makes the skipper get his act together, too: he'll find out how long it takes the trimmers to get the genoa in and get hiked out. He'll probably get things in motion earlier for the real start, and get his verbal signals sorted out."

Dakron said, "And last on the list: *Heavy Air, Dinghy Start: Be dialed in right off the line.*"

"Speed, speed, speed in dinghies," McBatten said. "When it's really honking, height off the line can't hold a candle to blistering pace. To get the jets requires doing your homework: plenty of speed testing with a partner before the start to tweak the rig and slot into the fastest sail and boat trim. All your settings should be quantifiable, too, so you can sheet in to your marks (on the jib sheet, vang, traveler) immediately. After the gun you'll need to sail the waves and the breeze, not have your head inside the boat, pulling strings. As far as positioning your boat for the start, make sure you set yourself up so that there's plenty of space to leeward to jump into and crank up the speed. This, by the way, means not getting so tight on the layline to the port end that you have to scrape to make it: you'll be rolled, and in heavy air those two extra tacks will be costly. Deadly, even; there's nothing like a capsize right off the starting line."

"Your customers don't just buy a sail, they buy you, mentor and coach," Deep Dakron said.

"Their success is my success," McBatten confirmed. "I'll do anything to help them win."

"Then mind if I make a suggestion? I think you need to put all of these details you've just told me into these boxes. People aren't going to get it if they just read, 'Don't get bunched.'"

"Hmm," said McBatten. "That would make it two, three, even four sheets of paper."

He considered for a moment, then shook his head. "Why, that'd cost me a fortune."

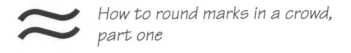

*How to round marks in a crowd,
part one*

# PARTNERS IN THE WALTZ

**D**eep Dakron wasn't sure how he came to be slumped on the office couch of McBatten Sailmakers—he must have driven there in a daze, and somehow made it up the stairs before he collapsed. But there was Kent McBatten seated across from him, waiting for an explanation.

McBatten tested the edge of his scissors—dull already, that Kevlar was wicked stuff—and wondered idly what Dakron's latest trauma might be. Boat speed? Crew trouble? Windshifts?

"Marks," moaned Deep Dakron, coming out of his trance. "Every time we got near a mark this weekend we lost boats. Even while *rounding* the mark we lost boats. At one mark four boats passed us. *Four boats.*"

Dakron spat the last out, the catcalls still echoing in his ears.

Ah! An easy one! thought McBatten. "At which marks did these shameful performances take place?" he asked.

"The weather mark, the reaching mark, and the leeward mark," Dakron said. *"Marks.* I hate 'em all," he added.

"Well," said McBatten, "without delving into the sordid details of each particular rounding, I'd say your problem stems from *premature culmination.* Simply, you commit yourself too early and too deeply to the rounding maneuver, and consequently you don't have anything left for post-rounding afterplay, which experts tell us is the most meaningful part."

"What?" said Deep Dakron.

"Allow me to enlarge on that," said McBatten. *"The most important part of any mark rounding is not the rounding itself, but your position afterward*, when all the curse words have dissipated and you are sailing on the next leg of the course. Sounds simple, but it's too often flubbed by the amateur, and forgotten by the veteran. After rounding the mark, ask yourself: Am I better off now than I was before the mark? Or better still, consult the McBatten Agony Help Line whenever you are approaching a mark rounding in the company of other yachts."

Deep Dakron levered himself into something resembling a sitting position, and listened; Kent McBatten had raced Olympic classes in the no holds barred European circuit, and he'd survived, even profited from the sort of mass mark roundings which drove International Juries to tears.

McBatten said, "Agony Help Line Tip #1: **Know thy partners**. First, establish with whom you are entering this shared experience, this tête-à-tête, this *waltz* around the mark. Who your 'partners'— the people steering and crewing the other boats—are is as big a determinant of your tactical approach as are the relative positions of the boats, the wind strength, or the location of the next mark. Once you consider their skill level and psychological makeup relative to your own, certain moves will be ruled out and others will become more attractive.

"The first of my people categories are those **looking for trouble**. These I classify as the sea lawyers, the aggressive types, and the tailenders bent on match racing the nearest boat. A second type of mark rounding neighbors are those **likely to have trouble** with the rounding. These boats are habitually out of control, due to poor helmsmanship and/or crew work. On occasion, everyone qualifies for this category: *you* may skipper the boat with the jammed halyards that is taking everyone ten lengths beyond the mark.

"If you're lucky, you'll be dealing with the third type, known as the **friendly marshmallow**. They are fine sailors but lack killer instinct, and thus are perfectly harmless and able to be bluffed, cajoled, or otherwise reasoned with in your favor. Finally, you may find yourself rail to rail with one or several of your fleet's **top dogs**. They are astute boathandlers and rule quoters, and won't negotiate any of your demands. Whichever type or types of partner it is your karma to be paired with, each should be given a different flourish in the mark rounding dance. Get it?"

"Get it, and I've gotten it," said Dakron, wondering which category he fell into.

"First, the looking for trouble types, my least favorite. Basically, these guys (and, nowadays, even ladies) are a pain in the posterior. Everyone in the fleet knows it, and looking for trouble types take pride in their reputations. Typically, they start in with verbal abuse and threats well before the mark, when they should be concentrating on sailing; it's no wonder you've caught up to them, and are now threatening their mark rounding. Never become entangled verbally with them. If possible, maintain as nonthreatening a posture as practical. Remember, as soon as you've overlapped them, either to windward or leeward, they consider you fair game for every rule interpretation buried in the appeals book.

"Therefore, I prefer to make my move—either to grab the inside overlap or else roll over the top of them and take their wind—as suddenly and as devastatingly as I can. If they see that you've surfed a killer wave to an undisputable, unbreakable overlap, or that you've unexpectedly snapped up to windward and done a *gotcha* on their wind, they have little choice but to relent. They'll still be screaming, of course, 'You can't *do* that,' but for them the show is over. If I can't make my move in a devastating fashion it's not in my interest to even try it, because they'll gladly take me to the protest room on the slightest pretext. So, the tactic with those looking for trouble is to make your move suddenly, or else stay clear and don't get into a skirmish, because they'll cost you places and time in the race.

"Next, and easiest to deal with, are the **likely to have trouble** types. Simply, these sailors self-destruct, and all you have to do is make sure you aren't caught in the explosion. At weather mark roundings they are likely to keep reaching high of the course to the next mark, while they struggle to untangle their mainsheet. Don't round on their windward side, unless you are far forward enough to roll over them, because they'll take you up with them.

"At the gybe mark, they either sail past in the throes of foredeck problems (if you are overlapped to windward of them you go, too) or else crash-gybe and park next to it, sails flogging (plan your escape route around their roadblock). At leeward marks they are notorious for either a very early or a disastrously late spinnaker drop, and a wide, *wide* rounding into which the next five boats can sail through abreast. *Never* get caught on the outside of a likely to have trouble at the leeward mark. Wait, go behind him if necessary, then sail through the gap between him and the mark.

"The **friendly marshmallow**, sadly, is a much rarer find today, and nearly extinct in some classes. These wonderful fellows are inclined to give you the nod when your overlap call is dodgy, are moved when they hear how badly you need to do well in this particular race, and generally sail in a gentlemanly fashion. Don't abuse the marshmallow's goodwill, but do remember that he is likely to give you a break when you need it, and will only be moved to protest if you shatter his teak toerail."

"Watch the toerails," said Deep Dakron.

McBatten continued, "Lastly, how do we deal with a **top dog** at a mark? Knowing that these pros have superb crew work, a thorough grasp of the rules, an abhorrence of the protest room, and want to pass you very badly, what's your approach? Keep it straightforward. If your boat is correctly placed, if you are fast enough to win the overlap, then you've got the advantage during the rounding: fair is fair. Don't try any cutesy stuff with them because they have seen it *all.* But don't get rattled, either; they have to take the racecourse one mark one at a time, just like the rest of us."

The telephone interrupted McBatten.

"Probably the Sultan of Brunei desiring a quotation on his America's Cup wardrobe," said McBatten, bounding across the office. "Don't go away. I'll be back with Agony Help Line Tips #2, 3, and 4."

"You'd better," said Deep Dakron, still contemplating his place in McBatten's Agony lineup. How about top marshmallow?

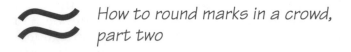 *How to round marks in a crowd,
part two*

# TURNING POINTS

**"W**here were we?" said Kent McBatten, flopping onto the office couch of McBatten Sailmakers, next to Deep Dakron.

"Lacking knowledge of how to round a mark, I came seeking enlightenment," said Deep Dakron, "and ran into something called Agony Help Line Tips, #1 of which was **know thy partners.** Dare I ask what the rest involves?"

"Ah! Mark roundings! Moments of truth in yacht racing!" said McBatten. "You ask, *why* must we round marks? Well, not only does it keep us out of the Race Committee's hair for a couple of hours, giving them time for lunch, rounding a mark is the only verification of whether we are ahead or behind the boats around us. Given Fate's fickle winds, all else is conjecture. In effect, the boat race begins anew with each rounding. But you knew that, right?"

"Hmm," said Deep Dakron.

"And so we meet Agony Help Line Tip #2: **Garbage in, garbage out.** You don't need an analyst to tell you that if you are in sad shape going into the mark rounding, you'll be in worse shape coming out. We've all done this: After finding ourselves abeam and on the outside of boats before rounding the gybe mark, we discover—after we've gybed and been blanketed by the inside boats—that not only are they now truly ahead of us, but the boats behind are in the process of sailing merrily by, too. We bemoan our wretched luck, but the look on our crews' faces says it all: What did you *expect* to happen, dum-dum?

"So, the way to avoid becoming garbage in, garbage out is to *anticipate.* Well in advance of the rounding, evaluate your chances of getting the inside overlap. If it doesn't look likely, start planning an alternate route that will minimize the disadvantage. This may mean slowing your boat down to *fall in line astern of the inside over-*

*lap boat or boats*, which, while giving up one boat length, keeps your course options and wind clear *after* the rounding. Also, it's a good defensive move when there are boats threatening from astern.

"When the next leg shows a lot of latitude for course variation—such as when the second reach of a triangular course is very broad, and may require gybing to reach the leeward mark—try to stay farther outside of the inside-overlapped boats to keep clear of their blanket after the rounding. In any case, the important point is to *anticipate.* Don't go around the mark and off a cliff, lemming-like. Visualize what will happen during and after the rounding if you stay in the present situation relative to your neighbors, and if what you see scares you, get yourself out of there.

"Now, closely related to this is Help Line Tip #3: **Leave yourself an out.** Even though rounding a mark forces us into close proximity with the scheming characters on the other boats, it doesn't have to mean that they have to control us. Approach any mark rounding as a defensive driver; leave yourself an out. Protect your freedom to maneuver *after* the rounding. The object is not to let *them* limit your options. It does little good to nip neatly around the mark if you find yourself pinned, going in a direction you don't want to go.

"A classic example of this occurs at leeward marks. Say you've rounded right behind boat *Just Ahead of You*, and boat *Right Behind You* has rounded right on your transom. Once you're settled down on the wind, you try unsuccessfully to stay clear of the backwind of *Just Ahead of You*, which is pinching in an effort to squeeze you off, and you are unable to tack away without tacking too close and fouling *Right Behind You*. Suddenly you're trapped, the Velveeta in the sandwich, and all because you haven't left yourself an out, an escape."

"What would you do, or have done, or should have done?" asked Deep Dakron. "Besides change those awful boat names?"

"If I wanted to tack quickly after the mark, I'd have used some of the momentum of my rounding to luff up to windward half a length right after the mark. You know, take a swoop up and get myself above the line of both boats," said McBatten. "This gets me partly clear of *Just Ahead of You*'s backwind and gives me freedom to tack in front of *Right Behind You*, who isn't going to anticipate what I've done. This way I'm not pinned by either boat.

"My other option, if there is a goodly space of clean air and water in front of *Just Ahead of You, and* if he makes a bat-turn, dead-in-the-water rounding, is to peel around the mark with speed on and drive off through his lee. But I'll only attempt this if both of the above conditions are present, otherwise I run the risk of losing *Right Behind You.*

"You have to keep your freedom while rounding the windward mark, too, especially on windward/leeward courses and when turning onto the downwind run of an Olympic course. Say you round on the outside of a boat, overlapped about abeam. You want to gybe and break for the inside of the course but can't because he, as leeward boat, is controlling you. Had you *anticipated* him blocking your gybe, you would have allowed enough distance to swing your bow past his transom. Then, you could begin sailing your own race instead of being held hostage."

"The price of freedom," said Dakron, "can be measured in boat lengths."

McBatten wasn't finished. "The whole point is to anticipate who will be controlling whom after the rounding, and to position your boat so that you don't become controlled. Which brings me to my pet peeve, Agony Help Line Tip #4: **Whither now?** It's absolutely astonishing how many sailors round a mark with only a vague idea of where they're going. Oh, they know the next mark is somewhere over there, but a compass course? Forget it. And has anyone actually *seen* the next mark? Or thought to look for it? Hardly ever—unless you're on one of the Top Dogs' boats. They have their crews looking at the second leg while they're still halfway down the first.

"Before you get close to rounding any mark, you should ask yourself: What will the apparent wind angle be on the next leg? Should we attack it high or low? Are the boats around me likely to sail it high or low? Is the wind increasing or decreasing? Have we detected a recent windshift to the right or the left? Will being on the inside at the mark give me an advantage for the rest of the leg, as when the second reach of an Olympic course is a tight spinnaker reach?

"If you aren't attempting to figure these things out, you might as well close your eyes as you round the mark, given the amount of concern you've shown about the next mark."

"The bland leading the blind," said Deep Dakron, "or is it the other way around?"

McBatten said, "How often have you rounded the windward mark and reached up with the spinnaker, thinking you were going so fast, and two minutes later noticed a group of boats way below. 'Where are those guys heading?' you asked. 'To the mark,' said your crew, pointing to a buoy in line with your shrouds. 'The mark is down *there?*' you choked."

"I didn't know you were aboard that weekend," said Deep Dakron. "But the Race Committee didn't set the mark in the right place."

"Even so, there's no reason you shouldn't have been the first to locate it," said McBatten. "Get one of your crew to find the reach mark when you're sailing up the first beat. Think ahead! A little early work eliminates a lot of agony later on. And one of my crispy new spinnakers will get you to that reach mark fast," said McBatten, reaching for his price list.

But Dakron had already sprung from the couch, and was taking the stairs two at a time. The front door slammed.

He's anticipating, thought McBatten.

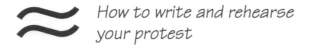 *How to write and rehearse your protest*

# TEXT, LIES, AND VIDEOTAPE

**D**eep Dakron planted both elbows on the yacht club bar.

"Give me a double," he ordered. "No, a triple. No, make that a kamikaze, cubed. No, just give it to me intravenously, right here, in this throbbing vein in my temple."

On the next stool, Zig Zag Brooke lifted an eyebrow. "Trouble?" he said.

Dakron mashed his lips together in a sour line. "Not until that guy on *Road Kill* signaled me with his Bravo flag, and followed that up with even more colorful hails and hand signals."

"Hmm, tell me more," Brooke purred.

"It happened at a mark," Dakron said.

"It usually does."

"There were too many boats."

"There usually are."

"There wasn't enough water."

"There usually isn't."

"Everyone yelled that they were right."

"They usually do."

"And of everyone, the guy on *Road Kill* picked me to give the evil eye to, and his protest flag was the only one that wasn't pulled down by the finish line, so we didn't take ours down either, and one of my crew happened to mention to the Race Committee that *Road Kill* may have fouled us, and, uh, I think I might be in a protest."

"You know, it's been a real slow day here at the club," said Brooke. "I was just about to head home and watch *Sports Bloopers* again, but I think I may stick around."

"Oh?"

"Yes. Nothing gets a yachtsman's blood pressure up like a blood red protest flag, and there's nothing more fun than watching yachtsmen bounce off the low smoky ceiling of The Room—the protest room. Quick, man! How much protest time is left?"

"Twenty minutes, about."

Brooke spirited Dakron's drink away from him. "Hustle down to The Room and get a copy of your assailant's protest—you are guaranteed one, if you ask—and get two protest forms for your defense. Hurry!"

When Dakron returned he was out of breath. Brooke had cleared a space among the beer bottles and had the rule and appeals books out. "Hand me your phone card," he said.

"Why?" Dakron asked, but Brooke snatched it and whittled out a boat template that fit the one-square-equals-one-boat length diagram on the back of the protest form. "It's as vital to have an accurate diagram," Brooke explained, "as it is to write legibly and spell correctly. Often, it's the diagram or a key word or phrase on the form that decides the protest. But first, the facts. Or fiction, as the case may be."

Brooke read the opponent's protest, had Dakron read it, and then made Dakron draw his diagram, write out his description of the incident, and write down the rules that Dakron felt made him right and the skipper of *Road Kill* wrong. Brooke read the form, asked a few pointed questions and said, "Thank you, Mr. Dakron. And now, Mr. *Road Kill.*"

Here Brooke assumed the part of Dakron's opponent and refuted every point of Dakron's case, from his verbal description of events to his diagram. He summed up by saying that Dakron's recollection of events was hazy, to say the least; the boats had been in a completely different position than what Dakron had led the Protest Committee to believe. And not only that, Dakron *knew* he was wrong, he had tried to get away with it and now he had made up this, this *preposterous story*, and he had a string of witnesses who were prepared to testify to the whole Dakron debacle.

Deep Dakron boiled over. "What! You can't say that! That's not what happened out there. That's a lie, that's—"

"That's quite enough from you, Mr. Dakron, *sir*, and you will kindly refrain from speaking until the Committee asks you to speak," Zig Zag Brooke intoned in a Committee voice, and then said, "Look, Dakron, you know that this is exactly what you're going to face in The Room. And you've reacted with exactly the sort of belligerence guaranteed not to impress the Committee. As soon as you get flustered or angry in The Room, you're history. Rule one is to stay calm, even if your firstborn child is trundled in to witness against you.

Maintain your poise, even if it feels like you're poisoning yourself.

"Yacht racing is supposed to be the last refuge of the gentleman sportsman—okay, I said *supposed* to be—and this code is expected to be observed in The Room. Respect your competitor and what he says, even if his form reads like science fiction and his performance begs for an Oscar. Now, let's go through these attacks on your case and get your defense straightened out. I'll take the part of the plaintiff, you'll be the defendant, and then we'll switch."

"Oh, I get it," said Dakron. "Trying the case beforehand. Playacting, like *People's Court*."

"You really catch on," Brooke sighed. "You're going to be a pistol in The Room."

Then they went at it, Brooke attacking Dakron's diagram and testimony, Dakron pointing out the inconsistencies and loose ends in *Road Kill's* case, and then vice versa.

"Look here, your testimony contradicts your diagram," Brooke said, "and the Protest Committee will not be amused by that. You tell us you had the overlap at four lengths to the mark, but on paper your four lengths looks more like two lengths. Let's redraw your diagram, make it a three-stage one, including the positions of boats leading up to the incident, and let's make the relative boat speeds and distance traveled per second reflect reality.

"Were you going three knots (five feet per second), four knots (six and a half feet per second), or five knots (eight feet per second)? Work it out. There, that's better. Now we see that *Road Kill's* diagram is off, too. He has himself clear ahead, but was he really traveling at eight knots (13 feet per second)? Hardly. Bring that to the attention of the Committee.

"Before you go into The Room, you had better have the speed/time/distance stats of every boat in the incident down cold, and their relationship to each other, and their relationship to the mark. Which boats were sailing a hot angle to the mark? Which were sailing by the lee, chutes collapsed? Now get that drawing done and file it, quick! Protest time is almost over."

Deep Dakron signed his name, dashed off and dropped the form in the slot. Shortly the skipper of *Road Kill* brushed by, frowning at his photocopy of Dakron's protest.

"You didn't mention contact, so I assumed there wasn't any . . . was there?" Brooke asked Dakron.

"No, but almost."

"So, there's hope. If there's no contact, most protests are disallowed, providing one party doesn't prove—or *convince*—the Committee that a foul occurred. That's why you should always avoid touching another boat, and why you should stay out of situations that place the onus of proof on yourself. Where does the onus fall here?"

"On him, then on me, or the other way around, depending whose protest form you believe," said Dakron.

"Looks like a toss up. Be glad I'm not on the Protest Committee— I'd throw you both out for ruining my happy hour. This might come down to witnesses. Whenever a Bravo flag goes up, note the potential witnesses right then and there, and when you get ashore pin them down as to how much of the incident they saw—as well as how much they didn't see. A witness can be a double-edged sword. How well does your witness know the rules? Is he/she neutral, or an interested party? Show the witness both protest forms. Are they clear on the incident? Who do they think was right? Which protest form do they think is closer to what they saw out there? If they're in doubt about the facts, if they're likely to blurt something which might cripple your case, forget it. Now, do you have any witnesses?"

Dakron fidgeted. "Well . . . I have a friend on *Bad Rap* who owes me one, who I think I can get to say—"

"Don't even try it," Brooke told him. "Protest Committees can smell collusion and coached witnesses a mile away, and then it's *phffft* for your case, and your credibility. Nowhere more than in The Room does the saying 'What goes around comes around' hold true. Abusive behavior, a rude attitude, angry comments, coached witnesses, the fabrication, grooming and/or stretching of facts, all of it will come back to haunt you. Even if you win your case using these kinds of tactics, word gets around, and it'll influence your next rules incident or protest. It's called negative pretrial publicity."

"Ask Mike Tyson about that," said Deep Dakron, "during visiting hours."

"So, you've got no witnesses, that hurts, but that doesn't mean you're a dead duck. You're armed with the main ingredients: you know your case, and you know your opponent's case even better, so well that you could switch sides and argue against yourself. You've anticipated his line of attack, his distorted view of the incident, so you won't be caught flat-footed and slack-jawed. You're prepared with facts and figures and a diagram in synch with what's going to come out of your mouth. You're ready to point out the inconsistencies of his case, and you've got some tough questions for him to answer on the spot."

"Can I have just one last sip of my kamikaze?" Dakron asked.

"No," said Brooke. "You're going to need a cool head, not a hot head in there."

A Committee voice boomed, "Skippers of *ROAD KILL* and *SNAFU.*"

"This is it," Zig Zag Brooke said. "Go in there and present your case—present your *facts.*"

Deep Dakron's hands shook as he slid off his stool. "You'll be here if I need you?"

"Wouldn't miss it," Brooke said. "I love protests."

*(Cue: organ music)*

Will Deep Dakron be disqualified, his scorecard splattered with alphabet soup from here to Tuesday? Is Justice on sabbatical from the smoky back room of the local yacht club? Will *Road Kill* collect yet another pelt? Tune in for the hearing . . .

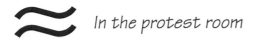 *In the protest room*

# TEXT, LIES, AND VIDEOTAPE: THE HEARING

$O$ur story so far: Deep Dakron and the skipper of *Road Kill* have protested each other over a mark rounding incident. Resident yacht club barfly Zig Zag Brooke, torn between watching *Sports Bloopers* and helping Dakron, has walked Dakron through the drawing of a proper diagram, showed him how to drill his opponent's protest form for loopholes, and briefed him on deportment in The Room. The hearing is under way right now and Dakron is on his own, arguing his case, defending himself in The Room and, hang on, here he comes:

The door to the protest room opened and the skipper of *Road Kill* strode out scowling, trailed by Deep Dakron, who looked as if he'd just had his measurements taken for the electric chair. Zig Zag Brooke ushered him onto a bar stool.

"They call that 'finding facts,'" Dakron groaned. "All they found were cracks in my facts. I'm doomed. Three six-packs of beer, 12 sandwiches, and one weekend—"

"What happened?" said Brooke.

Dakron looked shaken. "They had me trembling like a leaf. I was mumbling, incoherent, they cross-examined me to shreds." He reached for his kamikaze, but Brooke slid it out of reach.

"How did your protest form hold up? Is that still in one piece?"

Dakron looked up. "The diagram was great. It made sense when I didn't. Thank goodness for pictures."

"And *Road Kill's* form?"

Dakron brightened. "His form went off like a land mine he'd planted and then stepped on. He ended up pointing out the inconsistencies in his own artwork, like when his boat miraculously sped up from three knots to eight knots and broke my overlap. The Committee was amused by that."

"I'm sure."

"But still, I'm history. The skipper of *Road Kill* and his 'facts' . . . I hate to impinge on his reputation, but he's—"

"Lying?" said Brooke. "Ah, yes, the human side of protests. In any protest, there's always the question of perspective. And, to tell the truth, an incident often does appear completely different to the skipper of Boat A than the skipper of Boat B. Protest Committees have to allow for differing perspectives, and give each skipper the benefit of the doubt, and trust their testimony—and so must Skipper A and Skipper B trust each other. If we do anything less, there's no point in filling out our protest forms and sitting down at a table together."

Dakron looked mournful.

"But sometimes, we come up against the dark underbelly of the protest process. The rules book assumes that we yachtsmen will comport ourselves as gentlemen and ladies, as sportsmen, on the water as well as in The Room. I suppose that's why we're not required to take an oath or swear on the Bible before giving testimony. Though, these days, I doubt that would help. Sad, isn't it? People just need to win too badly.

"Yacht racing has always had its sea lawyers and cheats. We all know of sailors who have lied, or see nothing wrong with fudging the facts, shading testimony, coaching witnesses, stretching overlaps, completing tacks or gybes or hails a boat length sooner in The Room than on the water. Perhaps we've done it ourselves, under the guise of 'presenting our case.' Such demonstrations of poor sportsmanship—many of which ripple out of that grand dame of pettifoggery, the America's Cup, and down through the classes and into our young sailors—eat away at the foundation of our sport. If a little cheating, a little lie now and then is okay, if 'everybody does it,' if it's 'part of the game,' then what does that say about the participants in the game? And where will it end?

"Our protest flags will become battle flags. The facts of a rules incident, and the rules themselves will exist only to be tweaked and tailored. Why drop out, why ever admit that you're wrong when you can construct a case for yourself in The Room? And, of course, if you can't beat the other guy on the water, why not take a cheap shot at him in The Room?"

Dakron looked even more mournful.

"And you know the only thing we can do in the face of such dishonesty?" Brooke asked. "We can conduct ourselves as sportsmen.

Sailors know when other sailors lie. I believe that the members of the Protest Committee know when a sailor is lying. Even if they can't say so directly, they know, and these things have a way of catching up with people."

Dakron looked slightly less mournful.

Brooke asked, "How was the skipper of *Road Kill* behaving in The Room?"

Dakron looked relieved not to be serving on the Protest Committee. "He bordered on the condescending side of belligerence. He kept quoting rules to the Committee, telling them what they should throw me out on, and kept muttering and rolling his eyes during my testimony."

"Perfect. Protest Committees *love* to be told which rules they need to brush up on. And they particularly appreciate being sworn at."

"He was even surly to his own witnesses. I never thought I'd feel sorry for my opponent's witnesses."

"And how did you behave?"

"I already told you: I shook like a leaf and said, 'Yes, sir,' and 'No, sir.' I think they felt sorry for me. One of them offered me a glass of water."

Brooke ordered another rum and orange, and took a sip of Dakron's kamikaze. "Sounds like it could have gone worse. Why are you so worried?"

"Videotape," said Dakron dismally. "*Road Kill* has a videotape. The Committee is in there going over it frame by frame, just like the Rodney King trial."

"Perfect!" Brooke said. "This will wipe out his witnesses. We'll be back to the diagrams and the skipper's testimonies."

Dakron looked wiped out, eyeing his drink he couldn't get to.

The door of the protest room opened and a Committee member yelled, "Skippers of ROAD KILL and SNAFU. "

"Win, lose or draw, remember to thank the Protest Committee," Brooke told Deep Dakron. "These people are volunteers, and they've donated their time to the thankless job of deciding between two tales of a mark rounding. They've done the best they can with the toughest part of any protest: finding the facts."

"Thanks for getting me through this," said Dakron, who looked poised on the edge of a nervous breakdown. "I'm sorry to put you through such an ordeal."

Brooke said, "Ordeal? Forget it. I can watch *Sports Bloopers* any time. Besides, I love protests."

While Dakron was gone, Brooke took a few more sips of his kamikaze.

Fifteen minutes later, the doors to The Room flew open. The skipper of *Road Kill* made a brisk exit. Dakron moved unsteadily, as if given a last minute stay of execution. The Committee members pulled the door shut firmly behind themselves, looking like they'd had it with volunteering.

"See?" Brooke told Dakron. "They threw him out, right? No, first tell me about the videotape."

Dakron sat down, shaking. Then, out came a high-pitched laugh.

"The videotape! It showed that his main witness, the mastman on *Law of the Jugular*, had his head covered with spinnaker cloth during the incident. And then someone's shoulder got in the way of the camera, and the auto-focus didn't focus. The tape didn't help *Road Kill* much."

"And so they threw him out," Brooke crowed.

"Not exactly," said Dakron. "After the Committee gave us a lecture on the rules, they lectured us on grammar and spelling. I had three spelling mistakes on my protest form, and *Road Kill* changed verb tenses twice. Both protests were disallowed."

"Why is it," Zig Zag Brooke wondered, "that the best sports bloopers are never captured on videotape?"

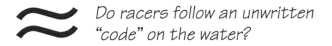 *Do racers follow an unwritten "code" on the water?*

# BREAKING THE CODE

Scratchen Sniff yawned, a major yawn that stretched his handlebar mustache. He laid the rules book aside and yawned again.

"No wonder it's never been a bestseller," he said. "A new edition, but still written in that *Satanic Verses* style of obfuscation, still loaded with more doubletalk than a political manifesto. And the worst part is, there's not a single word in it about the code."

"Code?" said Deep Dakron. "Not Morse code? Don't tell me. I was just getting my numeral pennants down."

Dakron opened the rules book. "It looks black and white enough to me, even if the numeral pennants are in color. Don't see anything about a code, though."

"For all the times I've read the rules book I still can't find those interpretations the rules ghouls manage to flush out from between the lines," said Sniff. "It's black magic, like the budget. Besides, I'd rather refresh myself on the rules by taking a sail through a computer rules program. Then you can watch the rules in action, see the situations developing and onuses changing, and get an incident analysis and a decision without being verbally abused or filling out a protest form. But even so, there'd be nothing in the software about the code."

"Code? What code?" said Dakron, leafing through the rules book. "You're right, it's not in Definitions, or in the appendices. Looks like your code doesn't exist."

"Oh, it exists, all right. Everybody knows there're two types of sailor: those who sail by the rules, and those who use the rules to sail."

"Sea lawyers, you mean," said Dakron.

"Worse than that. These days, a rules gulf has opened up between match racers and fleet racers," Sniff explained. "Match racing as practiced today is dog eat dog, a bagful of dirty tricks. Draw an infraction and cry foul, or just fake a foul, but trap them, get 'em any way you can, do the other guy dirty before he does it to you. Match racers have perverted the intent and the common sense behind the yacht racing rules, and with their twisted behavior they threaten the decency of the entire yachting world."

"Match racers have perverted the racing rules?" said Dakron. "I *thought* some of them were a little strange. The rules, I mean."

"Baby, you ain't seen nothing yet," promised Sniff. "Starboard tack boats hunting port tack boats to extinction, boats sailing backwards to disqualify each other, people taking their opponents beyond yesterday's layline, it's all in your future. Regattas will become more acrimonious than sessions of Congress. The code is being eroded even as we speak."

"You haven't divulged what this code is."

"It's no secret. The code is simply the unwritten, unspoken code that most sailors sail by and expect others to sail by, and when someone breaks the code it sends reverberations through the fleet."

"Reverberations?" said Dakron.

"The code is the universal code of fair play, and the reverberations are sending the very foundations of yachting, formerly a civilized sport, crumbling," Sniff said.

"Fair play? But that's addressed in the rules book. Fair sailing, gross breach of sportsmanship, and all that."

"Sure, it's in there, but to win a 'fair sailing' protest you'd have to prove that your shrouds had been hack-sawed, and provide the fingerprints." Sniff sighed heavily. "I suppose the code is better left out of the rules book. If it was reduced to black and white, the match racers would only make a mockery of that, too."

"I'm still not clear on exactly how this code works," said Deep Dakron.

Sniff said, "To most people the code means sailing to win by sailing—beating the competition with better tactics, windshifts, boat speed, crew work—not by using the rules to take cheap shots at them. To most sailors the racing rules function in the same way as driving laws; they spell out the right of way in an effort to prevent collisions. Well, not to match racers, they don't. They use the rules to take cheap shots at the competition."

Dakron said, "Cheap shots? But how? The rules are the rules, aren't they, and it's every sailor's responsibility to know the rules and use them to win . . . isn't it?"

"Sure, as long as you don't break the code doing it," said Scratchen Sniff.

Dakron sighed. "Now I'm confused. You're advocating a fuzzy double standard here, like not opening the restaurant door for your date but still getting stuck with the check. That's the problem with unwritten rules—they're not the same for everybody, and no one really knows what they are."

"Getting back to the code of yacht racing, here's an example. The rules book says that after the start, the leeward yacht may luff the windward yacht. A basic rule that everybody knows and respects, but the match racers have pushed things to an extreme: anytime, anywhere, no hail, no warning, they'll throw the helm hard down and wham! pop the other guy. This is the code match racers live and die by; things have gotten so bad that they *expect* the slam, surprise luff any time they get within a boat length of each other, so it's no surprise, or shouldn't be. But transpose the match racers' code into fleet racing and what happens?"

"Surprise!" said Dakron. "And wham! Splintered rails and a shattered weekend."

"You got it. Now suppose we take this slam, surprise luff and put it in a typical fleet racing context: you're rounding the weather mark onto the run, and a check through your mainsail window reveals that the boat in front of you is bearing away and hoisting his spinnaker. You're following suit when wham! the guy has nailed you with a surprise luff. No hail, just helm hard down, *smack*, you're out. Ciao, buddy! Gotcha. Guess you shoulda been watching. Too bad. You understand: I had to beat you in this race, and I just did."

"I'd tell the guy he's a sneaky, dirty, cheating son of a—"

"Cheating, did you say? He nailed you with a perfectly legal maneuver. He's right, and you're wrong," Sniff said.

Dakron grumbled, "The guy may be right, but he's got all the moral authority of a Heidi Fleiss, the Hollywood Madam, resorting to a sneak attack like that."

"Oh, dear, did that violate some sort of code of yours? What code is that? Can you show me in the rules book?"

"You know very well what code it is," Dakron said.

Sniff smiled. "So now you're starting to realize that there are plenty of times during the course of a fleet race, such as on the start line and when rounding marks and crossing tacks, when you're vulnerable to all manner of match racing dirty tricks, too numerous to mention, and most of which are unspeakable, anyway."

"Don't tell me. I wouldn't want to get any ideas," said Dakron.

"Now let's take that slam-luff-when-raising-the-spinnaker situation and ask, when would it *not* violate the accepted standard of fair play? Would it be acceptable during a club race? A national championship? A world championship? The Olympic trials? The start line of the Whitbread round the world race?"

"Not during a club race. You'd get a knuckle sandwich back at the club," said Dakron.

"But why? It's perfectly legal, right there in the rules book in black and white. Or is it somewhere between the lines? In any case, why *not* use it?" said Sniff.

"You know why," said Dakron.

"Okay, let's look at using it in, say, the Olympic trials. Top-level sailors, no effort spared in their physical training or boat speed programs, they should be ready for anything, right? In this particular class there are 25 entries, but only a handful have a real shot at winning. When to go after your arch-rival with a slam-dunk, sneaky luff? The second race? The next-to-last race? Anytime? Never?"

"I guess it depends on how badly you want to win," Dakron said.

"Olympic-class sailors want to win pretty darn bad," said Sniff. "The trials are a one-shot regatta, and everything comes down to winning it. There is no second place—kind of like match racing."

"Well, then, anytime, I guess, if it comes down to winning or not."

"Okay, and afterwards some of these same sailors borrow a boat and race in your fleet championships. Suddenly it's wham-bam-sorry-ma'am, and you find yourself eating lunch on the way back to the club, disqualified."

"Maybe the rules book is at fault, not the sailors," said Dakron. "The rule should be amended so that the leeward boat has to hail first, and then luff slowly."

"That might help," Sniff admitted, "but it's the attitude, the chucking of fair play in favor of winning at all costs, it's the erosion of the code that's at the root of the problem. The match racers, who live for the sound of crunching fiberglass, would only find some new clever way to subvert the new rule."

"Well, not everyone is into sneaky luffs. I haven't been nailed yet."

"*Yet,*" said Sniff. "Some code breakers might choose to play the onus game, another match racing art form. Here's an example: you're in a fleet race, and coming into the finish you tack into a tight lee bow position on a starboard tack boat that you need to beat. No contact, but he responds with academy award-winning theatrics. He screams and crash-tacks, throws up his hands and throws the Bravo flag at you. He claims you've tacked too close. He knows the onus is on you. He knows that you're in deep doo-doo unless you can somehow prove yourself innocent. He risks nothing by throwing the flag, and he has a good shot at throwing you out. What a break! You've just made his day! And it's your own fault: you made the mistake of getting within a half boat length of him, and you should have known that the onus was on you."

"Someone did that to me, once," said Dakron. "I tacked into a clean lee bow and lost in The Room. He must have been a great match racer."

"The erosion of the code of fair play, the decline of Western civilization as we know it," Sniff mourned. "Sailing will turn as petty and vicious as the fight over spaces in the K-Mart parking lot, and it's all due to that bastion of poor sportsmanship, the America's Cup, and the breeding ground that feeds it, match racing. May they fall on their own stilettos."

"I think you're a little paranoid about this," said Dakron. "It's not that bad out there. There's no conspiracy. I haven't noticed any rush to guerrilla tactics when yachts meet."

"You've been warned," said Sniff.

Dakron chuckled. "Guess I'll have to keep both hands on the tiller and both eyes on the boat in front of me when I set my spinnaker, in case he throws it hard over and tries to hit me. He might be sailing under some subversive code."

Sniff was not amused. "These days, you'd better watch your front *and* your back," he said.

Deep Dakron thought for a moment. "Uh, and say this guy does hit me?"

"There's no rule against it," said Scratchen Sniff.

 PART SIX

# HEAD AND HEART

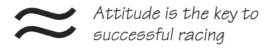 *Attitude is the key to successful racing*

# GRINNING IS EVERYTHING

**"I**'m so tense and nervous I can hardly steer," Deep Dakron groaned, and *Snafu*'s aluminum tiller extension vibrated on its universal joint.

Tactician Scratchen Sniff caught a "What else is new?" look on the faces of the crew, and whirled around and inspected Dakron. Sure enough, Dakron was showing the stuff of a Wall Street crash, not a sunny Saturday in the Weekend Warrior Series.

Sniff leaned close and studied Dakron. A vise of concentration, Dakron's face was painfully contorted. The corrugations in his forehead were pronounced, as were the deep creases from his squinted eyes. The wrinkles from his scrunched-up nose intersected with grimace lines from his mouth, and Dakron's jaw was locked, his lips drawn over his teeth in a snarl. Ligaments and muscle groups, on the verge of spasm, stood out from his neck.

Can't be much fun to steer in that condition, Scratchen Sniff mused. How can he see? How does he draw breath?

Sniff leaned back and studied Dakron's posture, a humpback spinal curvature compounded by a crick toward the transom. Dakron's shoulders were bunched, and his head dropped from his shoulders and twisted onto a nearly horizontal plane; Sniff wondered how Dakron would ever uncoil himself to tack.

Checking the competition, Sniff noted that the face of *Pigeon Kicker*'s helmsman appeared just as tense, his trunk afflicted with the same aft-leaning curvature as Deep Dakron's. Sniff chuckled. That posture—now universally revered as "fast" the world over—had originated out of the exploits of a group of Star and Snipe sailors from San Diego. Never mind that they were all sailmakers, and that these sailmakers all had bad backs, so bad that when they sailed they tensed, and then slouched. Their winning ways had been emulated by everyone, right down to the bad posture. Funny, how things go.

Sniff glanced over at the *wunderkind* female skipper of *Noxious*. Same tense posture, and—most unfortunate, this—same death-grimace. What this fleet needs is an osteopath, thought Sniff.

Sniff crept up behind Deep Dakron and dug his thumbs into the ridge of muscle between Dakron's neck and shoulders.

"Waaaahhh!" Dakron shrieked. "What are you *doing?*"

"Windward rolfing," said Sniff, working down the spine. "Gets you through a race's tight spots."

Dakron's back began to ease, his shoulders to drop. "Ooh. Ooh. Right there. *Ooooh.*"

"Just as I thought," said Scratchen Sniff, "there're no deformities, nothing's slipped. You suffer purely from self-inflicted nervousness and tension, which is quite normal considering that you are the bill-paying owner of a racing yacht. What concerns me, however, is that this is adversely affecting your motor mechanics and cognitive level."

"Huh?" said Deep Dakron. But his tiller extension was no longer rattling.

Sniff had reached the lower back and was starting back up, working his knuckles along Dakron's vertebrae. "Exactly. You believe you're wound up in 'concentration,' but your physical state is actually just a symptom of your nerves and tenseness."

Dakron said, "I know. Didn't I just *tell* you I was nervous and tense?"

Sniff began working on Dakron's shoulders again. "Right, but the important question is, Why? Let's tackle your nerves first. Listen, everyone gets nervous before a race. World champs have been known to throw up their breakfast on the tow to the starting line. Everyone has done the last minute rush to the yacht club toilet before the big race. Some have to go back a second, or a third time. But you can—you must—overcome your nervousness before the race starts. How? By getting yourself into the state of mind where you are *racing*, doing your job instead of worrying about doing it.

"For some people this means ultra-preparing their boat so they know that everything is as good as it can be; only then can they relax. Other skippers need to be out on the racecourse a full hour before the start to feel comfortable. For others, practicing tacks and spinnaker sets, or pacing with another boat is reassuring. Others require still other stimuli."

"One beer kind of helps me get into the flow," said Dakron, falling slightly off the wind.

Working on the neck just below the ears, Sniff increased the pressure until Dakron flinched. "Watch the telltales!" Sniff nagged. "Catamaran expert Randy Smyth says that he feels nervous until he gets that first wave in the face, until he gets his head wet, and then he snaps out of it and is ready to race. The lesson here is to study your nervous, prerace self and figure out which mental and physical triggers you need to pull to be 'ready to race.' Don't ignore it and don't leave it to chance. If you absolutely must have dried apricots and half a Diet Coke right before every start, so be it."

"Have you ever considered becoming a masseur?" asked Dakron.

Sniff grunted. "So, once you're racing and you find yourself becoming unbearably tense, what to do? Ask again: *Why* am I so tense? It's only, I repeat, only a sailboat race. There's always another race. Even the pros racing for the America's Cup realize that there's always a tomorrow, another Cup. So, relax. Do your best, that's all. *Enjoy* the race.

"My favorite 'Why do we race?' story concerns the great Danish sailor Paul Elvström. You know, four Olympic gold medals, more World and European titles in more classes than anyone will ever win again, just a yacht racing legend and an all-around inspiration. Well, a reporter asked Elvström, 'What's more important? An Olympic gold medal, or a world championship?' Know what he said?"

"Gold medal," said Dakron. "Everyone knows you can cash in on them later on."

Sniff dug a knuckle in hard, and Dakron jumped. "Elvström said: 'A good race, that's the main thing for me. I never liked the prizes. I like the race. I like to be on the water. That's my life.'"

"Wow," said Dakron.

"Exactly. Elvström revealed the secret of his success, a 'secret' overlooked by far too many of us: *enjoying the race*. But how can you enjoy the race when you're wound up like a bomb disposal expert? Think of the best races you've ever sailed. You weren't tense. You flowed. You concentrated, but you didn't crank your mind or your muscles into knots. You were able to see past the setbacks, see that in ten minutes or two legs you'd be back in the hunt."

"How does one begin relaxing and enjoying?" asked Dakron.

Sniff continued karate chopping between the shoulder blades. "Unwind yourself physically. Take a deep breath, and let the muscles in your face relax. Try it. Let your forehead go. Eyebrows. Cheeks. Mouth. You'll find you've been keeping your face tensed up out of habit. There, you're looking better without the snarl. Next, sit up straight, but relax your shoulders. Relax your neck. Relax your tiller arm. No more white knuckles. See how much effort it took to keep everything drum tight? That's wasted energy. You'll last longer and steer better when you're relaxed. You'll be more receptive to the touch of the wind, the sound of the bow wave, the heel of the boat. In other words, you'll be able to concentrate."

"Have you ever considered becoming a talk show psychologist?" asked Dakron.

Sniff said, "The relax and enjoy technique is used to advantage in other sports, too. Tennis, tiddlywinks, even boxing. Remember Muhammed Ali? 'Float like a butterfly, sting like a bee,' right?"

"Watch these hands!" said Dakron, dropping the tiller extension and sending two left jabs and a roundhouse right into the air. "Float like a butterfly and sting like a bee, that's me!"

"You just stick to the floating," said Sniff, "and leave the stinging to me."

 *Prerace homework that helps you win*

# WINNERS NEVER SLEEP

Vroom! Vroom vroom vroom! Nigel Mansell streaked by in the lead, a blur on the screen.

Zig Zag Brooke clicked the remote.

Ugggh! Yagggggh! Uhhh-yagggghhhh! Andre Agassi grunted a backhand volley.

Zig Zag Brooke clicked the remote.

Leap, *floooooooooooooat* . . . SLAMDUNK. The crowd roared as Shaquille O'Neal flew through the air.

Zig Zag Brooke switched off the TV, much to the irritation of everyone else in the yacht club bar.

"Oh, for the good old days," Brooke sighed.

"The good old days?" said Deep Dakron. "You mean before all the violence, the grunting, the big money deals in sports?"

"I'm talking about sailing," Brooke said. "These days, kids think that if they go out and buy a Shaq jersey and shoes, they'll *be* Shaq. Same goes for sailing."

"They'd have to shave their heads," observed Dakron. "Though that'd be better than going Rastafarian. Imagine Dennis Conner with dreadlocks!"

Brooke said grumpily, "And the same goes for grown up yachtsmen: no one wants to hear the awful truth about winners."

Dakron tried to think if anyone in his fleet had shaved their head. Did bald spots count?

*"Winners work harder,"* said Zig Zag Brooke.

"I'd work harder if I knew I was going to win," Dakron said.

"Winners *work*," Brooke said. "Perfect example, look at that bunch of losers out there. Disgusting."

Through the club's picture window a racing fleet milled about prior to the warning signal. "Why are they losers? They're not doing anything," Dakron said.

"Exactly. Only fifteen minutes to the start, and they're losing already."

A couple of boats were reaching back and forth aimlessly, others were still motoring, most hadn't got around to raising jibs yet. The crews were laying about in the cockpits, trading stories and laughing. Dakron wished he were out there.

"Look at 'em!" Brooke hissed. "Everyone talking about last night. There's a certain kind of sailor who's all bar talk on the water, and all race talk in the bar. Know what I call 'em?"

"Losers?" said Dakron.

Brooke clicked the remote at the sailors, trying to make them grunt, or float, or do anything besides yak. "Not a Shaq in the bunch," he said sadly. "Like every other race this season, they'll start this one as strangers."

"Strangers?" said Dakron.

"Strangers to their own boat, to the racecourse, to each other. First thing they should do is kill the damn motor, raise the jib and start *sailing*, getting the feel of things."

"Prerace homework," said Dakron.

"Right, but there's more to it than that. Lots of people go through a prerace checklist, but they're mostly just going through the motions. Before a race you have to feed your unconscious to get yourself ready to race. That means getting comfortable with the conditions, with how your boat feels, with how everyone is working together. The only way to do that is to sail—to turn off the stereo, cut the gab, and use the time to focus on the doubts and anxieties that will distract you from the racing."

"So when the race starts you can *race*, not worry about racing," said Dakron.

"You got it. If you're concerned about your boat speed, find a tuning partner and go to work on speed until you feel comfortable. If you're more concerned with the windshifts, use the time to concentrate on getting a handle on that. If you do it right, by the time the race rolls around, you and your crew will feel totally *ready to race*. Your sailing gloves will be broken in and your sunscreen will be sunk in. Everyone will be chomping at the bit instead of feeling nervous. When the race starts you'll cross the line and think, *I've been up this track before.* I know this wind, this sea condition, I feel comfortable with how the boat feels, how we've got our sails trimmed, our crew weight placed. We've got a plan of attack for the race and we are ready to race, so let the race begin."

"Are you hinting that I should leave the dock a little earlier?" Dakron asked.

"It might help," Brooke said, "but not if you just get out there to go through the motions. For example, if you want a tuning partner, arrange beforehand to meet well before the start, and don't just stick to a static, artificial tuning set-up either. Push your helming and your sail trimmers into shifting gears not only for the conditions but for race situations, such as going into 'squeeze' or height mode, or shifting into fast and low. Remember, once the gun goes you'll be in a race, not a straight-line tuning contest, and a race involves things like trying to build speed after a lee bow tack, or trying to lift clear of a lee bow tacker. Racing would be easy if it weren't for the other boats."

"Never thought of it like that," Dakron said. "So I should use the prerace tuning time to get my *racing* speed up to speed."

"And the payoff is, with prerace racing you'll familiarize yourself with the range of puffs and lulls you'll see after the start, and thus you'll know the range of adjustments you'll be using, and you'll be reaching for the right strings right off the bat, adjusting the sails and body weight quicker than the competition, cutting down on chatter, keeping you in the groove."

"Sounds too good to be true," Dakron sighed.

"It can be almost sinful. Especially when you hit a powerboat wake right off the starting line," Brooke said.

"Huh?" Dakron said.

"The jib goes out, the backstay off, mainsheet off, the weight comes off the rail and you power through while the losers who haven't done their prerace tune-up fall apart on either side of you. Sinful, all right."

"I never dreamed that a winner's work ethic included punching through wakes before the start. That's almost unethical! But what about tracking the windshifts?"

Zig Zag Brooke said, "An admirable pursuit, but don't fall into the trap of just writing down the numbers and thinking you've got it. Record the windshifts on both tacks with the compass, sure, but also observe the wind conditions you'll be racing in. Get a feel for the puffs: Are they streaky? Are they sharp gusts with holes behind, or are they gradual? Are they coming shorter or longer from one side as opposed to the other? Compass headings are fine, but they don't tell you which side or type of puff has the most velocity or lasts the longest.

"Get your head out of the boat when you're doing wind work, and use the other boats to help you assess the conditions. Periodically check the boats on the edges of the course. Anyone showing a lift or header you haven't recorded? Anyone getting more wind or less wind than you've seen? You can bet you'll see it during the race, when the fleet fans out."

"That's even sneakier," said Dakron, "letting the other boats do your work for you."

"And don't forget about downwind. A lot of people do. They put in a good tuning and wind session upwind, and then go ambling back to the starting line with their brains on hold, as if they won't have to sail downwind during the race. But the fact is, you can hook into a puff or lull for a longer period of time downwind than upwind, so that's all the more reason to get a feel for sailing the breeze downhill. Go out of your way to experience a major puff or lull downwind; it may turn out to have either less or more wind than what you expected, and that will drive home what you'll need to watch out for during the race. And there's nothing like riding a few streaks and leaving your tuning partner behind to pump everyone up about the run."

Dakron noted, "Of course, people would have to raise their genoas and actually start sailing, and maybe even try out their spinnakers to get to that stage."

"Not like this bunch," Brooke agreed, clicking the remote at the fleet idling about. The warning signal had gone up and still some boats had not brought a headsail on deck. The preparatory went up: five minutes. A few crews were still soaking up the sunshine.

Brooke shook his head at the boats and said, "Doing some prerace work gets your head into racing mode. Every day on the water is different, and when you go sailing you pick up a thousand conscious and unconscious signals. Start with the simple mechanics, and that leads you into doing things right come race time. Instead of going through a lackluster 'practice set' and a few listless gybes with the spinnaker, do a racing rounding of a mark, an imaginary mark if need be. Get everyone 'racing,' if only for a few boat lengths, and they put in more effort, they learn. The helmsman finds his downwind angles, the trimmers find out how far back to square the pole, how much pressure on the sheet the chute needs, and other things crop up: the mark on the spinnaker halyard is missing. We'll need to ease the main halyard, and someone will have to hold the boom out on the run. Gybe a few times, and the message emerges: this is how high we'll come out on the new gybe, trimmers, so anticipate."

"In essence, you're doing a little work before you go to work," Dakron said. "Overtime ahead of time."

"That's right. You push yourself a little, and at the same time you get yourself comfortable, get everyone tuned into the business of racing," Brooke said.

Boom! went the Race Committee's starting gun, and the fleet moved off the line. One boat hit a powerboat wake and stopped dead. He was quickly rolled by boats on both sides.

"Serves them right," Brooke said. "They have the best tans in the fleet."

Brooke turned away from the window and clicked the television back on. A downhill racer came whooshing through the finish gate, and everyone in the bar sighed; the TV was back on, full of winning sports heroes.

"How come you don't do any racing these days?" Dakron asked, nodding at the fleet sailing up to the window. "You could probably clean these guys up."

"Aw," said Zig Zag Drooke, "it's too much work."

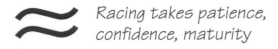 *Racing takes patience,
confidence, maturity*

# GROW UP AND WIN

"Somebody get that damn leech cord!" Deep Dakron hollered.

The genoa leech had begun motorboating with the start gun, a *whuppa-whuppa-whuppa* that shook *Snafu* like a fleet of Cobra gunships swooping out of *Apocalypse Now*.

Lisa Quick-Cam leaped to leeward. "I can't fix it! The leech line cleat is missing," she reported.

*"I can't fix it, it's missing,"* Dakron mimicked. "Oh, that's great. Just great."

"Lisa, lash it with a length of line," Scratchen Sniff suggested.

Dakron said, "Lisa, up forward, down in those compartments to starboard, there's some line. Get it and lash that leech cord. You're the lightest, Lisa."

Quick-Cam jumped below and began overturning bunk cushions, and finally emerged with a coil of dock line. "This?" she said doubtfully.

"No, not that! Try the port side locker, aft," said Dakron.

A series of mutters came from below, and Quick-Cam's gloved hand thrust a mildewed bundle of clothesline into the companionway. "You mean, this?"

"No, no!" Dakron cried.

"Well, that's the only spare line you've got down here," Quick-Cam said.

"Oh, that's just great," Dakron moaned.

"Try this," said Sniff, emptying a pocketful of Spectra, a variety of sizes perfect for lashing, pre-cut into handy lengths, from his foul-weather jacket.

In seconds, Quick-Cam had the leech cord lashed to the clew ring. "Hand it around the mast when we tack, and it should last the race," she told the Kid, who was doing foredeck.

Dakron spun on Sniff. "You had that line in your pocket the whole time," he said.

"Always bring a little string," Sniff said. "It can save your race when those untaped ring-dings work out of shackle pins, when that loose nut drops off your tiller extension, when you forget to replace your leech line cleat."

Dakron eyed the nut on his extension. "I detect an unfavorable shift in the karmic winds," he said. "Get on with it."

Sniff eased the traveler an inch and drew himself up. "Well, it may not seem like it, judging by the behavior of some of the top names in our sport, but winning sailors share three traits, three sides to their personalities that they have consciously worked at to improve their results."

Dakron waited, resigned.

"First, they have **paticnoe**."

"I don't have time for patience," Dakron snapped.

"Second, they have **confidence**."

"I'm not sure I can come up with enough confidence," Dakron said.

"Third, they have **maturity**."

"I can't see the point of maturity," said Dakron.

"Let's start with the toughie, **patience**. The sport of sailboat racing is only surpassed in frustration by two pursuits: golf and Rubik's cube. In racing there are races, there are regattas, there are *years* when nothing goes right. And you never know when you'll be tested to the limits of your endurance. The most innocuous-looking beat or reach or run can mushroom into a hellish eternity, piling indignity on indignity, a stress-load of humiliation and mental privation guaranteed to blow the gaskets of any ordinary mortal's patience, and yet you, Weekend Man, are asked to stay calm, to keep concentrating, to keep thinking rationally, to maintain a serene expression while you're rotating in a private wind vacuum and maelstrom of current, the boats you had put away long ago flying past on all sides, their crews catcalling and snickering into their sailing gloves. Brother, that's when you need patience."

"Well, I don't have it," said Deep Dakron.

"That's when you need to dig deep and come up with that inner stuff, that indomitable human spirit that says, 'Hey, this ain't so bad. This is *nothing*. I eat this kind of stuff for breakfast. Just wait till that next leg, that next race, that next regatta: We are going to lay waste to every one of you who guffawed into their fist. Like the Terminator, I'll be back.'"

"And Arnold did come back, just like he promised, and blew everyone away," Dakron said.

Sniff said, "And so will you. So, patience is a measure of your intestinal fortitude. Ask the mother of two-year-old quadruplet boys; you can only win by mining new depths of patience, not by mimicking Mt. Vesuvius. How to *get* patience? You build it. First, never forget that there's always another day, another shift, another race. Second, put the bad things behind you, even as they are happening. Don't dwell on the past; plan for the future. Third, remember: The sun don't shine on the same dog's rear every day. Your time in the sun will come; maybe five minutes from now with a new wind line, or next season, but be patient. Recognize that not being patient is counterproductive. Work toward your goals, and the arrows of misfortune will bounce off your shield of patience."

"So how did Schwarzenegger make out in *Terminator II?*" Dakron wondered.

"The next internal building block is **confidence**. Not everyone can be the winner, but one thing everyone *can* do is to sail to their ability. Most of us, listening to that tinny little negative voice telling us we aren't as good as the guy or gal in the next boat, routinely sail below our potential. Even Olympic level competitors, on that first or fiftieth trip overseas, have to overcome scary unknowns, debilitating tales of boat speed breakthroughs and government-sponsored teams. No one is immune to a confidence crisis.

"And what you, Weekend Man, have to do is to break down a similar bunch of unknowns. Go and see for yourself that the other teams are much like yours, that their equipment and techniques are not a level above yours. Of course, if they *are*, or if they are merely different, then make note, and learn and incorporate the good stuff into your program. But usually you will just find a similar bunch of humans in a similar boat, and if you sail to your ability you'll have as good a shot at beating them as they have at beating you. So, go out and race *them*, not yourself.

"Too, you have to break down any 'knowns' throwing you into a slump of confidence. Maybe it's a competitor who 'always' beats you, or a condition you do poorly in, like heavy or light weather. Don't attack a known that's beating you all at once; take it bit by bit. Someone's finishing ahead of you? Well, how? Are his starts better? His downwind speed? Study whatever it is, line up next to him, shower him with cold beer and questions, *learn.* Is it a wind or sea condition that's got you down? Pick out one aspect—your sail trim, or your steering—and work at and improve it, then step up to the next aspect. You can't tell yourself, bang! I'm confident! and expect to change that voice inside. Confidence comes from laying a foundation and building on it, and periodically going back to shore up any shaky areas. It's something you build inside, alongside your mine of patience."

"Getting pretty crowded in there," said Dakron.

"And lastly, we have saved room in our sailing hope chest for that staple of yachting's top talents, **maturity**."

"Maturity?" said Dakron. "You mean the America's Cup skipper who practiced in a blonde wig was demonstrating maturity?"

Sniff sighed. "Some things defy analysis. Anyway, maturity reveals itself in many ways. The greatest winner of all time, Paul Elvström, did some real trail blazing here. People thought he won because of his natural ability, but Elvström kept telling them it was his preparation, his practice, his physical conditioning that helped him to four gold medals and all those world championships. And finally, after he'd beaten everyone enough, the sailing world got the message. Now everyone is into preparation and practice and training—or at least they'll tell you they are."

"Some are more mature than others," said Dakron.

"That's right. I'll bet you can't name a top sailor who is lackadaisical in those areas, and even if you could, he or she won't be on top for long, not the way the sport is moving. Even now, most sailors don't put in a fraction of the training that, say, tri-athletes do—not yet, anyway. Thus, maturity translates into commitment, even on a weekend racer's level. A mature approach means that you chase down every last irritating detail, you prepare your boat and your body, you plan your schedule, you buckle down and do all that stuff when you'd rather be lounging in the glow of *Roseanne*. Maturity, plain and simple, means taking charge of your sailing. And you know what? You'll enjoy it a lot more when things don't keep going wrong."

"Maybe I need to start consulting a psychiatrist," Deep Dakron said, "instead of my sailmaker."

"Maybe you just need to grow up and win," Scratchen Sniff said, "and get a new leech line cleat."

*Why and how to keep
a racing notebook*

# BACK TO YOUR FUTURE

"Uh-oh," whispered Kent McBatten.

"What?" Deep Dakron hissed.

"Nothing," said McBatten.

The wind, iffy all day, had just gone extremely soft. *Snafu*, on the weather hip of a line of boats, had just been lifted 10, 15, and now 25 degrees, turning a neat circle inside everyone, and was now aimed straight at the finish line.

"We are so golden," Dakron cooed. "King of the hill."

Then the wind lifted even more, putting *Snafu* on a beam reach— and the boats below on a hot angle to the finish.

"Damn," said Deep Dakron.

Then everyone tried spinnakers. And then the wind died completely.

"Whew!" said Dakron.

On the far side of the course, a dark line appeared on the water.

"Uh-oh . . ." said McBatten.

Boats began tacking, their sails bulging with wind, romping for the finish as *Snafu* sat absolutely windless.

"Damn," said Deep Dakron. "Why did you have to start uh-ohing, anyway?"

"I had a flash," McBatten told him.

"A flash from the crystal ball? A flash of precognition?"

"Just the opposite: a flash*back*. I remembered other races where the wind died due to a new wind pushing in. You know, we sailors are always trying to predict the future, but we should be looking to our past. Unless we learn the lessons of our racing history, we are doomed to repeat them."

Deep Dakron sighed.

"In my hot shot days, when I really worked at this racing game, I kept a regatta notebook. I'd write up every race, what I did right and what I did wrong. It was hard, sitting down to do that every night, but I'd often surprise myself, devoting a whole page to a single pivotal leg, setting down the details of the wind, the tide, boat positions, sail trim, my mental state, what my crew and I discussed, how we saw the race and arrived at our decisions, what the winners did right, what the losers did wrong. Soon I'd have categories, lists—"

Dakron didn't doubt it. McBatten was a great one for lists; probably a spin-off of all that inventory sailmakers carried.

"And then I began to see patterns, winning and losing patterns, certain things I did over and over in my sailing. The great part was, I had this report card I could refer back to, so I didn't slip back into my old bad ways. You know, when I'd read: *Weather mark: lee-bowed row of starboard tackers—didn't make mark. Gybed around and tacked under next bunch, almost fouled out, didn't make mark again— too much current. Forgot to check current before race* and it'd bring the pain and humiliation of that incident right back, like an excruciating open wound."

"Wonderful," said Dakron.

"And by the time I closed my notebook I had a fresh resolve to check the current, because it wasn't the current that did it to me, it was *me* who did it to me. Why be your own worst enemy, when you've got a whole fleet of them out there?"

"I think I'd get writer's cramp, or writer's block," Dakron said.

"After I'd filled up a few notebooks I had a good picture of how I approached races and handled myself in regattas, so I reverted to three notebooks, **Trim, Tactics,** and **Rules,** in which I recorded things that made a difference.

"Into Trim went anything and everything I'd learned from myself or my competitors about going fast: sail shape, sail trim, rig tune, body position, kinetics techniques, developments in other classes and overseas. If it made the boat go, it was in there. And if a certain tuning spelled death when you were caught out with it, I'd note under what circumstances to avoid it, and when to employ it. Of course, I kept all my rig measurements and rig tension numbers in Trim; that meant I didn't lose my 'fast' when I changed boats, and I could evaluate a new sail or mast objectively. And I jotted down revealing comments heard and overheard during a regatta; after a few beers, the fast guys couldn't help but let slip the glorious details of how they'd depowered, vang-sheeted, changed gears, how their crews played the spinnaker, whatever. And I was right there, all ears, and later, a flying pencil."

Dakron observed, "Too bad you didn't start a Royals notebook; you'd have a bestseller by now. Would keeping a notebook have saved Di and Fergie?"

"In Tactics I set down instances of how the wind, the competition and my own actions either made or put paid to my race. Local knowledge stuff, like how a shore or point of land clicked under certain conditions but bombed under others. Crude drawings, you know, but when I went to a new venue I could pick out the similarities and avoid making blunders I wouldn't make at home. Of course, I couldn't help but include the height and type of clouds, land temps, air temps, things that tipped me off to a change. Always lots of question marks about the wind, which led me on investigations. Why didn't the sea breeze build on a certain day, for example? Well, I'd find out that some other breeze had been opposing it, and my grasp of the wind became better rounded by the exercise. The wind always makes sense, given perspective."

"Are we talking 20/20 vision, or infallible hindsight?" Dakron put in.

"My jottings in Tactics also pointed up how I and my combatants played the wind, and each other. Personalities came out: the Gambler, the Conservative, the Leader, the Follower, the Renegade, the Conformist. Each had their moment of glory, and I began to see when and why I should nudge my tactical style into a different frame when the wind and other boats behaved in a way that warranted it. I could change my *modus operandi* according to the wind and the flow of the game. It was liberating; I didn't have to lock myself into any certain style. I could sail however I wanted."

"It's a free country," Dakron noted, "and it takes all kinds."

"The Rules notebook was the hardest to buckle down to. It was stuffed full of old protest forms—mostly protests I'd lost. Know the good thing about losing a protest? You learn never to make the same mistake. And if you can bear to keep your protest forms, you don't forget what you've learned. I'd also note how other people's protests turned out; who the Protest Committee threw out and why, how sticky they were on details, like the size of the protest flag and how soon it was flown, and how different people interpreted the rules. Well, I never failed to learn something. Those how-to books on the rules are great, but there's nothing like what really happens during the buzz of a regatta, with the people factor muddying the black and white of the rules book.

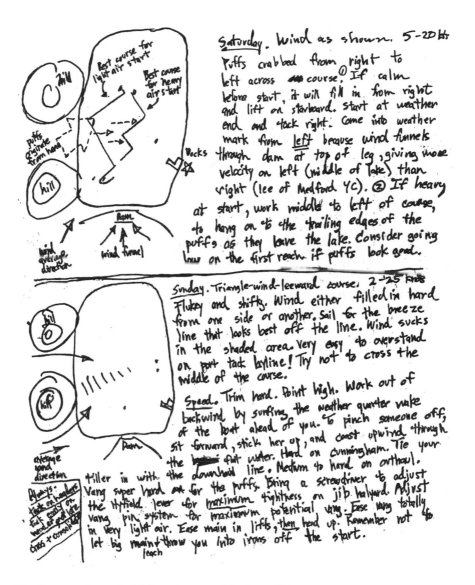

Saturday. Wind as shown. 5-20 kts
Puffs crabbed from right to
left across the course. ① If calm
before start, it will fill in from right
and lift on starboard. Start at weather
end and tack right. Come into weather
mark from left because wind funnels
through dam at top of leg, giving more
velocity on left (middle of lake) than
right (lee of Medford YC). ② If heavy
at start, work middle to left of course,
to hang on to the trailing edges of the
puffs as they leave the lake. Consider going
low on the first reach if puffs look good.

Sunday. Triangle-wind-leeward course. 2-25 knots
Flukey and shifty. Wind either filled in hard
from one side or another. Sail for the breeze
line that looks best off the line. Wind sucks
in the shaded area. Very easy to overstand
on port tack layline! Try not to cross the
middle of the course.

Speed. Trim hard. Point high. Work out of
backwind by surfing the weather quarter wake
of the boat ahead of you. To pinch someone off,
sit forward, stick her up, and coast upwind through
the flat water. Hard on cunningham. Tie your
tiller in with the downhaul line. Medium to hard on outhaul.
Vang super hard for the puffs. Bring a screwdriver to adjust
the Hyfield lever for maximum tightness on jib halyard. Adjust
vang pin system for maximum potential vang. Ease vang totally
in very light air. Ease main in lifts, then head up. Remember not to
let big main+throw you into irons off the start.

The three most important things about a notebook are (1)
start a notebook; (2) use it religiously at every regatta; and
(3) never—no matter how mildewed it becomes—throw the
notebook away. Writing racing situations down reinforces the
lessons learned, and rereading old notebooks gets us Into
the race before the racing begins.

"And by recording the significant bits, I'd learn. I'd also put my boat-to-boat battles on the starting line and at mark roundings into Rules, and I'd recognize chronic situations I shouldn't be getting myself into. I used to be a great tack-into-a-last-second-inside-over-lap-at-the-mark kind of guy, a-luffing-too-quickly-before-the-start man, a sticking-my-nose-in-with-nowhere-to-go-but-crunch kind of person. The Rules notebook—the report card on my exploits—cured me."

Dakron asked, "Where are your notebooks now? Might be fun to read one."

McBatten dashed below and rummaged through his duffel. "Here. One of my early works, before I branched into the three categories. Pick a page, any page."

Dakron stuck the tiller extension between his knees and opened the battered book. "Hmm," he said.

"Oh, that. That was a round-robin series on a little puddle, ages ago," McBatten explained.

"Hmm," said Dakron.

Dakron looked up. "I feel like I've sailed the regatta. It had me thinking, analyzing. That's amazing."

"A good notebook can do that. It puts you right back in the race. You relearn those old lessons, and more," said McBatten.

"Reading this is super, except for one thing," said Deep Dakron.

"What's that?"

"I wish we weren't still becalmed."

# GOOD NEWS THAT'S FIT TO PRINT OUT

"Oouuuuuff!" Deep Dakron grunted and heaved his wet #1 genoa and two spinnakers, equally soggy, onto the office floor of McBatten Sailmakers.

From behind his buzzing computer Kent McBatten's eyebrows rose only slightly. "Casualties?" he inquired.

"One collision resulting in a spinnaker pole through the genoa, one spinnaker wrap resulting in multiple stretch marks, one goosewing gybe resulting in confetti," sighed Dakron. "Otherwise, everything's fine."

"The usual," said McBatten.

"Another great weekend," Dakron agreed. "What's up? Taking inventory again?"

McBatten was surrounded by piles of continuous feed computer paper, and he was going over the printout item by item, underlining or adding a note or a question mark here and there. There appeared to be several thousand items in McBatten's inventory.

"Ahem," Dakron coughed. "What are you doing? Inventory?"

"In a way," said McBatten, and right then his printer spat out two more pages. "I'm putting together a list of ways to win sailboat races and regattas. You know, some good news instead of bad news. But there are so many ways to win, this is turning out to be a life's work."

Dakron scooped up six feet of printout. "Say, I might be interested in some of this. In fact, I might be an authority on this."

Dakron sank into the couch and began reading:

- Never, ever irritate anyone on the racecourse, especially someone on your own boat, or on an official boat.

- Never get involved in a rules situation where the onus falls on you to prove your innocence.
- Late in the race or series, always, *always* cover the boats you have to beat.
- Don't show up at an important regatta with sails, rig, blades or crew that haven't been tested and brought up to speed beforehand, especially when the regatta is overseas.
- Never anger anyone on the Race Committee, Protest Committee, or any of the host yacht club members.
- Always know the point scores going into the last few races.
- Don't diminish someone on your own boat by yelling at them, or taking over their job.
- Have everyone on the crew read the Sailing Instructions.
- Never arrive late to the starting area.
- Go one-on-one against a fast boat before the race to tune up for the conditions, and to get yourself tuned in.
- In dinghies, never forget that raw downwind speed is just as important as upwind speed. Work on your downwind technique.
- Stick to the basics with crew work, tactics, and sails.
- Never sail with bad equipment. All breakdowns are mental in origin.
- Don't take a flyer unless you're absolutely desperate to stay alive in the race or series.
- Trophies are not important: learning and improving your skills is the only trophy you really take home.
- Never scream at anyone on the racecourse, even fishing boats.
- Do not tack or gybe until the crew members are ready, and they say, 'Ready.'
- Don't make excuses. Make a comeback.
- If you need to make a radical change to your sailing style, make it . . . but work it out before the championships.
- Sail with as many good people as you can. *Learn.*
- Sail in as many different classes and types of boats and different types of racing as you can. *Learn.*
- Ego is good, but smarts is better.

- Don't stress out.
- Focus on the main issue at hand; don't work on the perfect roll-tack while letting the competition roll by you on a huge shift.
- Everyone must keep their eyes open at all times. Surprises on the racecourse usually come right after a nap.
- Always keep score.
- When you can cross your competition, you better gybe or tack and cross 'em.
- Use more than your eyes; use temperature, heel angle, the sounds of bow wave and stern wake, your sunburned ears to *feel*.
- Watch the other boats, then the water, *then* the compass.
- Never do anything automatically; before you act or speak, *think*.
- Never touch another boat, unless you're match racing.
- Throw your protest flag only in self-defense, and even then be prepared to lose half the time.
- Socialize after the race.
- Buy one of those books about the new racing rules, and go through it with a highlighter.
- Never quit a race—the only exception is if someone's life is in danger.
- If you capsize, get pumped and get into it. It's good conditioning.
- Pack a good lunch.
- In big fleets, play the percentages. In small fleets, play the players.
- Learn to sail in dirty air; learn to keep your boat moving, instead of moaning and falling apart at the tiller.
- If you get behind, make your comeback boat by boat, the smart tough way, not by taking a flyer and hoping you get lucky.
- Wear sunscreen and a hat. Don't get fried on the first day.
- When riding waves, always steer for the downhill part of the wave to catch it, and then trim across the face to keep your apparent wind hot.

- In a big fleet, stay away from the mess at the pin and the Race Committee boat; get a clean start somewhere in the favored one-third of the line.
- Keep updating your race commentary. Can we cross that boat on the other side of the course? Can he cross us? Judging the boats means that you are judging the wind.
- Never hit the Race Committee boat.
- Ask the winners why they won. It's always illuminating . . . and they're usually eager to tell you. If they aren't, find out why.
- Get a look at your sails from off the boat. Swap with a buddy when you go speed testing and get a look at his sails, too.
- Keep abreast of developments in other classes; sail shapes, rigs, techniques, it's all interconnected.
- Always clap for your competition at the trophy presentation.
- If you see yourself getting locked into a bad start, bail out early: tack, gybe, get out immediately, before it gets *really* bad.
- Mark roundings: Go for the rounding that puts you in the best position ten lengths *after* the mark. It doesn't pay to round inside if you round dead in the water.
- Don't be a maverick; use the same sails and gear the winners are using.
- Think twice before gybing or tacking away from a group of boats; you might lose contact with the whole bunch.
- Practice with your crew how to shift gears for choppy water and smooth water, lulls and puffs.
- Don't go out on a limb early in a race or regatta.
- Sail every regatta as if there is no throwout. Then, use the last race to throttle your competition.
- At starts and mark roundings in a big fleet, the ability to point and hang high is a lifesaver. Going fast and low means you end up tacking away from people's hips constantly.
- After a tack, get all the way out on the trapeze, pull the jib all the way in, *then* hook up.

- Get off the emotional roller coaster. Be consistent. Don't take big chances. Don't make big mistakes. Don't take yourself out of play; take someone *else* out of play.
- Being comfortable with your settings and knowing how to use your sails in all conditions is more important than buying every new whiz-bang sail that comes out.
- Get Deep Dakron to order a new "Spiderman" #1 genoa and two new "GhostBusters" spinnakers this season.

"What!" Dakron howled.

"You found it," smiled McBatten. "Now how about giving me some good news?"

 *How much of sailboat racing is luck?*

# LUCK! OR SKILL?

"**D**amn!" said Deep Dakron, banging his tiller extension on the cockpit coaming. "Damn, damn, damn."

From his perch on the windward rail, tactician Scratchen Sniff smoothed his mustache. "You are pinching," he noted, "and negative thoughts do not make a boat go."

"It's just that those guys," said Dakron, jabbing a finger over his shoulder at *Dirty Heir,* "are so damn *lucky.* Look at 'em!"

It was true. By carefully playing every shift and never sailing out of major velocity, Dakron and Sniff had ground up *Dirty Heir* and left them hung out to dry on their hip, nearly 100 yards astern. But in the last thirty seconds *Dirty* had rotated up and away in a breathtaking 25-degree lift and elevator-puff, and was winning the race. Gone, in fact.

"That's not luck," said Sniff, "that's—"

"Don't you dare!" Dakron cut in. "Don't you dare say, 'That's not luck, that's skill.'"

"*Dirty's* lift isn't luck," Sniff continued, "and I wouldn't say it's due to skill, either. I prefer to think of it as merely another episode in the yacht racing version of *Unsolved Mysteries.*"

"What's a tabloid TV show got to do with reaching the windward mark first?" Dakron puffed.

Sniff said, "That program is educational; it tells us know-it-alls that there are still phenomena that we do not understand. Which brings me to Sniff's fearless definition of luck."

"Just my luck," groaned Dakron.

"Luck," Sniff went on, "is merely the *unforeseen arriving unexpectedly.* This brings us back to phenomena, of which there are two kinds: **Phenomena we do not control** and **phenomena we do not understand**.

"Let's take the first category: all those things which we do not control on the racecourse. Whereas a tennis net and a basketball hoop are always in the same place, during a sailboat race the wind, current, and wave conditions (including that old favorite, the powerboat wake) are ever-changing. Throw in the unfathomable moves of the Race Committee and your competitors and you've got the potential for some real bad luck, I mean uncontrollable phenomena.

"The second type of phenomena are the many things which we do not understand. When we race, our world hinges on the changes in our micro-environment of wind and water, most of which we are at a loss to explain—and thus unable to predict when or to what degree they will take place. Can any of us really work out why the wind suddenly shifts left or right, dies or increases? We can only concoct an explanation afterwards, in the yacht club bar.

"Then there are the mysteries of our own boats, how they can suddenly come to life and just as quickly die out, seemingly of their own volition, even when we've got everything at the right settings. If we really understood our vehicles, then sailing would be as easy as driving a golf cart, right?"

"Er, right," said Dakron, watching the telltales. "Now that I know how to be a victim, is there anything I can do to improve my luck, or phenomena?"

"You may be in luck," said Sniff. "Personally, it puts me more in control of my destiny on the racecourse if I make the distinction between phenomena I do not control and those I do not understand, because the next step is to learn how to maximize the gains and minimize the losses from both categories.

"You've heard the cliché, 'Winners make their own luck.' Well, you can't really make your own luck, but there are ways to align life's molecules and start them flowing your way—or at least duck the worst of it when a nasty phenomenon doubles back at you.

"The first step is to **keep your mind open**. As a race progresses, we tend to close our horizons as to what is possible; we expect the wind to swing only within certain reassuring numbers on the compass, we assume that the wind won't get lighter or heavier than what we've seen, and so on. So when good or bad 'luck' strikes—the unforeseen arrives unexpectedly— we are taken by surprise. There's a relationship in all this that should set your alarm bells jingling: the bigger the 'luck' and the more surprising it is reveal the degree to which we've been dozing at the wheel, not keeping our mind and eyes open.

"The second way you can improve your 'luck' is to **duck luck**. Simply, the more often and deeper you place yourself in high-risk positions—on laylines, in corners, into situations where you *need* something to come through or *not* to happen—the more likely you are to experience bad luck, I mean unfavorable phenomena. Consult the averages of Murphy's Law and they'll reveal that conservative sailing might not win the race, but it *will* win the series.

"Lastly, whenever the unforeseen arrives unexpectedly, you've got to **love your luck**. By this I mean that good or bad, whether you like what's happened or not, you've got to accept it and get on with the racing. Think of it like Wall Street's ups and downs: Just when you had racked up a nice dividend, everything crashes and the scramble starts over again. Or, just the opposite, out of nowhere you're handed a windfall for your pitiful shares. But the thing to remember is that it's not luck, it's just a combination of phenomena. And no matter which way it goes you've just got to shrug it off by saying, 'That's yacht racing!' Put a grin on your face, open your mind and eyes a bit wider, and get back in the hunt."

Deep Dakron sighed. "After all the money and time and practice and beers that I've invested, you want me to grin like an idiot and say, 'That's yacht racing.'"

"Beers," came the shout from a crewman who had disappeared below some time earlier. Chilled cans came zinging out of the companionway. One hit Dakron in the chest, another flew overboard. Without even turning around, Scratchen Sniff reached his left hand behind him and caught one backhanded.

"Wow!" said Dakron. "That was lucky."

"Now *that*," said Sniff, one-handedly opening the pull tab with two passes under the lifeline, "is skill."

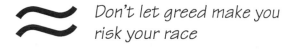
*Don't let greed make you
risk your race*

# GREEEEED

"**W**ell, I'd hoped we were through with that era," said Scratchen Sniff, sighing as he clicked the TV remote at a huddle of PR people outside a jury room. "Mercenary greed, blatant commercialism, a raw 'I'm gonna got mine' mentality, spying and dirty tricks, litigation, cheap talk, expensive champagne, boom and bust, the glitz of nouveau tycoons—"

"But that's what makes the America's Cup great," cut in Deep Dakron. "Did you see the promos for the après-Cup celebrity race, with celebrities from *Roseanne* and *Married . . . with Children*, with revolvers?"

Sniff wrinkled his nose. "America's Cup? I was talking about the Eighties. You know: the decade of greed. Well, it seems that Greed has returned with a capital G."

Dakron winced, remembering the Eighties. "I went bust, then boom, then bust. If only I'd cashed my chips in before that dark, dark Monday . . . How do you know greed is back? Where have you seen this monster?"

"In me. In you. All over our boat, last weekend," said Sniff.

"Black Sunday," Dakron agreed, remembering the drubbing they'd taken. "But were we driven by greed? I thought it was on the order of we have to try something."

"There's a distinction between putting in honest hard work to get ahead, and being greedy," said Sniff. "Remember the first race, when the wind went light and clocked around, making the second windward leg into a lopsided one-tack beat, and we were the only ones to tack out, chasing a puff?"

"We had to try something," said Dakron. "We couldn't just sit in *Ill Morrow*'s wake."

213

"And how, when we finally got the puff, dollar signs flashed in our eyes, and payoff money jingled in our pockets?"

"How were we to know that the puff would lift us 20 degrees, and that every boat in the fleet would come reaching in from underneath us?" said Dakron. "Who would have suspected we'd blow all our assets on one traded tack?"

"And what was our downfall?" prompted Sniff.

"That we didn't get the puff soon enough? That it shifted too much when we did get it?" said Dakron.

"*Greed,*" said Sniff, "with a capital G."

Sniff went on, "And remember the second race, when we split gybes with *Hysteria Kubed*, but saw right after we gybed that they had hooked into a puff, and we were headed for the Twilight Zone? Remember how we *still* kept going?"

"But we *couldn't* gybe back," said Dakron. "They would have been ahead of us."

"And remember how pride, brother of you-know-who, forced us into sailing off all of our assets, into speculating on an empty spinnaker? But what really prompted our downfall?"

"That we never got that puff," said Dakron, "but I think I know what you're going to say."

"*Greed,*" said Sniff.

Then Sniff said, "And remember how, near the end of the last beat of the final race, with only a run to the downwind finish to go, we could have crossed the fourth place boat, if only we'd tacked?"

Deep Dakron said, in pain, "We just needed one more puff, just a bit more of a header, and we could have had first place."

"Remember how third place would have been wonderful, but somehow not enough, and we held on, waiting for a bigger puff, for more header so we could *win* the race? And remember, while we waited, how everyone lifted up and away and the door of opportunity slammed shut in our acquisitive little faces?"

"Let me say it," said Dakron. "Greed."

"With a capital G," added Sniff.

"How appalling," said Dakron. "Greed *is* back. The fault lies not in our starry-eyed tactics, but in ourselves. How do we fight this insidious foe?"

Sniff said, "By using Sniff's anti-greed rules. The precepts of this statute prohibit snouts diving into troughs, the giddy running up of credit lines, and advocates negotiating from an asset-rich, *let's not gamble what we'd rather not lose* position. It's just what the Cup syndicates need."

"Hmm," said Deep Dakron.

"Rule Number One," said Sniff, "is to ask yourself, **what's the absolute worst that can happen?** This is the fundamental question we should ask before committing ourselves to any bright ideas on the racecourse."

"Kind of defeatist, don't you think?" said Dakron.

"Sobering is more like it," said Sniff. "Usually, when we think of a tactic we visualize only its success; the lift comes in and we cross the line of starboard tackers; we get the puff and break the inside overlap, etc. It can get to be a costly habit, counting returns before they're in.

"Looking at our tactic from the other way around forces us to assess the negative consequences. If the wind goes the wrong way, or goes the right way too much, will we be all night sailing back to the yacht club? Will we forfeit our dance cards entirely if our hoped-for puff doesn't arrive?"

"I believe the term is 'history,'" said Dakron.

Sniff ignored him. "So, assess your worst case scenario in boat lengths and places. Could we possibly lose five boat lengths? Ten? Twenty? So many that we blow ourselves out of contention in the race? In the series? How many boat lengths will it cost to pull off this move? Two extra tacks? Two extra gybes? How about places? Could those two boats pass us? How about those four over there?

"Figuring out possible losses in boat lengths and race places puts our motives under the bright lights for an interrogation. Okay, just which boats are we trying to pick off? How many? *All* of them? Remember: If you can't do the time, don't do the crime."

"Greed kills," Dakron agreed.

"Rule Number Two: **Protect your assets**. Simple math; can I afford this? Is this tactic in my regatta budget? Is it a necessity, or a luxury? Is it an impulse, a perk, a stab at status?

"In my present situation, does the attempt to gain three boats justify the risk of losing three? It could, if I'm asset-rich: if I have a cushion of sacrificial boat lengths; if I possess comeback boat speed; if I have some breathing room on my scorecard. It may not, if I'm asset-poor: if the boats behind me are ones I can't afford to lose to; if I've already used my throwout race; if my poor boat speed, crew work or other weakness could snowball a minor setback into a major loss."

"Deficit spending," said Dakron. "Imagine if the House of Representatives raced a world championship. They'd be into six- and seven-figure scorecards."

Sniff clicked the remote at Dakron, silencing him. "Rule Number Three: **The race finishes at the finish**. Is right now the best time to make your daring move? Or should you wait for a better opportunity? Think, reason, *feel*; are you tempting Fate? Could you be ignoring the warning tremors of a nautical Black Monday by acting too soon (for example, before the new wind can reach you)? Or by acting too late (after they've already got the new wind)?

"If you're not poised on such an abyss, consider the amount of racetrack available. How much time is left in the race? How many legs are left? How many and what kinds of opportunities for passing will be available? Will there be passing lanes on certain legs, but only parades on others? Will the wind continue fluky, or steady? You know your competitors; at what point will they go for the gold? When will they be most vulnerable? Will you be ready with a plan?

"In every race, in every series there's a time to fortify your position and a time to charge the enemy. There's no sense getting into a luffing duel on the reaches if it puts you out of striking range of the leaders on the next beat. And once back on shore, always remember to be outwardly nice, but sneaky. Never answer a direct question. Keep 'em guessing."

"I'm going to miss the America's Cup," sighed Dakron. "What else is on?"

The remote was a smoking gun in Scratchen Sniff's hand. "Here's a *Dynasty* rerun," he said.

"Perfect," said Deep Dakron.

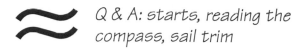 *Q & A: starts, reading the compass, sail trim*

# ASK DOCTOR DAKRON

Dear Doctor Dakron:

Please, Doc, you're my last hope! My private shame has been burning inside, my public humiliation twisting my crew apart for the last 20 years. Here's my problem: Right before the gun I look all set to get a great start, but in the last few seconds everyone leaves me in the dust. Doc, is it too late for me?

*(signed)* Desperate

Dear Desperate:

Whoa, big guy! Remember: Peter Pan couldn't fly until he thought those *happy thoughts.* And don't forget, you're not alone; this kind of thing happens to everybody, and it's nothing to get desperate about. Although, in your case, after 20 *years* of it, you are justifiably suicidal, and your crew is pardonably homicidal.

From my own experience, your problem stems from not knowing the exact moment when you can cross the starting line and not be over early, a direct result of not knowing how close to the line you are. Thus you are wavering, speedless, the jelly on the starting line muffin. But this is not entirely your fault. Just what is your bowman telling you with all those ridiculous hand signals, anyway? Too close? Not close enough? Too fast? Too slow? Fast-forward? Rewind? Eject? Some of these guys think they're directing the Pope's motorcade down Hollywood Boulevard!

It's time for a tough-love session with your bowman. No doubt he'll tell you some things that'll be tough to take, such as: *When you make your final run at the line, you set up too close to the line, and end up reaching down the line with the sails in tight, and then make a speed-killing bat-turn at the gun. And: Despite my 'too close' warnings, you get too close with five seconds to go and have to turn*

*down at the last moment, ending up too close to the boat to leeward.*
*And: You will continue to be left in the cheap seats unless you match*
*your boat speed to the boats around you before you go over the start-*
*ing line.*

Now, present your trusty bowman with your own set of demands:
*Give me a signal that means 'Come forward enough to keep your*
*nose up with the boats to windward and to leeward.' Give me a sign*
*that tells me I'm 'Going either too fast or too slow relative to the boats*
*around me.'* (Remember, it's the other boats, not the line or the gun,
that you're trying to ace.) *And finally, signal me if 'Our group is way*
*back from the line, or way over the line.'*

My last suggestion is to select a low-key race, give the helm to
one of your crew, and go up to the pointy end to get the bowman's
perspective. You'll find that judging time and distance on the starting line is a heavy responsibility, and orchestrating the helmsman
and string-pullers with hand signals isn't easy. After a few starts
you'll be glad to quit riding the nose cone of the Shuttle!

Dear Doc Dak:

I am a diehard class racer (and, I might add, something of a legend),
but I always seem to suffer when the wind picks up and it's time to
change from the genoa to the jib. As a result, I tend to hang onto the
genoa even when it's too windy, because I have such trouble down-
shifting to the jib. What am I doing wrong?

*(signed)* Power Failure

Dear Failure:

I've referred your letter to my trusty sailmaker, Kent McBatten, who
offers this two-weeks-late reply: "Dear Power Failure: You've stuck
yourself between the yin and yang of being overpowered and underpowered, and the clue to your failure lies in your own words. Think,
dum-dum! You mention 'genoa' twice, and 'jib' twice, but what's the
other sail you have up? Darn right, you've forgotten your mainsail,
you big silly!

"Now, I admit that it's a shock to the system, going from the
genoa to the jib, but what most of my customers forget in the switch
is their mainsail. No doubt when you had the genoa up the poor
main was bladed out with lots of mast bend, cunningham, outhaul,
and vang, depowered to the shallowness of my advertising budget.
That's great when you're overpowered, but when the little jib goes
up it's time to repower the mainsail shape.

"When you change to the jib it's likely you'll find yourself underpowered in the lulls, and your pointing and speed will suffer. Ease the backstay, let off some outhaul (the bottom of the sail does not need to be as flat as with the overlapping genoa, because there is less backwind), and pull the traveler up until the boat just begins to feel overpowered—that's the upper limit of powering up the mainsail. Then flatten it out slowly, and play the mainsail power to the conditions. With the small jib up, the mainsail assumes a more important role, that of boat speed and pointing 'throttle,' than it did with the genoa. Finally, if the wind drops way off, you should power up the jib by moving the lead forward and sheeting harder."

Dear Doc:

On our boat I'm in charge of reading the compass, and I hate the thing! I always write down the high and low port and starboard tack headings before the race, but once the race starts my headers aren't real headers and my lifts aren't real lifts. I'm about to throw away my grease pencil before the skipper throws me overboard!

(signed) Shiftless

Dear Shiftless:

Maybe you need reading glasses! Have you tried a pocket calculator? How about a Ouija board? Sorry—I passed your letter on to my personal wind fictician, Scratchen Sniff, and he had this to say: "I don't know about this guy's powers of addition and subtraction, but it sounds like he's spending too much time staring into the depths of the oil-filled crystal ball and not enough looking at the wind on the water. Literally, the wind is blowing in one ear and out the other! Shiftless has come unstuck because he's failed to note whether his prerace lifts and headers have occurred in puffs or lulls, and the compass numbers he's writing down reflect velocity changes more than windshifts. When he thinks he's headed he may just be sailing in less wind, and when he thinks he's lifted he may just be sailing in a puff.

"We all know that a boat will point higher in a puff and lower in a lull, and in light air it will point a *lot* higher or lower, fooling even the best of us into thinking the wind has shifted. The trick is to observe how much your boat angle changes purely due to wind velocity, and one good way to do this is to tack in a lull, and then tack in a puff as part of your prerace preparation. The difference can be astonishing to astute compass readers; the tacking angle can go from greater than 90 degrees to less than 80 degrees. Also, by testing both tacks in the same puff, lull, or windshift, you get a 'both tacks' compass number confirmation, and are less likely to be fooled during the heat of battle.

"Lastly, Mr. Shiftless, compass readings are made to be erased— that's why tacticians use grease pencil instead of chiseling them into the bulkhead. By revising your numbers as you go, you'll do better on each successive leg, and by the time you're back in the yacht club bar you'll know exactly what you should have done."

*Doctor Dakron endeavors to answer all letters, even if he has to wing it. Inquiries should be mailed with your daytime phone number and credit card details to: Doctor Dakron, Club Racers Anonymous, Agony Division.*

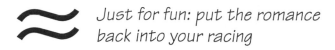

*Just for fun: put the romance
back into your racing*

# QUIVERING HEIGHTS

"**T**was a dark and stormy night," whispered a pale, trembling Deep Dakron, right out of the cover of a bestselling bodice ripper, about to sink into Scottish moors.

"Or at least it seemed like nighttime, after that fishing boat cut us off and we lost our sun, and our wind, and we plowed into his six-foot-high wake," said Scratchen Sniff.

*"Oh! My breast!"* cried Kent McBatten, trimming the genoa.

"Your breast?" said Dakron.

"Mm mmmm?" said the Mumbler.

"In my breast, deep in my heart of hearts, I know that this wrong will be righted!" McBatten declared, kindling the crew's inner fires. "Our passion for puffs, our love of lifts, our *lust* for laylines shall not go unrequited. Those daring white horses on the horizon will come racing in to our rescue. Verily, they will sweep us away!"

"Frankly, I don't give a damn," growled Zig Zag Brooke. "We're hardly halfway down the first page, I mean up the first beat, and we're already running out of exclamation points and italics. Let's save the romance for later."

"True love will wait forever," said Lisa Quick-Cam, hands clasped over her heart, "but sizzling romance must be resolved in 200 pages."

"Hark!" cried the Kid from the windward rail, the Kid who stayed ever-vigilant-without-being-reminded-every-two-minutes. "Puff coming down in five seconds."

"Ever seen a puff come up?" Sniff snickered. Ears pricked, brows clouded; what *was Sniff insinuating?*

The Kid called out, "And rubbish on your bow: a bunch of seaweed, 'biodegradable' plastic bags, one family tub of Colonel Sanders. Come down half a length—okay, you're clear."

"Our laminar flow plucked from the clutches of greasy chicken wings," said McBatten. "Bless you, Kid!"

"And waves: one, two, three waves coming. Five seconds! On your bow, *now.*"

Plucky, this Kid; orphaned, someday he will be a billionaire, owning these very waters, toying with all the people on the toy boats.

"He slices, he dices, he minces, pricking, puncturing, piercing," purred Deep Dakron, concentrating with surgical, serial precision.

"Lifted 10 degrees in a building puff," reported Sniff, swiveling his rakish mustache into the breeze. "We are back in this boat race."

"Twenty lengths to layline," McBatten hissed, kick-starting everyone's mental checklists. Who was on the spinnaker sheet? The afterguy? Brains raced, cogs clicked, tweakers were tweaked, suspicions aroused: Was it the maid, the butler, or the gardener? No: *the swimming pool man. Those kinky vacuum hoses, those pool chemicals, those sun-soaked suburban afternoons, our heroine sunbathing, top down and gate unlatched.*

"Get ready for a tack, and then a bear-away set," whispered Zig Zag Brooke to his railmates, knowing that with every four seconds another irretrievable boat length slipped by, grains of sand through the hourglass, the regattas of our lives. A late elbow, a loose knee would mean embarrassment, if not oblivion.

The Kid's eyes flicked over the foredeck, checking, doublechecking, and his finger flicked the jammed, and now unjammed, jib sheet.

"Move the jib lead forward one," he directed, anticipating the need for power out of the tack; a flat spot was coming. A sneer curled the Kid's lips; he already had the spinnaker hooked up.

Lisa Quick-Cam swung her legs up and in. *What a summer it's been!* she thought. *My skin, so golden, I'm hardly the same person. Does anyone see the poise, the confidence behind these same innocent brown eyes? Let them crash-tack! They'll never get these legs wet.*

*Snafu* tacked, poetry in motion, a symphony of sailors swooping on the mark.

"*Voilà!*" cried Dakron, powered up and moving, appraising his tiller extension as one would a glass of '71 St. Emilion.

"*Magnifique!*" echoed Sniff, kissing his fingertips.

The Kid raised his quivering pole and thrust it onto the mast ring, crying, "Topper!"

Quick-Cam anticipated him, bringing the lift up taut and singing against his chest, the pole cocked brazenly. They exchanged smoldering looks.

"They move so well together," sighed Zig Zag Brooke, misty eyed.

"Mmpggh!" said the Mumbler, wiping a tear away.

Laying the mark, Dakron kept it heated, but not too heated, as the spinnaker was hoisted, listening intently to the calls from McBatten.

"Down a touch, hold it there—the chute is filled. Now let's carve down smoothly, let's wind that afterguy back gently," McBatten cooed.

"Course to the next mark is down 15 degrees," Sniff reported from behind his binoculars. "I've got a visual on it. See that red spinnaker? Two of his spinnaker-lengths to leeward."

"Got it," confirmed Dakron.

Sniff continued, "Puff coming in ten seconds, let's heat up to get into it. We have four boat lengths of clear wind astern. Summer of the Bronze Birch and Firefly's Budding Promise are rounding the mark right now."

"Thank you," said Dakron, freed from having to turn and look behind, and then forward, and then behind: off-the-wind whiplash.

McBatten focused the crew on spinnaker trim, questioning, striving, never satisfied. "Can we try the pole up six inches, Lisa? What do you think about the afterguy coming back, Mr. Mumbler? Kid, what's the chute look like from up there? Zig Zag, is it breathing? Am I strapped? Dakron, your mainsail is perfection right about there, sir!"

McBatten used everyone's name, encouraging, empowering them, solicitous of each person's area of responsibility, careful not to diminish anyone, and soon these disparate individuals, thrown together by a fate cheaper than the plots of an airport book rack, pulled as one. As Quick-Cam raised her pole the Mumbler eased a touch of afterguy, maintaining the pole's fore and aft position. They winked.

Now the puffs came stronger, and the too-thin spinnaker sheet thrummed in McBatten's gloves, hotter than the first page of a Jackie Collins novel.

"Let's change before the gybe—I'll get the heavy spinnaker sheets," said Lisa Quick-Cam, diving below. Grasping the coils, Quick-Cam caught a glimpse of herself in the mirror. Is that person really me? she thought. I look so old. Those lines on my face, the wisps of gray. Just when I've got my sheet stoppers under my thumb, I'm thrown head over heels.

Coming into the gybe mark, everyone keyed on the Kid to assist him gybing the pole, for five seconds the toughest physical job on the boat, and the one most dependent on cooperation from the cockpit and helmsman.

"Trip!" yelled Deep Dakron, turning down to ease the pressure on the spinnaker. Quick-Cam eased her foreguy, ready to snap it back on if the pole kited. McBatten and the Mumbler worked sheet and afterguy, keeping the chute full, being careful not to let the spinnaker kite up and away. On the new afterguy, McBatten eased a goodly amount exactly when the Kid needed it. Zig Zag Brooke sprang forward and helped the Kid muscle the pole onto the mast.

"Made!" they shouted, and Dakron snapped the boat up onto a hard reach, following Sniff's directions to the next mark.

A gust seized them. In seconds the pressure on Dakron's throbbing tiller became too much, more than he could stand, leaving him aching for the release of—

"Vang!" cried Sniff.

At the ready, Lisa Quick-Cam freed it and the rope burned through her fingers.

*"Ohhhhhhhh,"* moaned Dakron, the pressure gone out of his tiller. When the puff died, he said, "Now, vang me hard."

Quick-Cam took it with both hands and yanked.

"Oh! Not that hard!" Dakron cried, and they roared away in a withering, rollicking blast of foam.

Barreling into the leeward mark, responsibilities discussed and assigned, trouble scenarios anticipated, the spinnaker people concentrated on the spinnaker, and the working sail people concentrated on the working sails, on keeping the boat fast and on its feet after the rounding. Tidying up would take a back seat to hauling butt up the windward beat.

"Traveler up, slowly now, as people come back on the rail," McBatten cautioned. "Now let's go to vang-sheeting," and he and Quick-Cam brought the sliding tubes of the vang together to the heavy air marks.

Sniff had writ the compass numbers of the first beat's headers and lifts in bold scarlet letters, and now he read them. "We're lifted 15 degrees," he announced, "and looking like a million bucks."

"Starboard tacker," McBatten cut in, a few tacks later.

"Dip, tack, or cross?" asked Dakron.

"Battle stations." Zig Zag Brooke alerted the rail crew, giving everyone five seconds of warning. Lisa Quick-Cam torqued her torso into line, measured the slack between her hand and the vang cleat, in case they had to dip the starboard tacker. *Now pop when I tell you,* she willed the cleat.

McBatten was semaphoring, sending an unmistakable query to the starboard tacker: *Can we cross, or would you rather we slam a lee bow tack in your face?*

Sniff broke in with a status report. "Still lifting, with more puff to come," he said tersely.

"Cross them," said McBatten. "They're waving us across."

"Thank you," said Dakron.

When they had broken free into open water Deep Dakron said, "Gee, do you think we can get through this entire race, do you think we can weather all these twists and trials and betrayals to realize our heart's desire: first place?"

Dakron clutched his bodice, or where his bodice would have been, had he been wearing one.

"Never fear," said Scratchen Sniff grandly. "These things always have a happy ending."